The Eucharist Today

The Eucharist Today

Essays on the Theology and Worship
of the Real Presence

Edited by
RAYMOND A. TARTRE, S.S.S.

P. J. Kenedy and Sons · New York

Nihil obstat:	Wilfred Thibodeau, S.S.S.
	Censor Deputatus
Imprimi potest:	Francis Costa, S.S.S.
	Provincial Superior
Nihil obstat:	John A. Goodwine, J.C.D.
	Censor Librorum
Imprimatur:	†Terence J. Cooke, V.G., D.D.

New York, New York
September 23, 1967

The *nihil obstat* and *imprimatur* are official declarations that a book or pamphlet is free of doctrinal or moral error. No implication is contained therein that those who have granted the *nihil obstat* and *imprimatur* agree with the contents, opinions, or statements expressed.

To my Father and Mother

Before the heavenly altar you now offer "the Lamb who stands as though slain." Your son joins in that same liturgy whenever he celebrates the Eucharist—a pledge and foretaste of our future life together with Him who was, and is, and will be forever.

Contents

ABBREVIATIONS

AAS   *Acta Apostolicae Sedis.* Rome, 1909– .

CSEL   *Corpus Scriptorum Ecclesiasticorum Latinorum.* Vienna, 1866– .

DB   *Dictionnaire de la Bible.* Paris, 1895–1912.

Denzinger   H. J. Denzinger, ed., *Enchiridion Symbolorum.* 1854 through edition by A. Schönmetzer (Freiburg, 1963).

LTK   *Lexikon für Theologie und Kirche.* 2nd ed., Freiburg, 1957–1965.

Mansi   J. D. Mansi, ed., *Sacrorum Conciliorum Nova et Amplissima Collectio.* 1757–1927; rpr. 1960– .

Pauly-Wissowa   *Paulys Realenzyklopädie der klassischen Altertumswissenschaft.* Stuttgart, 1893– .

PG   *Patrologia Graeca,* ed. J. P. Migne. Paris, 1857–1866.

PL   *Patrologia Latina,* ed. J. P. Migne. Paris, 1878–1890.

RAC   *Reallexikon für Antike und Christentum.* Stuttgart, 1941– .

ST   St. Thomas Aquinas, *Summa Theologica.*

PREFACE

The life of the Christian community is founded on a mystery. This means that it is founded on faith. The mystery we believe is that announced by St. Paul: we believe that God has formed a saving design for us and that this design becomes effective in the events of our earthly existence. The economy of salvation is incarnational: God presenting himself to men's faith in the shapes of this world.

It is one of the discoveries of the modern Christian—but this, surely, is simply a return to the original message of Christ—that the Mystery implies that salvation is for those who discern the features of the Incarnate Word in their fellow men and who give themselves to others in a service interpreting a love that transcends self-interest.

But in service to others the Christian holds no monopoly. The humanitarian is as dedicated as he—often more than he—to the betterment of his fellows. What distinguishes the Christian is that he sees Christ in others. Perhaps with difficulty, and without being able to discern any coherent design in his immediate situation, the Christian holds to the belief that the Mystery is being worked out through the complex patterns of personal relations and human society. He believes that he and his fellow men are involved in the unimaginable consequences of the Incarnation: God in Christ drawing the world to himself. The Christian's charity is founded on faith, finds its perspectives in hope.

Can we not discover here the significance of the Eucharist for contemporary Christianity? *This is my body.* Those who take and eat will become his body: a community, a communion; they will be Christ-in-the-world. Impossible to say who answers the invitation to eat; the influence of the sacrament goes far beyond those who can be numbered as communicants. What is important is that the sacrament is at the center, giving meaning to all the rest. Here Christ is the one for others: the very food they eat. Through eating this bread they have eternal life, sharing in Christ's sacrifice.

This is surely the point: that the Christian community is called to be a true community of men, acknowledging human values, yet sacrificing themselves to the Father. The paradox will be blatant to the humanist; it is one that the Christian is invited to live. The Eucharist—communion and sacrifice—stands as a clear denial of a radically secularized Christianity; it brings the Mystery among us, proclaiming the service that must be rendered the transcendence of God while, at the same time, calling to the task of being human.

The discussion centering on the Eucharist in contemporary Catholic theology is not an inward-turning withdrawal of attention from the mission of the Church to the world. That mission, as the Council stressed in several places, has its source and achieves its fulfillment in the Eucharist. The message that the Church has to preach and the task that every Christian has to carry out in the world cannot be properly evaluated if they are not seen as extensions of the mystery of the Eucharist.

The articles collected in the present volume go to the heart of the mystery when, again and again, they return to the theme of the Real Presence. This is the fundamental truth; its consequences touch every moment of Christian existence. It is not a truth to be isolated from its context: God's calling together of the community of man in Christ, the Savior. Yet if this truth is lost, the whole structure of the Church as the sacrament of Christ in the world is undermined. The Church is left without a sacrifice on its altar and Christians are not constantly summoned to review their existence in the world in the light of their relation with God.

The value of the essays lies, not least, in the eloquent testimony they bear to the faith of some of the most distinguished theologians of the Church in this fundamental truth of the Real Presence. That they can give an account of their belief belongs to their professional capacity as theologians. But beyond the professional competence, and sustaining it, there is the combined act of witness to the faith held by the universal Church; and this is more impressive than any scholarship.

Nearly every article draws attention to the manifold aspects of the Eucharist and underlines the difficulty of maintaining a balanced view of the integral mystery. One consequence of the Real Presence that is explored in depth—the visit to the Blessed Sacrament—might not seem to be the most urgent or "relevant" issue in the theology of the Eucharist or in the life of the Church today. No doubt this is true. Yet often it is only when seemingly less important things are eliminated that their significance is realized.

The intention of the article on the visit is to draw attention to one aspect of the Eucharistic mystery which tends to be overlooked in the new stress on the central importance of integrally active participation. An honest attempt is made to break out of the individualistic categories employed in too much of the literature on the visit, and to relate this private devotion to the principal themes of the liturgy. The pastoral importance of this effort cannot pass unnoticed. Authentic participation in the action of the Mass is constituted by a way of Christian living; and for this, personal devotion is unquestionably required. The *opus operans* of the sacramental encounter with Christ is the whole life of the community and the individual. Otherwise liturgy becomes a charade.

The individual, who has to find his own place in the Christian community, will also have to determine for himself his own attitude to the Eucharist. But the objective mystery always remains. It cannot be reduced to rational categories, even if that is the only way we have of

speaking about it. After the simple affirmation of Christ at the Last
Supper, *This is my body,* nothing more profound has ever been said
about the Eucharist than what is found in 1 Cor. 10:17: *Because the
bread is one, we, though many, are one body, all of us who partake of
the one bread*. This book calls upon us to meditate on these two texts of
Scripture.

COLMAN E. O'NEILL, O.P.

University of Fribourg
August 4, 1967
Feast of St. Dominic

The Eucharist Today

Introduction

For some time before the publication of the encyclical *Mysterium fidei* on September 3, 1965, new theological approaches to Christ's Eucharistic Presence had appeared in Europe, unsettling many of the faithful by their novelty. It was to clarify these issues that Pope Paul published the encyclical; and of course it received a mixed reception, some scholars praising it as a modern manifesto of Catholic faith, while others deprecated it as being out of touch with the phenomenalist trend of theology. It was thought that Pope Paul was concerned merely to maintain a *status quo* irrelevant to the mentality of this age.[1]

The consequences for paraliturgical popular devotion to the Blessed Sacrament began to be felt partly under the influence of these theories that seemed to belittle, as less than theologically correct, the worship of Christ's presence in the Blessed Sacrament.

Doubtless there is some truth in the accusation of overemphasis on private "tabernacle" devotion to the prejudice of the Mass, the central act of Catholic life and activity. Still, as in all movements aiming at reform, extreme conclusions were sometimes drawn from the centrality of the Mass liturgy—to the point where nearly all forms of Eucharistic piety were considered medieval relics and pietistic excrescences. To demonstrate that this was not so was one of the main thrusts of *Mysterium fidei,* which rejected a theology tending to minimize the objective, ontological Eucharistic presence of Christ. As Father Anthony Padovano, commenting on the encyclical, writes:

Most of our difficulty with Eucharistic adoration comes from either so strong an emphasis on the Mass as liturgical action and banquet that ideas of sacrifice and enduring Presence seem outdated; or from so strong an eagerness to return to primitive Christianity (which does not show the same interest in Eucharistic adoration) that we see it not as a guideline for future Christianity but as something one must ever repeat as perfectly as possible; or from a conviction that the practice has no scriptural basis. The first

3

objection is dogmatically unsound; the second mistakes the Apostolic age for the Parousia, calling a perfect age what was merely a glorious age, romantically demanding that Christianity forever relive its past and forfeit its flexibility in time.

The third objection is a little more sophisticated than the first two. Some comments in this area may prove helpful. It may also enable us to show that Catholic doctrine on Eucharistic adoration is not *only* the result of a reaction to Berengarius of Tours, or of a medieval misinterpretation of the Eucharist, or of an overly individualistic approach to the Eucharist. (*Paulist Press edition, p. 23*)

A number of contemporary theologians have been exercised to clarify and set in its true perspective the Catholic dogma of the Real Presence—that is, to situate it within the context of the total mystery of the Eucharist and of the Church. From their writings I have gathered here a few essays that provide solid theological background—biblical, speculative, liturgical, spiritual—on the two most misunderstood aspects of the Eucharistic mystery—the doctrine and the worship of the Real Presence. For, as Father Clark concludes his chapter, "These and other neglected truths must be restored to the doctrinal and devotional balance if the renewal of Eucharistic and liturgical life in the Church, in the postconciliar era to which we are all committed, is to come to its hoped-for fulfillment."

When dealing with so deep a mystery as the Eucharist, however, it becomes impossible for the human mind to grasp it in its fullness and complexity. As Father Jungmann observes in Chapter 10, on Eucharistic piety,

An imposing building remains the same although it may look different according to the side from which one views it. The same is true of the holy Eucharist. It is a sacrifice, a memorial, a thanksgiving, a sign of the new and eternal covenant, an epiphany and presence of Christ, a sacred meal. The human mind is too limited to grasp all these aspects simultaneously. Thus at different periods in the history of the Church, different facets of the Eucharist have been emphasized, as they corresponded to the need and atmosphere of each successive age.

The important thing, then, is to hold on to each aspect and, however enthusiastic we may be about one viewpoint, to take care not to minimize the others. The Eucharist stands and falls on the integration of its every part into the whole.

In a sense, then, this collection of essays is one-sided, in that it omits other aspects of the Eucharist—e.g., its sacrificial and nutritive elements. But it is not thereby intended to belittle the other considerations that enter into the composition of the Eucharistic mystery. The same complaint could be lodged against any book dealing with the Eucharistic mystery exclusively in terms of a sacrifice or of a meal—which accusation can be made of some works today. One point is as fundamental as any other, in as much as without the Real Presence there can be no real sacrifice nor real Communion of the body and blood of Christ.

It is true that the Eucharist was instituted primarily to be eaten and offered and not to be adored. It cannot be argued, however, that no other reason was in Christ's mind in making the Eucharist a *permanent sacrament* than that it should be present only at the time of the sacrifice or at the moment of Communion. To doubt this purpose of Christ "to abide forever with men," to refuse to do him some form of homage, to deny his intention to establish a personal, active *conversatio* after the liturgical celebration, would set at naught the very reason for the permanence of his presence. The Reformers, almost to a man, came to deny the reality of Christ's presence (and its worship) precisely because they viewed the Eucharistic celebration only as a meal that, once finished, no longer required the presence of Christ in the bread.

Properly understood, adoration and devotion to Christ in the sacrament are conceivable only as an extension of the worship offered at Holy Mass, into whose context Eucharistic devotion must be made to fit. There can be no real separation between the Christ of the altar and the Christ of the tabernacle if the theology of Eucharistic worship is to have any meaning.

To appreciate the value of Eucharistic adoration, its relation to the Mass must be brought out and its link with liturgical worship clearly defined. When we speak of the sanctifying role of adoration, of the personal intimacy with Christ resulting from it, we state a theological fact. The personal experience of strength and dedication gained from the Holy Hour is not a pious illusion. Pope John XXIII pointed out in his encyclical on the priesthood (*Sacerdotii nostri*) that the night-long vigils of St. John Vianney before the Blessed Sacrament were both the cause and the effect of his appreciation of the Mass as well as of his incredible zeal for souls.

On this point of Eucharistic prayer it is well known that, when he [John Mary Vianney] had only recently been made the parish priest of a little village in which Christian life was definitely languishing, he used to pass long and joyous hours of his nightly repose adoring Jesus in the Sacrament of his love. Thus the sacred tabernacle seems to have been the source from which he constantly derived heavenly strength by which he nourished and rekindled his own piety and provided for the effectiveness of his apostolic work.

The long and continuous prayer of the priest before the adorable sacrament of the altar has a dignity and an efficacy which are such that the priest can obtain them in no other way. There can be no substitute whatever for such prayer. Thus the priest, when he is adoring Christ the Lord and thanking him, when he is offering satisfaction for his own sins or for the sins of others, or finally when he is praying most fervently to commend to God the matters entrusted to him, burns with a more ardent love for the divine Redeemer to whom he has promised his fidelity, and for the men in whose favor he is exercising his pastoral care. And from the Eucharistic piety which is ardent, zealous, and effective, it inevitably follows that he will feed and nourish the interior perfection of his own soul, and that the supernatural strength, with which the strong workers for Christ must be equipped, will come abundantly to him in the carrying out of his apostolic responsibility. (*NCWC translation*)

It is a theological monstrosity to imagine that Christ, whose dynamic activity is exercised at Mass, becomes passive, inoperative, and inarticulate once the Mass is ended. It is perhaps this supposed passivity of the Real Presence that contributed to a less orthodox approach to the worship of the Eucharistic Christ. Christ became an object to be worshiped rather than a person identical with the Christ offered at Mass and received in Communion. The sacramental state prolongs Christ's sacrificial offering of adoration, thanksgiving, reparation, and petition. The sacramental effects (e.g., of spiritual Communion) through interpersonal relations had become obscured.

Devotion to the Eucharist cannot and should not be considered apart from the liturgical worship of Mass. The commendation of popular devotions by the Constitution on the Liturgy of Vatican Council II applies most particularly to devotion to the Blessed Sacrament: "Popular devotions of the Christian people are warmly commended, . . . [but they] should be so drawn up that they harmonize with the liturgical seasons, accord with the sacred liturgy, are in some fashion derived from it, and lead the people to it." (§ 13).

This is the area in which Eucharistic adoration must be "updated" and "adapted" for the renewal of the Church. Very few attempts have been made so far to integrate private or public adoration of Christ with liturgical worship and Christian living. The *res* of the Eucharistic sacrament is to foster charity for Christ, but this charity cannot be separated from charity toward his members. Eucharistic worship must lead to an active love for souls, under pain of becoming a purely subjective exercise in pietism.

Eucharistic devotion must have these two objectives: 1. Integration with the liturgical seasonal cycle and spirit; and 2. Inspiration to charity in all the forms under which it is manifested today: ecumenism, missionary effort, love for the poor and disinherited and the victims of segregation and other social injustices

It should be easy enough to endow Eucharistic devotion with the spirit of the liturgy as it unfolds each day in the Church's worship. The liturgical seasons and the sanctoral cycle provide fruitful matter for meditation in the presence of Christ, who either renews his sanctifying mysteries during the successive seasons or exemplifies them in the lives of the saints, our brothers, whose feastdays we celebrate through the year. Both as a preparation for Mass or as a more leisurely contemplation and "tasting" of Christ's mysteries, Eucharistic devotion can enrich the meaning of our daily Mass and seal it wondrously within the context of Christian life and activity.

Likewise, the ecumenical and missionary horizons opened by Pope John and Vatican II can be enlarged indefinitely when, as we kneel before Christ in his sacrament, his own great charity is poured into us and our strength is renewed. Then may we "come apart and rest awhile" in Christ's companionship of prayer and so be filled with his consuming zeal for the Father's glory and the welfare of the Church.

Far from being outdated, Eucharistic devotion will bring us fully into the liturgical spirit and ecumenical charity—the two pivots of the present Church renewal. Without Eucharistic devotion, neither *devotion* nor *devotedness* are possible. The importance of the Real Presence for the devotional life of the Church was attested by the Franciscan, Duns Scotus (the seventh centenary of whose birth was celebrated in 1966), when he asserted that "Unless indeed the body of Christ were present in the sacrament of the Eucharist, little importance would be given to the other sacraments, and *all devotion would die out* in the Church, nor would any worship of latria be offered to God."[2] And In *Mysterium fidei* Pope Paul emphasized the Eucharistic reservation as the spiritual center of the parish:

You realize, venerable brothers, that the Eucharist is reserved in the churches and oratories as in the spiritual center of a religious community or of a parish, yes, of the universal Church and of all of humanity, since beneath the appearance of the species, Christ is contained, the invisible Head of the Church, the Redeemer of the World, the Center of all hearts, "by whom all things are and by whom we exist" (1 Cor. 8:6).

From this it follows that the worship paid to the divine Eucharist strongly impels the soul to cultivate a "social" love (see St. Augustine, *De gen. ad litt.* XI, 15, 20; PL 34:437), by which the common good is given preference over the good of the individual. Let us consider as our own the interests of the community, of the parish, of the entire Church, extending our charity to the whole world, because we know that everywhere there are members of Christ.

The Eucharistic sacrament, venerable brothers, is the sign and the cause of the unity of the Mystical Body, and it inspires an active "ecclesial" spirit in those who venerate it with greater fervor. Therefore, never cease to persuade those committed to your care that they should learn to make their own the cause of the Church in approaching the Eucharistic mystery, to pray to God without interruption, to offer themselves to God as a pleasing sacrifice for the peace and unity of the Church, so that all the children of the Church may be united and think the same, that there be no divisions among them, but rather unity of mind and purpose, as the Apostle insists (see 1 Cor. 1:10). May all those not yet in perfect communion with the Catholic Church, who, though separated from her glory in the name of

Christian, share with us as soon as possible with the help of divine grace that unity of faith and communion which Christ wanted to be the distinctive mark of his disciples. (*Paulist Press edition, pp. 52 f.*)

In both the selection and the presentation of the present essays, I am deeply indebted to my colleague on *Emmanuel,* Father Ernest Lussier, S.S.S., Lic.S.S., who drew up the critical Bibliography, and to Mary Ellen Evans, editor of P. J. Kenedy & Sons, without whose kind understanding and thorough knowledge of manuscript editing this volume would not have seen the light of day.

Likewise, I extend my heartfelt thanks to the editors of the publications credited in the individual chapters for their permission to use their material, and to the several translators who, though anonymous, played so important a part in transmitting the original thought of the authors; to Father Eugene LaVerdiere, S.S.S., who prepared the Index; and to Louise Martinez and Mary Battista, who typed the manuscript.

RAYMOND A. TARTRE, S.S.S.

New York, August 3, 1967
Feast of St. Peter Julian Eymard

NOTES

1. See *Concilium,* v. 14 (New York, 1965), pp. 157–176.
2. "Nisi enim corpus Christi esset in sacramento Eucharistiae, parum curaretur de aliis sacramentis, et periret omnis devotio in Ecclesia, nec exhiberetur actus latriae Deo." (Rep. IV, d.8, q.1, No. 3 [Vivès 24], pp. 9b–10a)

I. The Real Presence in Theology

> The bread of the Eucharist
> is also the bread of faith.
>
> *Cathal B. Daly, Bishop of Ardagh*

Jacques Dupont, O.S.B.

1   "This Is My Body . . . This Is My Blood"

The symbolic interpretation of Berengarius in the eleventh century and of some Reformers of the sixteenth century forced the Church to affirm with greater accuracy that the body and blood of Jesus Christ are present in the sacrament of the Eucharist "in their natural properties and in their substantial reality" (Retraction of Berengarius), and that "Jesus Christ, true God and true Man, is truly, really, and substantially contained . . . under the appearances" of the consecrated bread and wine (Trent). The Magisterium thus confirmed the meaning of the affirmations of Scripture and at the same time developed a more definite terminology in order to stave off erroneous interpretations the more effectively. This course of action is no different from that followed by the Council of Nicea, which added explicitness to Scripture by asserting that the Son is "consubstantial" with the Father.

Henceforth, the exposition of Catholic doctrine on the Real Presence was to involve two phases. The first elucidates the teaching of the scriptural texts concerning this dogma. The second shows how a more definite terminology makes it possible to keep this teaching abreast of the new problems that call for a more exact definition. Here and now we deal only with the first phase. Exegetical research sets forth the reality of the presence of Jesus Christ in the sacrament, and thus lays the groundwork for further explanations on the manner and nature of that presence. We shall concentrate on the fundamental text: the account of the institution of the Eucharist, and more particularly the words spoken by the Lord over the bread and the cup: "This is my

13

body—This is my blood." We shall try to reset this text in its proper perspective and thereby be led beyond to what is strictly essential to the question of the Real Presence. The Real Presence, in fact, is but one aspect of Eucharistic doctrine. In order to give real meaning to the dogma of the Real Presence, we have to understand the place it holds in the entire economy of the Eucharistic dogma; if we isolate it we run the risk of distorting it.

Four accounts in the New Testament report the actions and words with which Christ instituted the Eucharist at the Last Supper. The account of Matthew (26:26–29) is identical with that of Mark, except for a few unimportant variants. Luke (22:15–20) takes both after Mark and after tradition as reported by Paul in the first epistle to the Corinthians. In spite of the literary style that lends a personal touch to Luke's account, it seems difficult to classify it as an independent witness. So that we are left with two independent witnesses: Paul in the first epistle to the Corinthians (11:23–25) and Mark (14:22–25). Written between A.D. 55 and 57, the first epistle to the Corinthians is prior to Mark's gospel, which was written probably in the 60's. By its context, however, the tradition of Mark seems, on many points, to belong to an earlier period and to be closer to the Aramaic sources than that of Paul's version.[1] We shall therefore follow Mark as our guide, but referring on occasion to the account of Paul and even to those of Matthew and of Luke.

I. THE CONTEXT

A brief survey of the context will prove helpful, for some of the over-all coloring of Mark's Chapter 14 is bound to be reflected in the verses that concern us.

In the episode of the anointing at Bethany (14:3–9) the action of the woman was interpreted by Jesus as something done in anticipation of his coming burial, and thus it became a prophetic action that foretold and foreshadowed the death of the Savior. The pericope, or passage, on the preparation of the Passover (12–16) calls attention to the prophetic intuition of Jesus, who knew beforehand all that was to take place. The betrayal of Judas (17–21) and, after the institution of the Eucharist (22–25), the flight of the Apostles, the denial of Peter (26–31)—all these incidents were known to Jesus; none of them was to take him by surprise. We have further evidence of the same prophetic spirit in the agony of Gethsemane (32–42). Thus, aware of the outcome of the drama in which he had become involved, Jesus was stricken with fear, but he did not falter; with full knowledge and in obedience to God, he went freely to his death.

A few comments are in order at this point.

1. The pericopes that precede and follow the account of the institution of the Eucharist underscore the prophetic foreknowledge of Jesus: he had freely accepted his sacrifice, aware of all that was to happen. It is natural that the context should draw attention to the prophecy contained in the Institution; there again Jesus manifested the knowledge of events about to take place and indicated beforehand to his disciples the meaning he gave to these events.

2. We are dealing here not with a continuous narrative that relates the sequence of events progressively, but rather with a series of episodes somewhat loosely connected. Each pericope records a memorable saying of the Lord with the background that explains it. The series of events is linked together obviously enough by literary devices of the writer. Notice in particular in verse 18 the opening of the pericope that foretold the betrayal of Judas: "And while they were at table eating"; then in verse 22, the pericope of the Institution: "And as they were eating." These are mere transitional phrases that enable the writer to insert incidents already known to him; the Evangelist did not invent these incidents but merely set them in their proper order without modifying the traditional form in which they had been handed down to him.

3. The question may be asked here and now: Through what channel did Mark receive the information he reports in the pericope of the Institution? Concerning Paul the matter is clear; the first epistle to the Corinthians refers directly to liturgical usage. In the course of their communal meetings, the Christians celebrated the "breaking of bread," commemorating on such occasions the actions and the words of the

Lord at the Last Supper. The exegetes generally agree that Mark also
relied on this Eucharistic celebration: the account of what Jesus said
and did in the presence of his disciples shortly before his arrest has
come down to us through a liturgical ritual. As Father Benoit summa-
rizes the question,

In the one as in the other [in Mark as in Paul] we find a text that is
unadorned, terse, and reduced to essentials, a text that does not pretend to
record down to the last detail everything that happened at the Last Supper.
Not that it distorted the facts, but that it simplified them. When reenacting
the Supper of the Lord, our first brethren retained only the important
actions and dropped the rest.

Father Benoit stresses the importance of that remark:

That literary observation has a twofold importance. First of all, by identifying in the accounts of Mark and Paul the very formulas used by the early
communities in celebrating the Eucharist, it confers on these texts [Mark's
and Paul's] an exceptional value of authenticity and authority. Then, if
we grant that these formulas do not pretend to tell us everything about the
last meal of Jesus, it justifies our searching elsewhere for a re-structuring of
the historical framework in which the formulas were inserted and from
which they drew their meaning. In other words, we feel impelled to go
beyond the liturgical commemoration to the concrete reality of the last meal
of Jesus.

The liturgical text is an asset; not only Mark and Paul vouch for it
but also the entire community. It is also a liability, for instead of
reporting a detailed account it supplies only the bare essentials. It is an
abridged narrative; in order to interpret it, we must take into account
whatever information may have reached us through other channels.

II. THE ACCOUNT OF THE INSTITUTION

Verses 22–24 of Mark read as follows: "As they were eating" (a
literary link that corresponds to Paul's introduction, "On the same
night that he was betrayed") "he took some bread." *Paul:* "Jesus took
some bread." *Mark:* "When he had said the blessing" (that is, when

he had pronounced the blessing); *Paul:* "And [he] thanked God," which is more after the Greek manner and, besides, corresponds to what Mark himself said concerning the cup. In a variant of the Roman liturgy, the priest makes the sign of the cross over the bread when he pronounces the blessing. This action may be misleading as to the real meaning of the blessing uttered by Jesus; what the priest blesses is not the bread but God; he addresses a formula of thanksgiving to God, beginning with these words, "Blessed be you. . . ."

After the participles denoting two preliminary actions, Mark uses three principal verbs, in the indicative, which he merely juxtaposes: "He broke it [bread], . . . gave it to them, . . . he said." Matthew and Luke also have the three verbs, but (as the original has it) they make one of the three a subordinate by using it as a participle: *Matthew:* "He broke it and, giving it to his disciples, . . . he said"; *Luke:* "He broke it and gave it to them, saying." Paul omits the verb *give:* "He broke it, and he said"; and in the words that follow he does not have the verb *take,* which expresses an action complementary to that of giving. On this point, Luke is in accord with Paul.

A parallel difference exists concerning the cup. Mark points out the two complementary actions: Jesus "gives" the cup, and the disciples "drink from it." Paul and Luke do not refer to these two actions. These are evidently nonessential details. On the other hand, all four witnesses call attention to the breaking of the bread: "He broke it." This action was considered so characteristic that the first Christians habitually designated the Eucharistic rite under the name of "breaking of bread." The breaking of bread is the outstanding action, the one that is stressed.

There was nothing unusual about the actions of Jesus as he presided at a Jewish meal; they owed their special meaning and importance to the words accompanying them: "This" (the broken bread) "is my body." Beneath the Greek formula the exegetes endeavor to rediscover the Semitic substratum. Concerning the verb *is,* it is enough to note that the copulative verb is not used in Aramaic, so that the phrase runs, "This, my body." Different translations have been proposed for the word *body.* The meaning that Father Bonsirven[2] and J. Jeremias, among others, have adopted would seem the one to be retained. The word "body," pronounced over the bread, is not to be considered independently of the word "blood," pronounced over the cup. We are dealing with two words that are correlative, in the Semitic vocabulary: *bisrâ'* and *'idmâ'* in Aramaic; *bâsar* and *dâm* in Hebrew. In Greek the word *bâsar* is most often translated as *sarx,* "flesh." In fact, the word "flesh" is the one we find toward the end of chapter six of St. John (6:51-56), who was certainly alluding to the Eucharist; we find it again in Ignatius of Antioch (*Smyrn.* VII, 1; *Philad.* IV, 1; *Rom.* VII, 3) and in Justin (*Apol.* I, 66). The Greek-speaking Christians generally preferred *sôma,* "body," possibly because the word "flesh" could easily convey a pejorative shade of meaning, although it is without doubt a more literal translation of the word used by Jesus.

In any case, what is essential is to realize that Jesus made use of two words that are correlative. The body lives by the blood, which is its vital principle; the two together designate man as an entity. In the context of the Passion, there is question of the body that was to be put to death and of the blood that was to be "poured out." The Pauline tradition (Paul and Luke) specifies that it is the "body [given] for you." Mark is not that specific concerning the body, but he has the equivalent concerning the blood, "which is to be poured out for many."

Mark: "Then he took the cup"; Paul and Luke add, "after supper." *Mark:* "When he had returned thanks"; Paul and Luke do not repeat the giving of thanks. Practically speaking, there is question here of a benediction addressed to God. *Mark:* "He gave it to them, and all drank of it"—an accessory detail, corresponding to the one Mark had already jotted down for the bread; it is lacking in Paul and Luke.

Mark: "And he said to them, 'This is my blood, the blood of the covenant, which is to be poured out for many.'" The last words, "poured out for many" (that is, for the multitude, for all) are not found in Paul, who says equivalently, but for the body only, "[given] for all." Luke combines Mark and Paul by saying of the blood, "poured out for you." Matthew is more explicit: "poured out for many for the forgiveness of sins." I shall not tarry over these details in spite of their interest and importance; the essential words are those indicating the contents of the cup: *Mark,* "This is my blood, the blood of the covenant."

From the grammatical point of view this is a peculiar phrase. The word "blood" is determined by two genitives back to back: the possessive *mou,* "my blood," and the object *tes diathékes,* "of the covenant." Problematical enough in Greek, the structure of this phrase is no less so in Aramaic, which does not attach a determinative object to a substantive with a possessive already appended to it. Thence the doubts raised against the one or the other of these two determinatives. Jesus would have simply said: "This is my blood," [3] or else, "This is the blood of the covenant."

These hypotheses have the merit of supposing that Jesus respected the rules of grammar and did not take with them the liberties he now and then took with the law of Moses. The fact is that the expression, adopted by Matthew in spite of his bent for grammatical correctness, includes the same elements as the more elegant tradition of Paul and Luke: "This cup is the new covenant in my blood" (Luke 22:20; Paul, 1 Cor 11:25). Matthew reverses the construction: the word "blood," with its possessive, qualifies the covenant instead of being determined by it, and it is specified that there is question of the *new* covenant. And so we grant priority to the less correct and more difficult expression, and we note that its parallel tradition repeats the same elements. We must recognize that the two determinatives in Mark and Matthew go back to the early days of the Church. If, from that time on, the Christians used a formula that was none too correct grammatically, we do not see why we should attribute it to them rather than to Jesus himself.

Compared with the Pauline tradition the text of Mark has the advantage of repeating the biblical expression of Exodus 25:8. In order to make the covenant between Yahweh and his people, Moses immolated bullocks, casting half of the blood on the altar and the other half toward the people, saying to them: "This is the blood of the covenant that Yahweh has made with you." [4] By reviving the expression "blood of the covenant," Jesus wanted to signify that there was equally question of a blood through which God was making a covenant with man.

It was not, however, by having this blood sprinkled upon them that the disciples were to share in this covenant, but by drinking the contents of the cup. Jesus specified that this "blood of the covenant" was his own blood: "my blood." The three gospel narratives specify still more, "which is to be poured out." [5] This detail is essential for understanding that Jesus was referring to the sacrifice of the cross. In this context it is evident that the immolation of Jesus on the cross took on the importance of a sacrifice and, to be more specific, of a covenant-sacrifice. Jesus was about to offer his blood to God (somewhat like Moses casting on the altar half of the blood of the sacrifice of the covenant); and by drinking from the cup, the disciples shared in the covenant.

We must examine more closely the sum and substance of these words of Jesus.

III. THE MEANING OF THE WORDS OF JESUS

1. The words of Jesus over the bread and the cup cannot be separated from the actions to which they give a specific meaning. The actions and the words constitute together what we may call a prophetic action.

We have already stressed the insistence of the entire context on the foreknowledge of Jesus; he knew what to expect, he foretold it, and he went to his death of his own free will. We come upon the same train of thought in the pericope of the institution of the Eucharist. Here again Jesus foretold his death, and he did so not only with words; he enacted it, as it were, in a symbolic action before the eyes of his disciples. That is what we find first of all in that pericope: *a prophecy in action*.

This manner of proceeding recurs frequently in the Bible. We come upon prophets who are not content with delivering an oracle but who mimic their prophecy and represent in symbols what they prophesy. We are familiar with that quaint personage of the New Testament, Agabus, who, by way of foretelling to Paul that he would be arrested, took Paul's girdle and tied his own feet and hands with it (Acts 21:11). In the Old Testament Jeremiah bought an earthenware jug and broke it in the presence of the assembly, saying: "Yahweh Sabaoth says this: I am going to break this people and this city just as one breaks a potter's pot irreparably" (Jer 19:11). But certainly the outstanding master in prophetic actions is Ezekiel. To quote two passages from his book:

Son of man, take a brick and lay it in front of you; on it scratch a city, Jerusalem. You are then to besiege it, trench round it, build earthworks, pitch camps and bring up battering-rams all round. Then take an iron pan and place it as if it were an iron wall between you and the city. Then turn to it; it is being besieged and you are besieging it. This is a sign for the House of Israel. (4:1–3)

Son of man, take a sharp blade, sharp as a barber's razor; take it and use it on your head and beard. Then take scales and divide the hair you have cut off. You are to set fire to a third in the center of the city, while the time of the siege is working itself out. Then take another third and toss it by swordpoint all round the city. The last third you are to scatter to the wind, while I unsheathe the sword behind them. Then take a few hairs and wrap them in the folds of your cloak; and of these again take a few, and throw them on the fire and burn them. From them will issue fire, and you are to say to the entire House of Israel, "The Lord Yahweh says this: This is Jerusalem, which I have placed in the middle of the nations, surrounded with foreign countries." (5:1–5)

We have certainly noticed the expression "This is Jerusalem," *zô't Yerushâlaim*. Grammatically it corresponds exactly to the formulas we are interested in: "This is my body. . . . This is my blood." In the prophecy of Ezekiel we must of course understand that the hairs represent or denote Jerusalem. More exactly, they signify Jerusalem by what happens to them; the fate of these hairs symbolizes the fate of Jerusalem.

We now see in what sense we may say that at the Last Supper Jesus performed a prophetic action before his Apostles. He showed them figuratively what was to take place on the following day. The bread he broke and gave signified his body which was to be given; the wine in the cup was the sign of the blood he was to pour out on the cross in order to establish the covenant God wanted to make with man.

2. The concept we have of a symbol or of a sign does not correspond to everything a Semite is inclined to see in it. For him a prophetic action is normally efficacious; it not only represents what it foretells but, in a certain way, produces it as well. Again, instances of this are

many. Jeremiah placed a yoke on his shoulders to signify the yoke that was to be imposed on Jerusalem; but false prophets took the yoke off the neck of Jeremiah and broke it, imagining they would thereby prevent the prophecy from being fulfilled (Jer 27 and 28). Having made himself iron horns, the false prophet Zedekiah declared to Ahab: "With these you will gore the Aramaeans till you make an end of them" (1 Kgs 22:11). The prophet Elisha told King Joash to shoot an arrow towards the east, and said: "Arrow of victory over Aram! You will defeat Aram at Aphek completely" (2 Kgs 13:17). Then he told the king to strike the ground; the king struck the ground three times, and the prophet grew angry: "You should have struck half a dozen times, and you would have beaten Aram completely; now you will only beat Aram three times" (*ibid.*, 19).

That is more than enough to caution us against the tendency to attach a purely intellectual meaning to the symbol. The prophetic sign may well be, and often is, an efficacious sign. That is the perspective in which we should place the account of the Institution. When Jesus said over the cup, "This is my blood of the covenant," he meant to signify that by drinking this blood the Apostles were to share in the covenant as really as the Hebrews in the desert shared in the Mosaic covenant on being sprinkled with the blood of the victims. The wine of the Last Supper was not an empty sign, the mere symbol of a covenant to be effected later; it had then and there in itself the efficacy of the blood poured out as a sacrifice. The blood that was in the cup not only signified the covenant but imparted it. The sacrifice of the following day already produced its effects through the sign that represented it at the Last Supper. Thanks to the prefigurative rite, the disciples really shared in the redemptive covenant.

If that is true of the prophetic rite of the Last Supper, it is still more so, we may say, of the repetition of the rite after the oblation of the sacrifice of Calvary. Paul says that every time the Christians celebrated the Eucharistic rite, they proclaimed the Lord's death, but as an event of the past. From prophetic the rite had become memorial. It recalled the cross not as an empty sign or mere symbol; for when they drank from the cup, the Christians shared in the covenant God had made with man through the blood Christ had shed on the cross.

The apologists of the dogma of the Real Presence tend now and then to disregard or tone down the symbolic and figurative character of the Eucharistic rite. It may well prove detrimental to the doctrine they profess; for the symbolic aspect is the first one to appear and to be stressed in the accounts of the Institution. In saying of the bread he broke, "This is my body," and of the wine in the cup, "This is my blood which I will pour out," Jesus foretold with a prophetic action the sacrifice he was to consummate on Calvary. It was an efficacious sign, however, for by eating of this bread and drinking of this cup, the Apostles really shared in the covenant to be sealed by the sacrifice of Calvary. After the Resurrection the meaning of the rite remained the same; by participating in it the Christians participated in the sacrifice of the new covenant.[6]

3. It is from the symbolic rite that we must take off to settle the issue of the Real Presence. The symbolism of the rite is not exclusive of its realism, at least in the order of action; for the Eucharist is a means of participating effectively in the sacrifice of the new covenant. We might go still farther and assert that this realism extends even to the Eucharistic elements, which are to be transubstantiated into the body and blood of the Savior.

a. By way of proving that, some scholars resort to arguments from grammar. They stress the verb *estin:* "This *is* my body. . . . This *is* my blood." The argument does not seem conclusive to us. We shall not insist on the fact that the Semitic original did not use a verb. By saying "This is my body," Jesus did not necessarily affirm that the substance of the bread was changed into the substance of his body. Considered according to the manner of thinking of a Semite and of the Bible, the obvious meaning would be: "This signifies my body—This represents my body." We have only to recall Ezekiel's saying of the hairs, "This is Jerusalem"—that is, "This is the symbol of Jerusalem," a symbol in the order of action. What happened to the hairs was to happen to Jerusalem. Hence we need not hesitate to discard an oversimple argument that proves nothing at all.

Neither would it help much to insist on the present tense of the participles: "This is my body given for you," *didómenon* (Luke), "This is my blood poured out for many," *ekkhunnómenon* (Mark and

Matthew; see Luke, "poured out for you"). We cannot conclude from the present tense that what the disciples looked upon was the body of the Lord actually given even then, or was his blood actually poured out even then. The authors of the New Testament hardly ever used the future participle; they used the present particularly when there was question of an impending future, or of a future that was certain. *O erkhómenos* is not "he that has [actually] come," but "he that is to come"; *oi sozómenoi* indicates not those actually saved, but those destined to be. By making use of the future the Vulgate translated according to the meaning: *sanguis qui pro multis effundetur.* It is a question of the body that is to be given, of the blood that is to be poured out.

b. The meaning of the rite offers something more deserving of consideration. We have said that by communicating to the sacramental species, the disciples shared in the covenant Christ made by the sacrifice of his body and blood on the cross. This efficacy of Communion does not make much sense if all we receive is a mere imaginary sign of the body put to death and of the blood poured on the cross. From the viewpoint not of an abstract logic but of the very concrete logic of the sacrificial cult, it is to the victim of the sacrifice we must communicate in order to share in the effects of the sacrifice. A symbol is not enough; it is essential that it be the victim itself, its flesh and blood. At the time of the covenant of Sinai Moses sprinkled the people with the blood of victims offered to God; we can hardly imagine he could have been content to use a symbol of that blood. This consideration is important, if only indirectly so.

c. The New Testament foundation of Eucharistic realism is found in Paul and John. The sense in which Paul understood the rite is unmistakable when we listen to his explanations: "The blessing-cup that we bless is a communion with the blood of Christ, and the bread that we break is a communion with the body of Christ. . . . Anyone who eats the bread or drinks the cup of the Lord unworthily will be behaving unworthily towards the body and blood of the Lord" (1 Cor 10:16; 11:27; see 11:29). It is well to note that in thus expressing himself Paul was teaching nothing new but merely expressing the accepted interpretation with which his readers were supposedly familiar. That interpretation is certainly most realistic: the bread and wine of the Eucharist are not only the sign but the very reality of the body and blood of the Savior.

John is no less a realist in the last part of his Chapter 6: "If you do not eat the flesh of the Son of Man and drink his blood, you will not have life in you. Anyone who does eat my flesh and drink my blood has eternal life. For my flesh is real food and my blood is real drink. He who eats my flesh and drinks my blood lives in me and I live in him" (53–56). These lines were written at the end of the first century for Christians who could not but refer them to the Eucharist. They stress an interpretation presenting itself as that of Jesus himself. We see no reason to deny any foundation to that opinion. Jesus himself, not necessarily in the synagogue of Capharnaum, may well have explained to his disciples the meaning of the rite to which he was initiating them.

If we take these explanations of Jesus for granted, we understand at the same time the concordance of the interpretation stressed by St. Paul and by St. John, each on his own, starting with the formula "This is my body"—an interpretation not borne in upon them offhand or founded on any subtlety of a questionable nature. We do not *deduce* the Real Presence from the formula Jesus used; it could be understood otherwise. We accept the words in their literal meaning because Jesus himself gave them that meaning. We should therefore admit that, as John gives us to understand, Jesus not only pronounced the formula of the Institution but also determined the meaning to be attached to it.

An obvious objection comes up: How is it that these explanations of Jesus were not taken up in any of the four accounts of the Institution? The answer lies in what we have already said about the literary character of these accounts. They are not complete and detailed accounts; they merely report a liturgical rite limited to what was essential in the actions and words of Jesus. It was not necessary to repeat the same explanations in the course of every liturgical celebration.

To summarize:

1. In order to find a foundation for the doctrine of the Real Presence, we need not insist on the grammatical meaning of the expressions used

by Jesus: of themselves, these expressions may signify a symbolic as well as a real identity.

2. We can do better by drawing on the efficacy of the Eucharistic rite, which expresses a participation in the covenant that was sealed by the bloody sacrifice of Calvary; in the logic of sacrifice, there is no real covenant without a real communion to the victim itself.

3. The decisive argument is found in the concordant testimonies of Paul and John; they express the common faith of the early Church and seem to be based ultimately on the interpretation Jesus himself gave to his own words.

IV. ESCHATOLOGICAL PERSPECTIVE

We have as yet said nothing of verse 25 in Mark, which places the Eucharistic celebration in its eschatological perspective: "I tell you solemnly, I shall not drink any more wine until the day I drink the new wine in the Kingdom of God."

Except for a few slight differences of wording, the text of Matthew corresponds to that of Mark. That of Luke, however, is quite different. Here the eschatological phrase comes before the Institution, not after. Moreover, it is said twice: once over the bread—or, to be more exact, over the Passover, then over the wine. So that the text of Luke sets up two antithetical tableaux: on the one hand, Jesus will not eat the Passover again and will not drink wine until the coming of the Kingdom; on the other, he institutes the memorial of the new covenant in his body and in his blood. To sum up, the antithesis opposes the Jewish paschal rite to the Christian Eucharistic rite; the Kingdom of God in which the Jewish rite finds its fulfillment is no longer the Kingdom of the end of time, but the Church is.[7] In Mark and Matthew the phrase in question in verse 25 creates a different antithesis: it opposes the Eucharistic meal to the eschatological meal.

This verse 25 does not seem to form part of the liturgical rite recorded in the preceding verses. We may be dealing with an independent *logion,* or saying of Jesus,[8] inserted in the account of the Last Supper possibly because it also spoke of a meal. The connection, however, may be closer than that. Mark inserted the phrase in this spot perhaps because he knew it had been said by Jesus in the course of the farewell supper—which is indeed what the text points out: Jesus was taking the Last Supper of his earthly existence. There is also a possibility that the phrase was placed in the context because its eschatological content corresponded very well to the general orientation of the Eucharistic celebration among the early Christians. They renewed the memorial of the Lord *donec veniat* (1 Cor 11:26), and the anticipation of that coming added a note of joy to the breaking of bread, *agalliasis* (Acts 2:46); the assembly closed with the wish, *Marana tha,* "Come, Lord Jesus" (1 Cor 16:23; Apoc 22:20).

In verse 25 Jesus declared first that he would drink no more of the fruit of the vine, which is equivalent to saying that his death was imminent. He added that he would not drink of this wine, but a new wine, in the Kingdom. That was a reference to the very common metaphor that portrayed the happiness of the world to come under the symbol of a magnificent banquet; [9] by speaking of his drinking the new wine, Jesus was foretelling his entrance into the Kingdom. As such, this verse does not seem to be related directly to the Eucharist. But, be it said once more, it is not by chance that the Evangelist inserted it in that spot, for its eschatological tone corresponds to that characterizing the Christian celebration of the Eucharist. The joyous anticipation of the Lord's coming in glory seemingly takes on its full meaning if we keep in mind that the Eucharistic rite already implied a presence, a real presence though veiled, of the one who was to come. The invocation *Marana tha* already received a first realization, a first fulfillment of a presence that anticipated the coming in glory and thus became a promise that filled this anticipation with sentiments of joyous confidence.

The Eucharist thus appears as a synthesis of the economy of salvation, for it represents the redeeming sacrifice of the cross and enables us to participate in it; it guarantees the permanent presence of Christ among his own, not only a spiritual but a real presence of his body and blood; it foretells and prefigures at the last the glorious return of the Lord, of which it is, so to speak, an anticipation in mystery.

NOTES

Dom Jacques Dupont, O.S.B., a noted biblical scholar, is a monk of the Abbey of St. André, Bruges, Belgium. The present chapter comprises the text of a lecture that served to introduce the more doctrinal studies pursued during a symposium on the Eucharist and the Real Presence, and appeared first in *Nouvelle Revue Théologique* in 1958.

1. See J. Jeremias, *Die Abendmahlsworte Jesu* (2nd ed.; Göttingen, 1949), pp. 94–98.

2. J. Bonsirven, "Hoc est corpus meum. Recherches sur l'original Araméen," in *Biblica,* 29 (1948), pp. 205–219; J. Jeremias, *op. cit.,* pp. 203ff. These two authors, working independently, reached the same conclusions. See also P. Benoit, "L'Eucharistie dans le Nouveau Testament." Les récits de l'Institution, *Lumière et Vie* 31 (1957), p. 65.

3. An opinion shared by J. Jeremias (*op. cit.,* p. 99) and by many others (see *ibid.,* n. 5). The philological argument of Jeremias seemed conclusive to A. Vogtle, *Das offentliche Wirken Jesu auf dem Hintergrund der Qumranbewegung* (Freiburg-im-Br., 1958), p. 19.

4. This text is quoted in Heb 9:20: "This is the blood of the Covenant that God has laid down for you."

5. Mark (followed by Matthew) specifies, "for many"—an allusion to Is 53:12. Luke writes, "for you." We might readily relate this to Luke's fondness for the use of the second person, but the fact that "You" is already found in the words said over the bread in Paul as well as in Luke, induces us to link its use to an earlier tradition.

6. To define the efficacy of the sacrament, we say that it effects grace *ex opere operato:* it is an action of God and a gift of Christ, like the sacrifice of Calvary of which it is a prolongation. This does not mean that it produces its effects automatically without the personal acceptance that makes man receptive to grace.

7. For more details see Benoit, "Le récit de la Cène," *Revue Biblique* 48 (1939), pp. 381 et seq.

8. See V. Taylor, *Jesus and His Sacrifice,* p. 139–142; *The Gospel According to St. Mark* (London, 1952), pp. 543 and 547.

9. The metaphor recurs frequently in the New Testament. A fine summary on this topic, starting with Matthew 8:11–12, is found in J. Jeremias, *Jesu Verheissung für die Völker* (Stuttgart, 1956) pp. 47 et seq.

Marie Joseph Nicolas, O.P.

2   "Do This
in Remembrance of Me"

My task is to explain to you the words of our Lord, "Do this in remembrance of me," and to offer my reflections on the underlying meaning of the Eucharist as a memorial.

It is with trepidation, however, that I set out to explain in human words and with human concepts the Church's belief in the Eucharist. First of all, I must remind you that the Eucharist is a mystery of faith, and that the human intellect must make every effort to approach it with an attitude of faith—yes, that certainly—but also with a kind of reserve. Now, to say that the Eucharist is a mystery of faith means three things:

1. It means in the first place that the Eucharist is above all rational explanations, that it is inaccessible to the senses, to experience, to physical science, and even to pure metaphysics. As St. John Chrysostom says, "In all things, let us render to God what is his due, and let us not contradict him, even if what he says appears to contradict our reason and our intelligence" (*In Mat. homil.* 82, 4; PG 58:743). To attenuate what the Word of God proposes to our faith in order to make it more comprehensible is to empty it of all meaning. In the presence of the Eucharist, therefore, the mind must above all else preserve its sense of mystery, of divine mystery.

2. If the Eucharist is a mystery of faith it can be understood only within the context of the other truths of the faith, that is, in the light of the entire economy of the Incarnation. The Eucharistic mystery re-

mains incomprehensible to anyone who does not *first of all* believe that God exists and has revealed himself to man, that he calls man to the most intimate union with his own being, and that the body of Jesus is the body of God made man, of the Word Incarnate. God has assumed a body only in order to be present to men, to offer this body to them as the proper and necessary mediation between our very carnal being and his divinity.

3. Let us go even farther. In the Eucharist we find, in a living and concrete form, the total object of our faith. Christian faith, in fact, is not mere intellectual consent to a truth. It is total loyalty to someone, to Jesus Christ, to someone who, as our God, loves us, becomes man, gives his life for us, saves us, and unites us to himself. Now, the Eucharist is the very fulfillment of this whole mystery and, through the Eucharist, we commune with Christ in the very act of his death and Resurrection. A purely intellectual faith in the Eucharist is hard for anyone who does not also commune with his whole being in the whole reality it contains.

THE MEMORIAL IN THE LIGHT OF ITS INSTITUTION

Since the Eucharist is a mystery of faith, we can know it only through Revelation. Everything we believe about it is founded on the accounts that St. Paul and the Evangelists have left us concerning Jesus' last meal. But the primitive Church practiced and lived the Eucharist before the account of the Last Supper was written down by the Evangelists. This account was first of all fixed in a liturgical form, and afterwards transmitted by living tradition. It was by doing in commemoration of Jesus what Jesus himself had done, that the Church transmitted to us the memory and the signification of what he did. The Eucharist of the Church is nothing else than the repetition of the Last Supper until the end of the world and the return of Jesus.

The Last Supper was undoubtedly a paschal meal, and therefore a ritual and religious meal that had its own specific meaning before the Eucharist came into being. This signification was nothing else than a commemoration filled with gratitude for the deliverance of Yahweh's people, Israel, from the bondage of Egypt, and of their trek to the

Promised Land through the desert under God's own guidance. It is the essential theme of the Old Covenant, the typical image of salvation. Until the Last Supper, Jesus had taken part each year in this celebration that was certainly a memorial to the history of Israel, but in his eyes also the figure of what he would finally do himself before he departed from this earth, for the sake of a New Covenant.

And now the moment had come for the last meal, filled with the most complete and decisive intimacy. This was the end of Jesus' life with his Apostles, as well as its consummation. It was the moment when a man wants to leave everything of himself to those he loves. This last earthly meal was to close with a mysterious gesture, the act that was to constitute the whole Eucharistic mystery. There was nothing new in the gesture of taking bread and breaking it, taking a cup, blessing and sharing it. That was already done at Jewish ritual meals, and even at ordinary meals. Jesus had often done this with his disciples, and it is certain that he had already filled the simple gesture with meaning. What was new on this solemn occasion were the words: "This is my body . . . This is my blood," spoken as he was giving his Apostles to eat and drink what appeared to be bread and wine.

In Matthew's text as well as Mark's, the words "This is my blood" are followed by an extraordinarily important amplification: "of the new covenant, which is being shed for many unto the forgiveness of sins" (Matt 26:27; Mk 14:24). To understand the meaning of this text we must juxtapose it to Exodus 24:7-8, where the covenant between Yahweh and his people is consecrated by the blood of victims: "And taking the book of the covenant, [Moses] read it in the hearing of the people, and they said: All things that the Lord hath spoken we will do, we will be obedient. And he took the blood and sprinkled it upon the people, and he said: This is the blood of the covenant which the Lord hath made with you concerning all these words."

We can be sure that the Evangelist was deliberately making this striking comparison, and that the first Christians understood perfectly what he was doing. The full impact of this comparison was to be felt a little later when the epistle to the Hebrews compared the two covenants, showing that the powerless and merely figurative blood of the ancient victims had been replaced by the all-powerful, eternally offered blood of Jesus Christ.

Luke, in addition to several precious details that I am omitting, adds these vitally important words to those of the first two evangelists: "Do this in remembrance of me" (Luke 22:19). St. Paul, moreover, does the same, and with even greater insistence. "In remembrance of me" means first of all: in remembrance of what I am doing at this moment, at this last meal. When the first disciples gathered together for the breaking of bread, they were acting not only in the name and by the power of the risen Lord, but in memory of what he himself had done on earth, by repeating the gestures and words he himself had used. The very heart of the Eucharistic rite, of what we call the Mass, is the repetition of the Last Supper by Christians.

But it is impossible not to give a broader meaning to the remembrance of this farewell repast. It is the remembrance of Jesus' entire life on earth among men. Thus, "in remembrance of me" also means: in remembrance of my own person, since I am about to leave you. And especially, as St. Paul clarifies in a most important commentary: "For as often as you shall eat this bread and drink the cup, you proclaim the death of the Lord, until he comes" (1 Cor 11:26). Therefore "in remembrance of me" means in the third place: in remembrance of my death for you. Of my death, and of my resurrection—inasmuch as Jesus is alive today and his death was but a passage to glory. That is what the Canon of the Mass expresses when, immediately after the Consecration, the priest says: "Wherefore, Lord, in memory of the blessed passion of the same Christ, your Son, our Lord, of his resurrection from among the dead and of his ascension to heavenly glory, we your servants . . . offer to your sovereign majesty . . . a victim perfect, holy and spotless, the holy bread of everlasting life and the chalice of everlasting salvation."

Whereas, through the ancient Pasch the people of Israel commemorated their deliverance from Egypt and, together with it, all of God's blessings, the Christian people commemorate through the Eucharist the history of their salvation accomplished by the death and resurrection of Christ.

Is the Eucharist, then, merely a remembrance, like the Jewish Pasch? Is it only a memory of the past and not a present reality? A memorial in whose name the eternal covenant with God is reaffirmed, but which cannot be identified with the reality recalled? Is the Eucharist merely a "representation" of the body and sacrifice of the Lord, of his body given for us, of his blood "shed" for us?

You well know that such is not the case at all, that according to our Catholic faith, based on the very texts of the Eucharistic institution, the Eucharist is a memorial of the past that preserves it, forever present and real, for every man who comes into the world. And that is indeed unique, miraculous. That is truly a "mystery," the mystery of Christ himself, of this God-made-man whose being as a man, whose human life have not been swept away by time as in ordinary human beings.

But before considering this mystery in itself, I should like to show you that human memory alone, through its own laws, its own efforts, tends to restore a presence to the past. It fails to achieve it, but it strives toward it. And the Eucharistic rite, by giving memory the power to restore past reality to life in all its current reality, is merely the triumph of this striving on the part of memory.

THE PAST RECALLED

Have you ever reflected on the meaning of the words "to remember"? I am not speaking of the phenomenon of simple repetition through which I remember a name, a lesson learned, or repeat a gesture already performed. I am speaking of calling to mind an experience one has lived in the past, an experience whose image, in rising before us, seems to contain something permanent. What we grasp first of all is ourselves, of course. We are aware of ourselves as seeming to experience something that is beyond time. We also grasp the underlying being of things, their meaning, and in a sense their soul. An impression such as this gives us a strange joy—as if reliving the past with the savor of the present made us conscious, of a continuity, a permanence, of a victory over time, almost of a resurrection.

Memories are sometimes unleashed by a sudden shock, by the unexpected awakening of a sensation experienced in the past. We sometimes keep as relics things that once had no value at all but now have the power to resurrect a memory. Does not everyone have some such memorial of his past life? But nothing can take the place of a deep, inward, and sometimes difficult effort to recover lost time and, together with it, the realm beyond time. And this effort proves futile in the case of purely human things. Our power to relive in a certain way what we have lived before does not bring these things or these persons back. At best it revives a state of soul. To remember is an effort to grasp what is no more, but this effort cannot, of itself, be successful. We can truly say of every turning point in our life, and especially of every real being that disappears from our life: "Never more, never more!" Could the disciples of Jesus, and Jesus himself utter this famous, touching, and so human lament at the close of the Last Supper?

True, we have been speaking merely of the personal memory that vanishes so quickly for each one of us. Groups, more durable than individuals, also seek to preserve the memory of the past through the generations. A sort of collective memory comes into being that is not simply the transmission of acquired habits and knowledge, but seeks to be a memorial, a conscious permanence of the past in the present. In every age men have held in remembrance great events and great men, celebrating them by commemorations, singing and writing about them in poems, stylizing them in representations that have the power to unleash the forces of sentiment and kindle an awareness of continuity.

In this regard, religions have always had a mysterious power to call past events to mind. And Christianity, more than every other religion, because it was founded on historical events, on the history of a man, has been able not only to call them to mind, but to make them relive for its faithful in sacred writings and actions that we call the liturgy. The Jewish Pasch was already a sacred memorial of the flight from Egypt; and almost all the sacred places, feasts, and rites of the ancient religion were remembrances. The Christian liturgy is simply the unfolding of the life and mysteries of Jesus in a form that expresses their full meaning. The Christian believer is not content to contemplate and sing praises of God's works accomplished in Jesus Christ and through him. He relives them in a certain way, for Jesus lived them on earth in his name and, by anticipation, with him.

In certain cases the liturgy even becomes dramatic and emphasizes this aspect of the past's resurrection. We have examples of this throughout Holy Week. Think of the procession on Palm Sunday, and of the Mass that follows, with the account of the Passion by three voices; the washing of the feet on Holy Thursday, the watch at the repository; the solemn adoration of the Cross. Think also of the Paschal Vigil when the great symbolic candle is lighted, and then all the candles of the faithful are lighted from its flame. At such moments, there is much more in question than a profane commemoration. The events called to mind have an eternal meaning and efficacy, into which one enters through faith. They belong to the past as events, but each of us must reproduce them in the mystery of his own life. The least word of the Gospel that we reread in a celebration is at once a thing of the past and of the present. We know that it was pronounced and lived by the Word made flesh. And we also know that it governs our life today.

Yet, while the liturgy enables me, by means of remembrance, to rediscover the very essence and spirit of Jesus' life on earth, it cannot by itself give me the absolute reality of Jesus as a human being and of the acts through which he accomplished my salvation. Christ will never, never again enter into Jerusalem amid the singing of Hosannas. He will never, never again repeat the words or gestures that the Gospel has recorded for us. Never again will he be nailed to the cross or bow his head and give up his spirit.

MAKING THE PAST PRESENT

Now we know that such is not the case at all for the Eucharist. Holy Week represents the passion and resurrection of the Lord only once a year. The Eucharist represents them every day. But it does so in the strong sense of the word "represent," namely, to render present.

If the Eucharist is a memorial, it is not so in the same way as any other liturgical ceremony. And that is why it is the summit and source of the liturgy. The Eucharist is exactly what our Lord did. In it he is as truly present among us in his body as he was when he lived on earth. Through it the saving sacrifice is as truly offered up from this point in time and space where we are, as it was on the cross, and before that at the Last Supper. And that is why the Eucharist is not celebrated merely at one moment of the liturgical cycle, as are Holy Week and Easter, but, on the contrary, every day of the year. It is a permanent presence and a permanent action of Christ among us, through his body and his blood.

In this connotation, therefore, the word "memorial" is too weak. Or rather, only here does it take on its full power, the plenitude of its meaning. It is a memorial that contains the very presence that it commemorates. It is such affirmations of our faith that we must justify and explain; and we must do so, bearing in mind the three ways in which the Eucharist, as we have already seen, is the memorial of the Lord:

1. A memorial of his presence among us on earth;
2. A memorial of his death and resurrection for us;
3. A memorial of the act by which he gave himself to his Apostles as food.

MEMORIAL OF CHRIST'S PRESENCE

When Jesus said that the bread and the wine were his body and his blood, he was speaking in the strongest terms. There was a real identity between "this" (this thing Jesus held in his hands and gave his disciples to eat) and his own body.

The objection has been made that there are many instances when the verb "to be" does not express identity, but rather "representation." Jesus' words, then, would mean: this represents my body, my blood. But Jesus does not limit himself to saying that he is the true bread, the true vine, that the bread and the wine can serve as symbols to express an aspect of his life-giving role. He says that this bread, this wine, that he is giving as food, are his body, his blood. He does not invite us to rise from the symbol of the bread and wine to the knowledge of a hidden reality. He says: Eat this bread, this wine, for this is my body which is given for you, and this is my blood that is shed for you. And my flesh is real food, my blood is real drink.

When John places the following words on our Lord's lips: "The bread that I will give is my flesh" (Jn 6:52); and again: "He who eats my flesh and drinks my blood has life everlasting and . . . abides in me and I in him" (Jn 6:55-57), he clearly understands these words in their realistic sense, and it is because of this realism that the Pharisees were scandalized: "How can this man give us his flesh to eat?" (Jn 6:53). Certainly, there is question here of a "spiritual" manducation, one that gives "spiritual" life. But the food that is to be eaten in this spiritual manner is indeed the real flesh of the Lord, with which the bread of the Last Supper is mysteriously identified.

And when Paul, after giving an account of the Supper, tells us that anyone who eats this bread and this wine as if they were ordinary food fails to distinguish the body and blood of the Lord, and anyone who eats unworthily eats and drinks his own judgment (see 1 Cor 11:29), it is evident that to his mind the presence of Christ and of his sacrifice does not depend upon our faith, but is just as real for those who do not pay proper respect to it. For them Christ's presence, far from giving them life, is their condemnation.

Now if Jesus, at the Last Supper, took bread and wine and made them into his own body and blood, while telling us to "Do this" in memory of him, then, when we obey we are doing the same thing that he did. When we "do this," we are taking bread and a chalice of wine and making them into his body and blood. That is what we do at every Mass. It is a *memorial of the Lord,* yes, because it reminds us of his historical life among us. But at the same time it is really the Lord, because his life has never ceased being present within the very heart of our human history.

The Catholic Church insists on this realism as being of her very essence. There would be no Church, no Mystical Body of Jesus Christ, if the Eucharist were not the physical body of Jesus Christ which the Church offers up to the Father, having first received it from him, and upon which the Church feeds in order to become incorporated into him and to belong to him. We must not confuse this faith with any explanations we might try to make of this Real Presence.

Some may even ask: Why bother explaining? Is it not enough that we believe Christ is God made man so that he might live among us? Must not every man be able to make contact with Christ and participate in his sacrifice personally, in order to join his own sacrifice to Christ's? Can the Incarnation be merely a historical event, and must it not become a living reality in each human life? If Jesus is really God made man, he must extend his coming and his influence in the flesh to every man. The body he has assumed must serve as an intermediary to make contact with us, who are so profoundly incarnate. When we consider the Eucharist from within the mystery of faith, it becomes normal, so to speak. It is easy for anyone who really believes in the Word Incarnate to believe in the Real Presence, in real communion with his body, and real participation in his sacrifice. He does not need to understand how these things are possible.

Moreover, the Church has no official explanation of the Eucharistic mystery. And the doctrine of transubstantiation must not be taken to be an explanation, but rather a more precise affirmation of it.

What does the Church mean by this word "transubstantiation"? We know that the term offends modern philosophical ears. The reason, of course, is that the word "substance" is one of those that causes the most profound division among philosophers. And certainly it is possible to make the mystery of the Eucharist more intelligible by means of a philosophy of substance. St. Thomas succeeded in doing it in a most inspired way. But in her definition, the Church uses the word "substance" only in the least philosophical, the simplest, and the most currently accepted way. If there is a philosophy involved here, it is the philosophy implied in the universal language, in the spontaneous institutions of the human mind. Substance is what is deepest, most real, and most essential in a being. Christ is substantially present in this consecrated bread. That means he is really, objectively there, independently of what I may think and of any human thought. I find him there because he is there.

Well then, is the consecrated bread no longer bread? I see the appearances of bread, and conclude that the consecration has not annihilated its physical and chemical properties. Everything that allows one to say of a thing that it is bread remains in this consecrated bread. And yet I say: It is no longer bread. The reason is that the underlying being that manifests itself in the physical and chemical properties has been changed, although there is no external evidence of this change. And it has been changed into the risen body of Christ. That is why the color, the taste, the nutritive properties of bread reveal to me and really render present to me not the bread that was formerly there, but the body of Christ.

It is therefore possible to say that the appearances of the bread have changed their signification. Naturally speaking, they signify bread with its function of providing me nourishment. Now they signify the body of Christ as the food of my soul. But they signify it because he is there, because he has mysteriously taken the place of their natural substance. They contain what they signify. Through these appearances it is the body of Christ that is in my hands and even within our beings after Communion.

The risen body of Christ is the whole and entire Christ. But his presence is not spatial and in no way disturbs the relations among bodies. Because it is substantial, interior, it is as invisible as the presence of a spirit. And yet it is the presence of a body. It is not multiplied with the number of hosts. In each individual host we possess the same body whole and entire, the same risen Christ, in the precise state in which he lives today and which will some day be ours as well.

Instead of picturing Christ to ourselves as descending from heaven and dwelling in a multitude of places, it might be preferable to think of distance as being annihilated. Each one of us, through each host, has contact with the physical presence, communes with the same body of Christ, with the same Christ as he is in heaven.

All the Church asks of her theologians, whatever their philosophy, is that they conclude to a presence of Christ that is as real, as objective, as substantial as his presence here on earth during his mortal life, through which he made contact with his Apostles, and that consequently when

I eat what was formerly bread, I am united to Christ himself, in his objective and substantial reality.

To believe in the Transubstantiation means to believe that what was once bread is now the body of Christ. It simply means, therefore, to believe in Jesus' own words: this thing I am holding in my hands and am giving you to eat, something that was bread when I took it from the table, has become my body.

MEMORIAL OF THE PASSION

To say that the sacrifice of the Mass is not only the memorial of the sacrifice of the cross, but also its reality, its actualization, may appear even more difficult to accept.

For after all, the body of Jesus exists, it is risen. The mystery lies in the fact that we can make it present, not that we restore it to existence and life. The sacrifice of Jesus, on the other hand, appears to be a past event. In order to become present, it would have to be accomplished all over again. Now, the risen Christ cannot die any more. And why should we repeat something that has eternal efficacy? Can the Mass be anything but a memorial of the past in whose name we receive God's gifts?

St. Paul gives us a very different answer: "As often as you shall eat this bread and drink the cup, you proclaim the death of the Lord, until he comes" (1 Cor 11:26).

To proclaim does not mean merely to call to mind, but to affirm as a presently active and efficacious reality. "This cup is the new covenant in my blood" (1 Cor 11:25). Each time we consecrate it we enter into communication with the very act that seals the new covenant. A Mass is as it were the presence and consummation here and now on earth of the act that reconciles God with man, with each one of us.

But the Church has never taught that the sacrifice of Christ is accomplished again at each individual Mass. Nor does she oblige us to believe that the Mass turns back time to bring us into the presence of the drama of Calvary, in its historical reality. The truth is that the act by which Christ offered himself in sacrifice is completed only by the Resurrection, and has been forever fixed and perpetuated there, in this leap beyond death. The fact that he offered himself once and for all does not mean that this offering is past, but that there is no need of repeating it because it still endures.

The risen Jesus is perpetually offering up his human life once immolated for us. His suffering and death are over. What still exists is the fact that he suffered and died for us, a fact that is incorporated into his risen state. It is in the name of this continuing reality that he intercedes for us, to use the words of St. Paul, who shows us Jesus entering the holy of holies by virtue of his own ever-efficacious blood. He is eternally the One who died for us, and he offers himself as such in his risen being. To make him present by his blood is to make him present in this very state of oblation, with the full efficacy of his sacrifice.

To make my thought clearer I should like to cite a few memorable lines by one of the greatest modern exegetes, Father Pierre Benoit:

Christ's past is not closed, as if he were merely a creature that belongs to earthly time. It is perpetuated in a contemporary history that is rooted in the new time inaugurated by the Resurrection. God's act forgiving men because of the Cross is eternal, just as God himself is eternal and transcends all the epochs of our human time. So too, Christ's act imbedded in the becoming of human history, goes beyond this history because it closes the ancient era and inaugurates the new. By his Resurrection, the life and death of Jesus opened out into a new world whose eternal present participates in a certain way in God's eternity. . . . The risen Christ lives a new life in which his past remains present. . . .

MEMORIAL OF THE LAST SUPPER

Finally, when we say that the Mass is a memorial, not only of the Passion and very presence of the risen Jesus but of the Last Supper, we always mean that this memorial is a current reality. It would be an understatement to say that the priest is the man who repeats the words and actions of Jesus. Jesus himself acts within the priest at the altar. We often say: The priest consecrates, the priest offers Christ. That is as if we were saying: This violin is playing a Beethoven sonata, when we know the violinist is playing it.

True, the priest is conscious and free in the hands of Christ, in contrast to the violin in the musician's hands. It is Christ who, through the priest, offers himself on the altar, in time. When Christ makes himself present in the Eucharist he is not offering himself up anew, but his eternal offering is in a sense "temporalized," incorporated in this point in time and space in which we are living.

In assuming this sacramental form through our instrumentality, Christ's sacrifice becomes ours, and the perfect host assimilates our personal offerings into itself. Bread and wine, taken from the works of creation, are the symbol of everything that men have received from God and must return to God. The total conversion of the bread and the wine into the being of Jesus Christ himself expresses the total assumption by Jesus Christ of all we have and are. Only God, by becoming man, could realize the perfect Host. But what he does is assume everything human into himself, incorporate into himself all men, the whole Church, molding them into his body, into the prolongation of himself.

When we celebrate the Eucharist in remembrance of Jesus, therefore, we are doing much more than merely repeating what he once did. We are lending ourselves to his invisible action so that he himself may repeat it. And what he once did was to make himself personally present, offer himself in sacrifice, and give himself as food, that is to say, in intimate and assimilative communion.

ETERNAL PLEDGE

In as much as Jesus actually lived and died on this earth of ours, the Eucharist is a remembrance. But the remembrance of his bloody death is consummated in the current reality of his sacrifice and of his living presence in our hands and hearts.

This present reality is filled with his earthly life and death. We can even say that when he lived, suffered, and died, it was for me, and he remembers it; and when I join him today, I am rejoining the One who loved me and delivered himself up for me, the One who "shed a specific drop of blood for me." The Eucharist does not merely give me the ever-real and dynamic present, but also the past in which this present is rooted.

It also gives me the future. We announce the death of the Lord until he comes, as St. Paul has told us. This return of Christ toward which human time is progressing, is already signified, announced and sacramentally realized by the Eucharist. The admirable thing about God's plan is that the One toward whom we are advancing and whose Parousia is awaited by the entire universe is also the One who is now leading us from within, who makes us grow every day in his image. The Eucharist is not only the actualization of a past but an ever-efficacious and operative mystery. It is already the beginning of Christ's Return. As the memorial of his earthly life among us and of his bloody sacrifice, it is the pledge of his eternal Presence and of our communion with him. It is really its sacramental realization, that is to say, a realization that is hidden, imperfect, and progressive.

"Until we all attain . . . to perfect manhood, to the mature measure of the fullness of Christ" (Eph 4:13), the Eucharist is our food, that is to say, it nourishes each Christian and it nourishes the Church. When the human race will have attained to the perfect measure of the fullness of Christ, he will appear as he really is and not under alien appearances. The sacraments will cease to exist. The Eucharistic veils will be torn away. The reality that the Eucharist had been hiding and yet giving us will be consummated definitively and perfectly: Christ Jesus in his glory, and we united to him in the same glory.

NOTE

Marie Joseph Nicolas, O.P., a member of the faculty and regent of the Dominican college in Toulouse, France, is the author of *L'Eucharistie* (translated as *What Is the Eucharist?*) and other studies in this field. His chapter in the present book appeared first in *Parole et Pain,* 14–15 (1966), a review published by the Blessed Sacrament Fathers in Paris.

3   The Sacramental Christ

THE WORD WAS MADE FLESH. The supreme era in the history of salvation was the time when the Word was made flesh, when Christ brought out of the shadows the pilgrim Church that until then had been living under the dispensation of the law of nature and of the Old Law, awaiting his coming. It was when Christ drew the Church to himself in order to bring her forth once again, as it were, and communicate to her the life of the New Law. As long as he was visibly present in her midst, she remained as though hidden in his light. She seemed to come forth from him without yet being separated from him, but progressively revealing her definitive structure.

Those were the blessed days when Simeon held the infant in his arms (see Luke 2:28), when the Savior waited for the Samaritan woman at Jacob's well (see John 4:6), when the disciples acclaimed with palms the gentle King who came forth to meet the daughter of Sion (see Matt 21:5). As the Evangelist wrote later on: "What was from the beginning, what we have heard, what we have seen with our own eyes, what we have looked upon and our hands have handled of the Word of Life . . . we announce to you, in order that you also may have fellowship with us" (1 Jn 1:1–3). "For God so loved the world that he gave his only-begotten Son, that those who believe in him may not perish, but may have life everlasting" (Jn 3:16).

Was the bodily presence of the Word-made-flesh in our midst snatched from us on Ascension day, when Christ, in his risen body marked with the stigmata that the Apostle Thomas had demanded to touch, passed to another world—a world parallel to ours in a certain respect and yet beyond the scope of our imagination, the world of the great beyond, of the end of the world and of God's glory?

What are we to answer? If it is true that God so loved the world that he *gave* it the bodily presence of his only-begotten Son, are we not permitted to think that—unless it were intrinsically impossible—he could love the world enough to *leave* with it the bodily presence of that same only-begotten Son?

And if it required the bodily presence of the then passible Christ to gather men around the redemptive sacrifice that he intended to accomplish, can we not say that—again if it is not intrinsically impossible—the same bodily presence of the now glorious Christ is just as necessary in order to multiply in a mysterious way among us and render efficacious at every moment of time, the *presences* of the redemptive sacrifice accomplished once and for all on the Cross? For after all, must not the bloody emanations of this sacrifice unceasingly penetrate every layer of the world, amid great shocks and explosions, to proclaim the death of the Lord and the forgiveness of sins, to gather up within it the City of God and tear down the City of evil?

But since Ascension day, when Christ entered the glory of heaven where he now dwells in his own natural condition, it is certain that he cannot have been corporeally present to us in time on earth except under appearances different from his own. From that moment, Christ necessarily had two kinds of presence—one manifest, the other hidden, mysterious, sacramental. It is somewhat as though one mother could be present simultaneously in two ways: manifestly to her seeing child, and in a hidden way to her blind child.

Such things are sheer folly according to human views. And yet the Church has a right to yearn for them and to think of them as desirable. Are they true? Are they even possible? Who was to tell her? Opening the Scriptures, she came to passages where it is noted that "before the feast of the Passover, Jesus, knowing that the hour had come for him to pass out of this world to the Father, having loved his own who were in the world, loved them to the end" (Jn 13:1); and that "the Lord Jesus, on the night in which he was betrayed, took bread, and giving thanks broke, and said, 'This is my body which shall be given up for you; do this in remembrance of me' " (1 Cor 11:23–24). In reading such things, could the Church fail to be deeply moved? Could she help whispering softly: "I had a presentiment of it, yet it is even more than I had intuitively foreseen!" [1]

It was all clear to her now. The love that had pressed the Son of God to come among us as a man pressed him to remain corporeally with us. To refuse to accept the mystery of the Eucharist, we would have to misapprehend the meaning of the mystery of the Incarnation.

DISCOURSE ON THE BREAD OF LIFE

Although John did not repeat the factual account of the institution of the Eucharist, which had already been given by Paul and the synoptic Gospels, the primary purpose of Chapter 6 of his Gospel, with its discourse on the bread of life, was to announce beforehand the institution of the Eucharist. And, as we know, the Eucharist was actually instituted at the moment when Jesus, about to enter upon the bloody sacrifice of his Passion, made this sacrifice sacramentally present under the appearances of bread and wine, so that his followers might participate in it not only through love but also by actual eating, after the manner in which the Jews united themselves through eating to the sacrifices they offered up to God.

The discourse on the bread of life becomes fully intelligible to us only when read in the retrospective light of the institution of the Last Supper. The discourse has three high points. Verse 35, when the mystery of the *Incarnation* is called to mind: "I am the bread of life. He who comes to me shall not hunger, and he who believes in me shall never thirst." Verse 52, where the mystery of the *Redemption* is foretold: "The bread that I will give is my flesh for the life of the world." And verse 54, where the very manner in which Jesus wants us to participate in his bloody sacrifice is announced: whence the Eucharist and the solemn urgings of the discourse on the bread of life, verses 54–60:

Amen, amen, I say to you, unless you eat the flesh of the Son of Man, and drink his blood, you shall not have life in you.

He who eats my flesh and drinks my blood has life everlasting and I will raise him up on the last day.

For my flesh is food indeed, and my blood is drink indeed.

He who eats my flesh, and drinks my blood, abides in me and I in him.

As the living Father has sent me, and as I live because of the Father, so he who eats me, he also shall live because of me.

This is the bread that has come down from heaven; not as your fathers ate the manna, and died. He who eats this bread shall live forever.

These things he said when teaching in the synagogue at Capharnaum.

There were some who murmured among themselves, saying: "How can this man give us his flesh to eat? . . . This is a hard saying. Who can listen to it?" (Jn 6:53, 61). From that moment, many of his disciples turned away and no longer accompanied him. "Jesus therefore said to the Twelve: 'Do you also wish to go away?' Simon Peter therefore answered, 'Lord, to whom shall we go? Thou hast words of everlasting life'" (Jn 6:68–69). The Eucharist, the supreme sacrament of unity, began with separations. It was not unity at any price that Jesus was seeking.

He had added: "It is the Spirit that gives life; the flesh profits nothing" (Jn 6:63). One of the memorable exegetical misconstructions of these words—which occur in the Gospel of the Word-made-flesh descended among us—seeks to prove the uselessness of the Word-made-flesh remaining in our midst. But what did Jesus really mean? He meant that there is a carnal sense in man opposed to the spirit of faith; and since this sense is incapable of acceding to the mystery, it serves no purpose. This, according to St. John Chrysostom, is the immediate explanation. "Does Jesus say this of his own flesh?" he asks. "God forbid! But he says it of those who understand his words in a carnal way. . . . What is necessary is that we contemplate all the mysteries with interior eyes, that is, the spiritual way. . . . You can readily see that the words 'the flesh profits nothing' do not signify the flesh of Jesus, but their carnal manner of listening" (PG 59:265). The commentaries of St. Cyril and St. Augustine penetrate into the heart of the mystery. Thus Augustine writes: *"The flesh profits nothing,* if it is alone. . . . But if Christ has come to our rescue by becoming incarnate, how can the flesh profit nothing? . . . The flesh has been the vessel: consider what it contained, not what it was" (*In Ioan. Ev. VI, 64,* Treatise 27, no. 5).

ACCOUNT OF THE INSTITUTION

What was being done in the year 55, in the Church of God at Corinth? St. Paul speaks of a table that is an altar, of a bread that is the body of the Lord, of a chalice that is the blood of the Lord, of a union of the faithful to this body and this blood through the act of eating, in the manner in which the Jews partook of the sacrifices of the Mosaic Law, and the Gentiles of the sacrifices of their idols. But neither the sacrifices of the Gentiles nor those of Israel were permitted any more, for fear of arousing the Lord's jealousy (see 1 Cor 10:14–22). A little farther on, Paul writes:

For I myself have received from the Lord what I also delivered to you, that the Lord Jesus, on the night in which he was betrayed, took bread, and giving thanks broke, and said, "This is my body which shall be given up for you; do this in remembrance of me." In like manner also the cup, after he had supped, saying, "This cup is the new covenant in my blood; do this as often as you drink it, in remembrance of me. For as often as you shall eat this bread and drink the cup, you proclaim the death of the Lord, until he comes." Therefore whoever eats this bread or drinks the cup of the Lord unworthily, will be guilty of the body and the blood of the Lord. But let a man prove himself, and so let him eat of that bread and drink of the cup; for he who eats and drinks unworthily, without distinguishing the body, eats and drinks judgment to himself (1 Cor 11:23–29).

The Church adds nothing to the meaning of these words. She accepts it in its fullest sense. She announces it to her children. Here is what St. Ambrose preached in Milan around the year 390:

Perhaps you say: *This is my ordinary bread.* But this bread is bread before the sacramental words. As soon as the consecration occurs, the bread becomes (*fit*) the flesh of Christ. Let us therefore establish this fact. How can what is bread be the body of Christ? By words is this consecration accomplished, and whose words are these? The words of the Lord Jesus. Indeed, all the rest that is said before, is said by the *priest:* he offers praises to God, he prays for the people, for rulers, for all other men. But when he is about to produce, *ut conficiatur,* the venerable sacrament, the priest no longer uses his own words, but the very words of Christ. Therefore the words of Christ produce this sacrament. What are these words of Christ? The very words by which he has made all things. . . . If, then, there is such power in the words of the Lord Jesus, that what did not previously exist has begun to exist, how much more efficacious must those words be in causing things that already existed to . . . be changed into something else (*in aliud commutantur*). . . . To answer you, therefore, before the consecration it was not the body of Christ; but *after* the consecration, I tell you that it is immediately (*jam*), the body of Christ. (*De sacramentis* 4:13–20)

THE TRANSUBSTANTIATION

St. Augustine tells us that the Eucharist contains what we *see* and what we *believe*. What we *see* is the appearances, the physico-chemical properties—in short, the "species" or "accidents" of the bread. After Christ's words, under these unchanged appearances of bread, what *is* there is the body of Christ. A profound change has occurred. There has been a change from one *reality* to another, from one substance to another. In a word: transubstantiation.

The Church has always believed and the Council of Trent has declared anew that "because Christ our Redeemer has said that what he offered under the species of bread was truly his body, through the consecration of the bread and the wine, a conversion of the entire substance of the bread into the substance of the body of Christ our Lord occurs, and of the entire substance of the wine into the substance of his blood . . . conversion that the Catholic Church rightly calls transubstantiation." [2]

The distinction between a subject or substance and its modifications or accidents is an evident reality for everyone of us. We all make the distinction between the permanence of our underlying and substantial ego and the mobility of our accidental dispositions or states. Within man there is one subject that is affected diversely, that passes from childhood to old age, from sadness to joy, from error to truth. The same tree sheds its leaves in the winter and burgeons again in the spring. The same elements of the universe are joined and separated, composed and decomposed. In all of nature we must distinguish between the substantial subject and its modifications.

Let us come back once again to the Eucharist. It is the substance of the bread, as we already said, that is affected by transubstantiation, not the accidents or physico-chemical properties of bodies that alone are governed by the laws of the physical and chemical sciences. All these sciences demand of us is that we should not impinge on their domain. They do not argue as to whether or not these properties have a subject, as we all tend spontaneously to believe, or whether, as certain Buddhist metaphysicians think, it is possible for motion to exist without a body in motion, whether there can be changes without anything to be changed, accidents without substance. That is of no concern to them. Similarly, the whole mystery of transubstantiation remains, by definition, outside their field of inquiry.

THE TECHNICAL FORMULATION

Only transubstantiation makes the real presence of Christ possible under the unchanged appearances of bread. Such is the teaching of the Church. In the name of Scripture, she announces things from another world, that "eye has not seen or ear heard, nor . . . [have they] entered the heart of man" (1 Cor 2:9). A doctrine from above, from far above our human ken, and yet so consoling to us because it opens up our souls to the horizons of the God who is Love—how can it fail to appear on first impact to be a scandal, a gauntlet thrown down to the endless arguments in which our minds are embroiled? It asks us to believe in the mystery of the one God subsisting in three Persons, Father, Son, and Holy Spirit; the mystery of the Son of God who became man and died on a cross; the mystery of his permanent presence among us in the Eucharist.

Each time, objections have been marshaled against these unimaginable revelations; each time, argumentative reason has striven to diminish them, to bring them down to its own level—namely, the level of a "religion within the limits of reason," and to reduce them to theses acceptable to itself, comfortable theses that would no longer scandalize it. And yet each time these temptations have been dashed against a small word that is not even in Scripture but that reconciles within itself those aspects of Scripture that have been seized upon to ruin and tear asunder the transcendent unity of Revelation. Such, for example, is the word "Trinity," used to affirm at once the unity of nature and the irreducible distinction of persons in God; the word "consubstantiality," to affirm the absolute identity of being between the Father and the Son; the term "hypostatic," or personal union, to affirm the unity of person and the duality of natures in Jesus; the word "transubstantiation," to affirm the presence of the body of Christ under the appearances of bread.

These words have been defined for all time. Even though each succeeding generation of thinkers strives to unravel their meaning, they will never be able to corrupt it.

These are precise, technical words. As interpretations multiplied, tending to minimize their meaning, or to find loopholes or subterfuges in them, it was necessary to clarify them technically, to maintain the sublimity and purity of Revelation. The terms used for this purpose were sometimes borrowed from the terminology of a philosophy that was already well developed. But this could be done only after taking them out of their immediate philosophical context, verifying and checking them, and subjecting them to the purifying light of divine faith that used them and molded them to its own ends.

Faith would have forged these terms when the need arose if they had not pre-existed. And this it actually did in certain instances. It is clear, therefore, that these technical terms do not enslave revealed dogma to any one system. It has recently been said that "orthodox Christian thought has chosen in Hellenic philosophy those elements that seemed usable to it; it has rejected metaphysical theses that seemed incompatible with its own principles, *it rejected the most original and unchanging theses of ancient metaphysics,*" [3] such as the thesis of the eternal duration of the world.

Even after they were technically formulated, the great mysteries of the Trinity, the Incarnation, and the Real Presence remained accessible in a certain measure to the faith of the masses of the faithful. We teach them to children in catechisms, for we do not think little children are unworthy to approach these revelations of God's love. There is no esoterism about Christianity.

Let us also make it clear that the revelation of the Real Presence of the Christ-God in the Eucharist has been accepted with the same profound faith, the same love, by the entire Church, both in the East and in the West. But where attacks against it were more subtle, more calculated, more violent—and this is true of the West—the formulation of this doctrine quite naturally became more technical.

NON-CATHOLIC APPROACHES

At the present time the attraction of the Eucharist for many of those who, outside the visible boundaries of the Church, claim as we do to be followers of Christ and of his Gospel, seems to be making itself felt with increasing force and—instead of growing weaker—to become almost irresistible. The time is past when Protestants spoke of the Eucharist as if it were a magic rite, a survival from mythical and pre-logical ages. They reread with renewed attention, in the Synoptics and in St. Paul, the account of the Last Supper—an account at once so unexpected, so simple, and yet so solemn and strangely moving. They are impressed by the fidelity with which the first Christians perpetuated the act inaugurated by our Lord. "Do this in remembrance of me," was his command, and the Apostle added: "until he returns."

The celebration of the Supper was the privileged moment for the Christian community when it encountered Christ, who had promised to return and who might well appear suddenly in glory to announce the end of the world. This ceremony had the mysterious power of unifying the Church on the highest level, the level of the Eucharist, by refocusing the Church, the body of Christ, on Christ who is its head. Should we not rejoice profoundly that all these things are being rediscovered by those of our brothers whom we cannot yet consider as belonging fully to the Church?

Several of our Protestant brothers, emboldened by these increasingly enlightened approaches to the mystery of the Last Supper, are beginning to *speak,* as we do, of a "real presence," of a "body of Christ," indeed of a "transubstantiation," to designate things that we do not consider to be such at all. Whence an inevitable source of confusion.

For us "This is my body" means: This is no longer bread, it is my body in the real sense of the word. For us, this is the *immediate* presence, the real presence, the *substantial* presence. And that is the transubstantiation.

For them "This is my body" means: This is bread that mediates my body, that is presented as a sign of my body, as having the power, if consumed with faith, of uniting to my body which can be only in heaven now. It is bread in the real sense; it is my body, only in the improper sense, through the figure of style that gives the same name to the means and to the end, to the sign and to the thing signified. It is a *mediate* presence, the presence of a *sign,* the presence by *interposition* of another reality, of another substance. And in that case there is not the shadow of a transubstantiation. When a mother gazes fondly at the photograph of her exiled son, this is for her the presence of a *sign;* but when there is a knock on the door and her son clasps her in his arms, that is a *real* presence, a *substantial* presence.

Surely we should welcome as a promise, as a reason for hope, the great devotion with which the Last Supper is celebrated by those who have not yet been able to discover in it anything but the presence of a sign of the body of Christ. In this respect these progressive approaches to the Eucharistic mystery are blessed, they are rising toward greater light. When Jesus asked his disciples what people thought of the Son of man, they answered that some thought he was Eliah, Jeremiah, or one of the prophets. And Jesus did not blame those who held these views. To them apply the words: "For he who is not against you is for you" (Mk 9:39). Then, turning toward his disciples, Jesus said to them: "But who do you say that I am?" (Mt 16:15).

THE RATIONALIST APPROACH

The same search that leads some upwards can cause the descent of others. The doctrine of the true, real, immediate presence of Christ under sacramental appearances seems too lofty to certain of our brothers who are sons of the Catholic Church as we are, but who have been seduced by easy solutions. Why not, they ask, substitute the very simple doctrine, free of mystery and scandal, of the mediating presence of a sign?

According to them, we could even keep the same terminology, we could continue to speak of the "real presence" of Christ in the celebration of the Last Supper, and give the faithful "the body of Christ." And everybody would understand when we explained that it is possible to make a profane use of bread, in order to feed our bodies; and that we can also make a sacred use of bread, to unite ourselves to Christ. Corporeally, Christ is in heaven and nowhere else; on the altar there is bread and nothing else. But if you eat this bread with faith and desire to be united to Christ, the signification, the destination, the finalization of the bread are no longer profane. You have changed them, and they have become sacred. While these things are *naturally* profane, they have now become *functionally* sacred. A *transignification,* a *transdestination,* a *transfinalization* of the bread has occurred. And if we concede that things have less value by reason of what they *are* than by reason of the *use* to which we put them, why not go so far as to designate this "transfinalization" by the venerable and traditional word of "transubstantiation"?

While such a view would draw us away from the Church, it would seem to bring us closer to those who, we have just seen, are approaching her. Nevertheless, it is better to ascend than to descend. This could be an instance of what our Lord meant when he said: "He who is not with me is against me, and he who does not gather with me scatters" (Matt 12:30).

THE FAITH OF THE CHURCH

Now, the Church did not invent these incomprehensible mysteries of the triune God in three divine Persons, of the corporeal coming of God's only-begotten Son at the moment of the Incarnation, of the continuation of his corporeal presence among us under the Eucharistic veils. Rather, she has accepted with awed humility and adoration these revelations of the transcendence of a God whose nature and plans remain hidden within himself, but who, she knows, is defined as Love (see 1 Jn 4:8). She proclaims these truths to everyone, to the most disinherited as well as the most learned, as good news, as *the* good news from another world, in whose light all the insoluble problems of this earth can be understood. She does not think it is necessary to hold it back from the poor or even from little children, for she knows the affinity of humble hearts, of pure hearts, for the mysteries of God.

In every historical era there have been minds of considerable stature, men who were almost always well intentioned and often great thinkers, who have proposed very simple explanations of these revealed mysteries, adapted to men of ordinary intelligence and to the needs of what nowadays we would call "the man in the street." In the fourth century the Arians agreed with us in saying that Jesus Christ *is* God, but they added that he is so *by mandate,* because he acts in the name of God and by his authority. The Nestorians, a century later, certainly agreed with us that the Son of God and the Son of Mary are *one and the same* person, but only in the sense that an ambassador is one with the prince he represents.[1] And today the *body* of Christ is given as food, but with the idea that it is *bread* representing the body of Christ. Through the ages the Church has always rejected such explanations.

In this purview we should cite here the solemn words of Pope Paul VI at the Eucharistic Congress of Pisa on June 10, 1965:

The sacred signs of the Eucharist are not merely symbols and figures of Christ, proofs of his love, or of his action on behalf of those who share in his Supper. They actually contain him, the living and true Christ, they designate him as present, as he now lives in eternal glory, but represented here in the act of his sacrifice, to show that the Eucharist reflects in an unbloody way Christ's bloody immolation on the cross, and that it makes those who worthily receive the body and blood of Christ clothed in the signs of bread and wine, participate in the benefits of the Redemption. It is so, yes, it is so, *cosi è, cosi è. . . .*

We say this to dispel uncertainties that have arisen during recent years, in a question of such vast importance, in the train of efforts to propose interpretations that elude the traditional doctrine and authority of the Church. We say this also to invite all of you, men of our century, to fix your attention on this ancient and ever-new message that the Church has never ceased repeating: The living Christ, hidden under the sacramental sign that offers him to us, is really present. . . . The Eucharist is a mystery of faith, a very strong, very gentle, and very sure light for those who believe. But an opaque rite for those who do not believe. Oh, how decisive is the theme of the Eucharist when it thus becomes a line of separation! Whoever accepts it takes sides. He is taking sides with the same enthusiasm as St. Peter once did: "Lord, to whom shall we go? Thou hast words of everlasting life" (Jn 6:68).[5]

To these sublime words I should like to add three beautiful testimonies borrowed from diverse times and places.

1. First, here is the solemn profession of faith in the Real Presence at the conclusion of the Mass according to the Coptic rite of Alexandria:

Amen, Amen, Amen. I believe, I believe, I believe. Until I draw my last breath, I shall confess that this is the life-giving body of your only-begotten Son, of our Lord and our God, of our Savior Jesus Christ. This body he received from our Blessed Lady and our Queen, the most pure Mother of God. He united it to his divinity, without mingling, fusion, or change. . . . I believe that his divinity has never been for a single moment separated from his humanity. It is he who is given to us for the remission of sins, to bring us life and eternal salvation! I believe, I believe, I believe that all these things are so!

2. At the end of the funeral oration for Anne of Gonzaga, Princess of the Palatinate, who had lost her faith and later regained it, Bossuet cites these intimate notes of the princess:

It is altogether believable that a God who loves infinitely should give proofs of it proportionate to the infinitude of his love and to the infinitude of his power. And what belongs to the omnipotence of a God far exceeds the capacity of our feeble reason. That is what I tell myself when the demons strive to perplex my faith. And since it has pleased God to make me feel that his love is the cause of everything we believe, this answer convinces me more than all the books in the world.

Whereupon Bossuet concludes:

Cease asking what it was that united heaven and earth in Jesus Christ, and the Cross with all its grandeurs: *God so loved the world!* Is it unbelievable that God should love and that his goodness should be communicated? Think of the feats to which love of glory inspires courageous souls; to which love of wealth incites the most vulgar souls; and finally to which all that bears the name of love impels all men. Nothing seems hard, neither perils, nor labors, nor sufferings: and such are the prodigies of which man is capable. Now, if man who is so weak attempts the impossible, will not God do something extraordinary to satisfy his love? Therefore let us give as the only reason for all the mysteries: *God so loved the world. . . . And we have believed the love that God has in our behalf* (1 Jn 4:16). That is the whole of Christian belief; it is the cause and the summing up of the whole Creed. It is here that the Princess of the Palatinate found the solution to her former doubts.

Bossuet also records these words of hers:

If God accomplished such great things in order to declare his love in the Incarnation, what would he not have done to consummate his love in the Eucharist, to give himself not merely *in general* to human nature, but to each Christian *in particular?*

3. In *La Messe Là-bas* Paul Claudel is reminded of those who, like Rimbaud or Mallarmé, in their efforts to elicit from poetry a power that it was not in its nature to give, ended by making poetry impossible. And yet there exists a form of verbal expression higher than poetry, the words that the priest pronounces at the moment of the Consecration, which, by virtue of divine omnipotence can instrumentally *accomplish* what they *signify:*

Rimbaud, why do you go away, and why are you once again, as in the
  picture books,
The child who runs away from home, going out toward the pines into
  the storm?
You were seeking so far away an Eternity accessible to every sense in
  this life.
Raise your eyes and keep them fixed before you, and look at the Azyme
  in the monstrance—for that's where it is.
Furious spirit dashing against your cage, full of screams and blasphe-
  mies,

It is by another road that we shall turn our feet toward Jerusalem.

You were not mistaken when you thus devoured things, poet devoid of the priest's power.

This is, are words suddenly capable of serving as a veil to Being.

This object amid paper flower decorations is really Supreme Beauty,

These words, so worn that no one hears them any more;—it was in them that Truth resided.

Can the words that restored the dead to life wear out or die?

Whenever the priest pronounces them, this bread suffices to make them endure.

To receive within us the Word that is the whole man, the man who is God as well as man,

We need only open our lips,

At last I see with my own eyes that supreme possession is possible!

Possession of the One who became flesh of our flesh, possession of the First Cause present in a body accessible to me.

And it is possible not only for my soul, but for my body!

Possible even during this life for the whole man who knows that he is more powerful than death!

The veil that conceals things has become transparent to me at one point.

I finally embrace Substance through the Accident.

IN CHRIST'S HOUSE

St. Francis of Assisi says in his *Testament:* "The Lord gave me such deep faith in churches that I prayed in this simple way, using these words: 'We adore you, O Lord Jesus Christ, in all the churches throughout the world, and we bless you because you have redeemed the world by your holy Cross.'" A church is Christ's house, even more than it is the house of the Christian people. Even the poorest Catholic church is filled with a mystery, a presence. It is inhabited. It does not receive its life primarily from the movement brought to it by the ebb and flow of crowds. In its own right, anteriorly, it is the source of life and purity for those who cross its threshold. It possesses the Real Presence, the corporeal presence of Christ, the "place" where supreme Love has touched our human nature in order to contract with it an eternal marriage, the powerhouse capable of illuminating the whole drama of time and of the human adventure.

Every man, woman, and child can enter there and meet the Jesus of the Gospels personally, silently, intimately. Everyone, however abysmal his ignorance, however great the sins that burden him, and whatever his secret interior anguish, can dare to approach him, as did once the sinful woman in the home of Simon the Pharisee. Everyone can cry out to him like the blind man of Jericho: "Lord, that I may see!"

When a sincere man inquires of you what he must do to find the Truth, ask him to go and sit a moment each day, with the Gospels in his hand, in a church at a time when no one is there. Ask him to do this perhaps even before you explain the catechism and the Christian mysteries to him, and also before casting him into the crowd of believers among whom he would feel like a stranger and where the Church might seem to him a community group like all the others. Later on he will be able to understand that the Real Presence is the underlying reason for the Church's permanence in space and time until the Parousia.

There are so many ugly churches at present time that we hesitate to speak with the psalmist of the beauty of God's house. We eagerly desire this beauty. But we are speaking of something else when we speak of a soul's encounter with the sacramental Christ. Such a meeting can be a great delight, a moment of paradise. It can also be the cry of a wretched and helpless creature; and it can be a sort of battle, a kind of agony. Then too, it can be a sudden and sometimes savage attack, a splinter from the bloody cross that tears the soul to its depths.

NOTES

Charles Cardinal Journet, archbishop of Fribourg, Switzerland, and a noted theologian of Vatican Council II, is the author of several important works, including *The Mystery of Evil* and *The Church of the Word Incarnate*. The present essay originated as a Conference of St. Louis of France held in Rome in 1965, and was translated from the French text appearing in *Nova et Vetera* (Fribourg), 4 (1965), pp. 275–289.

1. "If we announce the death of the Lord, we announce the remission of sins. If, each time his blood is shed, it is shed for the remission of sins, I must always receive it in order that my sins may always be forgiven. I who

am always sinning must always have a remedy" (St. Ambrose, *De sacramentis* 4:28).

2. *Denz.*, 877 and 884.

3. Claude Tresmontant, *Les idées maîtresses de la métaphysique chrétienne* (Paris, 1962), p. 15. Now available in translation as *Christian Metaphysics,* trans. G. Slevin (New York, 1965).—*Ed.*

4. According to Rudolf Bultmann, "the formula *Christ is God* is false, if it implies that God is an objectivizable entity. . . . It is correct when God is understood as the event of God's action." In other words, Christ, in announcing the beginning of the era of salvation, was the eschatological event by which the encounter between God and men took place. "The Lord-being of Christ, his divinity, is never more than an event" (*L'Interprétation du Nouveau Testament* [Paris, 1955], p. 231). That is why Bultmann reproaches the Ecumenical Council of Churches for its action at Amsterdam officially recognizing "Jesus Christ as God."

5. *Osservatore Romano,* June 12, 1965.

Francis Clark, S.J.

4   The Real Presence
and "Ontological Reality"

It would be unfair to suppose that the recent controversy about transubstantiation took its rise merely from a desire to make the hard saying of the Eucharistic presence softer for the modern mind to bear. There are several reasons, some of them theologically serious, why in recent years a current of disquiet and criticism, directed against the traditional understanding of the Church's dogma, has been making itself felt. I propose first to summarize these reasons, leaving comment on them until later.

This particular controversy must be seen against its general background—that is, the whole new outlook in Catholic theology, which, especially since the war, has been seeking to renew itself by a fruitful return to the sources and by a new methodology. In Eucharistic theology this has led to a reaction against the too-often arid and technical "cosmology" of the Real Presence in the Scholastic textbooks of yesterday.

And so there has arisen a contrary emphasis on the so-called "dynamic" conception of the Eucharist: the insistence on the communal meal, ecclesial and eschatological in its meaning; and on the liturgical action and on the participation therein of the People of God. There is the new imagery of the sacraments as primarily encounters with Christ in an interpersonal dialogue of faith and love. The Real Presence, some now say, is only a relative value, subordinated to those dynamic values. And some criticize the so-called "static" theology of the Presence,

61

together with the cult of the reserved Sacrament, as an exaggerated development in the Latin Church, one that promoted an individualistic, antiliturgical, and even superstitious piety.

In retracing the history of the doctrine of the Real Presence, some writers have alleged an opposition between "Augustinian symbolism," by which the bread and wine are essentially a *sign* of a supramundane reality, and "Ambrosian physicism," which, with its excessive realism of substantial change, led to a theology which contradicted the axiom, *"Sacramentum est in genere signi."* (This objection may remind some of you of the 28th of the Anglican Thirty-nine Articles, which declares that transubstantiation "overthroweth the nature of a sacrament.")

Another source of disquiet arose in a different quarter. Neo-Scholastic authors woke up to the realization that, in the light of modern science, it was no longer possible to call bread and wine homogeneous substances, according to the categories of Aristotelian-Thomistic cosmology. In both there is a physico-chemical multiplicity of great complexity. Where then is *the* substance of bread or of wine, of which the Council of Trent speaks? [1]

The reply of some authors was to rephrase the dogmatic expression in the terms of modern science. The substance that is changed, they explained, is really the whole multiplicity of physico-chemical substances: of microcrystals, molecular complexes, molecules, atoms, electrons, protons and what not, leaving unchanged the accidents of extension, of mass, of magnetic, electric and kinetic energies, and so on. But this reply, far from reassuring, served to make many more uneasy. After the controversy that ensued on these questions in the 'fifties, especially between Carlo Colombo and Filippo Selvaggi, some began to say that Colombo had not gone far enough in removing the Eucharistic doctrine beyond the reach of "physicism," and to ask whether the supernatural event that occurs at the Consecration could not be placed in the purely spiritual or intentional order, leaving the mundane reality quite unchanged in its own nature.

Harmonizing with this line of thinking was the influence of modern philosophical theories, which a number of Catholics thought could be usefully applied to Eucharistic speculation. The perspectivism that in various forms had found favor since the time of Nietzsche declared it nonsensical to speak of the nature of a thing in itself; its reality was its meaning for man, "for me." Adapting this to the theological sphere, a kind of "supernatural perspectivism" is proposed, according to which the Real Presence is a reality insofar as it is perceived by faith—not indeed merely individual faith, but the faith of the ecclesial community.

Similarly, according to existential phenomenology the deepest meaning of things is said to be their human significance, their finality and use as expressions of interpersonal relations, and it is suggested that this could be called their "substance." Bread and wine are "anthropological realities." Could it not be said that, because Christ uses them to express his self-giving and divine hospitality and so changes their deepest significance, this sign-change is transubstantiation?

TREND TOWARD TRANSIGNIFICATION

The seeds of almost all these ideas had already been sown in an unpublished work called *La présence réelle,* which originated in 1936 as the manuscript record of a private discussion. After the noble death of its author, Yves de Montcheuil, S.J., in 1944, it was multigraphed and in the following years had a widespread though underground circulation. It was in fact the source of the error about transubstantiation against which Pius XII gave a warning in *Humani generis* in 1950. (See Denzinger—Schönmetzer 3891.)

In 1955 came the book of the eminent Calvinist scholar, Franz Leenhardt, *Ceci est mon Corps.* Written in an eirenic and persuasive style, it seemed to provide a biblical justification for the same reinterpretation of transubstantiation that others were urging from the very different premises of perspectivism, existential phenomenology, and Augustinian Neo-Platonism.

Leenhardt argued that Christ's words at the Last Supper must be understood, not according to Greek thought-patterns, but according to the Hebrew mentality, for which things *are* to faith what the divine word destines them to be. At the Supper, Christ's own body was the instrument of his presence; but with deep prophetic symbolism he intimated that henceforth the bread and wine of his eschatological repast would be the instrument of that same presence, would *be* himself to his disciples eating thereof in the response of faith. And in this sense Leenhardt was prepared to say that the food was transubstantiated. His book made an impression, and some Catholics suggested that his ideas, and the similar ideas of others such as Max Thurian and the Anglican E. L. Mascall, opened a promising avenue toward ecumenical agreement.

Arising, then, from all these factors, a current of opinion began to appear openly from 1956 onward in some Catholic circles, particularly in Northwest Europe, toward a reinterpretation of the Tridentine dogma of transubstantiation in terms of transignification and transfinalization. These essays at reinterpretation were even disseminated in popular and devotional journals and aroused considerable dismay and protest. The cruder analogies with which they were sometimes illustrated did not help to reassure the faithful. One writer compared the change in the bread and wine to the change in a piece of cloth when it is adopted as a national flag; another likened Christ's presence to the personal welcome which a housewife incorporates in the tea and cakes she offers to her guests.

For the most part, however, the new opinions were carefully and reverently expressed. There is no point here in naming their authors, for whom I have indeed fraternal sympathy and regard. Opinions advanced conjecturally before the issue of the papal encyclical *Mysterium fidei* would no doubt be modified today. An inquisitorial mentality is abhorrent to us, and our concern should surely be not to seek *adversarii* to fix labels to, but simply to have a care for the faith of the flock of Christ.

Inevitably when this discussion got out into the marketplace, it underwent a blunt simplification there. There was bewilderment, incipient doubt, much inarticulate distress of heart; and there were some bitter fruits in Catholic life and practice. Nor was that surprising: for why should one adore transfinalized bread, or reverently preserve it after its dynamic sign-function has been performed?

All this gives the background to the publication of *Mysterium fidei* in September 1965. The Holy Father explained there that he had been obliged to speak out, "so that the promise of a new flowering of Eucharistic piety which, as a result of the Council, is pervading the whole Church, be not frustrated by the spread of false opinions." While praising the theological diligence of those who had sought new insights into the mystery, he declared: "We cannot approve the opinions which they express, and we have the duty to warn you about the grave dangers which these opinions involve for right faith." So much, then, for the recent history of this question.[2]

G. K. Chesterton, that stout champion of the man in the street, once remarked that he had long found himself in that hopelessly outnumbered minority which is engaged in defending the convictions of the mass of mankind against the attacks of all men. To adapt his paradox, it would be understandable in these days if a puzzled shepherd of souls should sometimes get the impression that he is defending the beliefs of the whole People of God against the attacks of all the theological experts! But it would be a passing illusion. *Securus iudicat orbis terrarum.* So in our question, to keep a sense of proportion one must remember that the opinions I have described were proposed by a relatively small group, even an "in-group," who certainly cannot be taken as representative of the *sensus theologorum,* let alone the *sensus fidelium.* It is an occupational hazard of theologians to congregate into a mutual admiration society.

FAITH SEEKS UNDERSTANDING

Now I offer some reflections on the theological issue itself. If in the past the theology of transubstantiation has too often been presented as if it were a cosmological conundrum, in some recent writings it has too often been presented as if it were a linguistic conundrum. In both cases its religious value is obscured.

The truth of the Real Presence is one aspect of the whole rich Eucharistic mystery, and we must never lose sight of its integral connection with the other aspects—especially sacrifice and communion—and with the whole. The deep meaning of our Lord's words at the Last Supper has been unfolded to us first through the inspired interpretation of St. Paul and St. John, and then progressively through the believing, praying, and teaching Church down the ages. Namely, THIS which we take and eat, THIS which is the mysterious center of the Church's worship, *is* Jesus Christ himself, present in the very flesh in which he was born of the Virgin Mary, in which he died on the cross, in which he is now victoriously glorified.

The sacrifice of salvation is daily celebrated at our altars and the work of our redemption thereby made operative, because *what* is offered in the consecrated Host and chalice, he *who* offers himself there, is the High Priest and Victim himself. We truly participate in the sacrificial banquet because we receive there the same Victim of the unique sacrifice. *Dominus est:* this *is* Christ, not anything less. Whatever speculative theology may say further about the Real Presence must start and finish at that central truth.

Both historically and theologically, the defense and guarantee of that primary revealed truth is the complementary doctrine, implicit at first and later unfolded in the life of the Church, which we call transubstantiation. That long process of doctrinal unfolding from the Patristic age to Trent has to be traced and pondered theologically in order to appreciate the essential content of the eventually defined dogma.

The authentic witness of tradition is to a real conversion of the very constitutive being of the bread and wine into Christ's natural body and blood. Substance in this dogmatic tradition is not tied to the technicalities of Aristotelian philosophy, but means in general the concrete reality of created things—as, for instance, in the celebrated fifth-century homily *Magnitudo,* which had a considerable influence in the later crystalizing of the doctrine.[3] In the basic realism of this change of the terrestrial substance into Christ's, the Church finds the perennial safeguard of her belief in the realism of Christ's corporal presence.

Faith seeks understanding of why this is the way to the Real Presence; and the profoundest speculative answer, though obscured in post-Tridentine Scholasticism and seldom fully grasped by present-day critics, is still that of St. Thomas Aquinas. His further theological explanation is not of faith, but the Church has approved it as helping to illumine what is of faith. The Eucharistic consecration cannot transfer Christ from his place in heaven to our altars, cannot multiply him, or condense him or recreate him there. But in the full perfection of his manhood he becomes present at a thousand thousand places on this earth, really, corporally, and substantially, because at each a terrestrial substance has been wholly converted by divine power into his physical body—which neither increases nor leaves heaven.

Substantial reality, as such, transcends the spatial order of dimensive quantity, and thus the same individual reality, Christ's body, can be present under different localizing dimensions. Because of the intrinsic entitative continuity of the "wonderful and singular" conversion wrought by divine power in the Eucharist, St. Thomas explains, Christ is now the successor to the entity of the previous terrestrial substance, and so immediately begins to be present, without any distance or spatial transfer, under the localization of those empirical accidents that formerly located the terrestrial substance.

For St. Thomas, transubstantiation is not just an extra dogma, but the only possible way by which the dogma of Christ's Real Presence can be true. Although his elaboration of the doctrine belongs to the sphere of theological speculation, in which differing opinions may freely be held, it does at least point the way to avoid those crude difficulties that arise from too-naïve use of the imagination when reflecting on this mystery.

The Church does not impose any cosmological theory of substance, but she uses the term to refer to a concept that is drawn, to use Pope Paul's words, from "what the human mind perceives from universal and necessary experience of reality." But if no particular philosophical system is obligatory for expressing the Church's belief, there are some systems, such as mere perspectivism, which are certainly inadequate to do so. It is rather ironical that some who reject as outdated the help of Scholastic philosophy in elucidating these questions now insist that we should accept in its stead a far less universal and more ephemeral philosophy, existential phenomenology, as providing the sole key to the hidden meaning of the Catholic dogma.

WHAT IS "ONTOLOGICAL REALITY"?

In *Mysterium fidei* Pope Paul insistently reaffirms the Tridentine definition of the complete conversion of the substance of bread and wine as the way to the Real Presence of Jesus Christ. He goes on to explain that there is thereby a new significance and a new finality, not of the bread and wine but of the *species,* as a *consequence* of transubstantiation. These are his words in this key passage:

As a result of transubstantiation, the species of bread and wine undoubtedly take on a new significance and a new finality; for they are no longer ordinary bread and ordinary wine, but the sign of a sacred reality, and the sign of spiritual nourishment. But the reason they take on this new significance and this new finality is precisely because they contain a new "reality" which we may justly call *ontological.* Not that there lies under those species what was already there before, but something wholly other; and that not merely because the faith of the Church deems it to be such, but in objective reality, since once the substance or nature of the bread and wine has been changed into the body and blood of Christ, nothing remains of the bread and wine save only the species. Under these, Christ, whole and entire, is there in his "physical" reality indeed bodily present, although not in the same way that bodies are present in a given place.[4]

Here the papal magisterium offers us a new term to clarify the traditional terminology. In transubstantiation, we are told, there is a change of "ontological reality." How are we to understand this expression? Although it is new in ecclesiastical documents, it was already familiar from recent theological discussion. In particular, it had been used repeatedly as a key term in the writings of Msgr. Carlo Colombo, now a bishop and known to be a special theological consultor to Pope Paul VI.[5]

And here I must apologize for introducing three technical distinctions for the sake of clarifying the term in question. First, the order of ontological reality is contradistinguished from the merely ideal, intentional, or moral order. What has real concrete existence is ontological; what is merely a designation or mental construct, a new purpose or moral dignity attributed to a thing solely by an act of will, is not ontologically existent.

Secondly, ontological reality is either spiritual (for instance, an angelic spirit, the human soul, or the grace-participation of divine life), or else it is corporeal, belonging to the created order of material things. Certainly bread and wine belong to the order of corporeal ontological reality; and so does Christ's physical body, although now in a higher and glorified state. One must remark in passing that no explanation of the Real Presence that relies on the special "spiritualized" quality of our Lord's risen body can be adequate; for it fails to take account of the reality of the presence in its institution at the Last Supper, when his body was not yet risen. Pope Paul accordingly warns against the error underlying some of the recent speculations, which would explain the Eucharistic presence in terms of a supposed "pneumatic" and therefore ubiquitous body of the glorified Christ. *"Ave verum corpus natum de Maria Virgine."*

And our third distinction is this: Within the order of corporeal ontological reality we must distinguish between the empirical level of phenomena, and the metempirical level of ultimate substance, which we can conceive but cannot imagine. We are led to affirm the existence of this metempirical reality not only by the common reflection of mankind and all sane philosophy, which acknowledges that the flux of empirical phenomena cannot be identical with the abiding reality of things, but also theologically, inasmuch as this is necessarily implied in the Eucharistic doctrine of the Church and the further explanations of the magisterium. It is at this level of metempirical ontological reality, yet still within the corporeal order, that we must place the ontological change that occurs in the Eucharistic consecration.

People who scoff at the concept of metempirical substance (which they usually imagine in a crudely Lockeian sense) forget that even this material world confronts us with an ultimate mystery, which is the secret of the Creator. As mere human reason cannot comprehend how God creates and conserves this world in being, by what right can it conclude that it is impossible for God, in accordance with his own high purposes, to refashion and transmute the very constitutive being of his material creatures, in an order beyond the scrutiny of man? What Cardinal Newman wrote of transubstantiation in his *Apologia* is still relevant today:

It is difficult, impossible to imagine, I grant;—but how is it difficult to believe? . . . I cannot indeed prove it, I cannot tell *how* it is! but I say, "Why should it not be? What's to hinder it? What do I know of substance or matter? Just as much as the greatest philosophers, and that is nothing at all." . . . The Catholic doctrine leaves phenomena alone. It does not say that the phenomena go; on the contrary it says that they remain. . . . It deals with what no one on earth knows anything about, the material substances themselves. (Chap. 5)

Among Scholastic authors there is a besetting temptation to confuse the theological concept of substance with their own cosmological theory. I suggest that confusion chiefly arises because they do not sufficiently distinguish two quite separate questions: First, "*Is* there ultimate substantial reality, not identical with the empirical phenomena of this world?" And second: "What are our philosophical criteria for discerning substantial unities in the realm of an inorganic matter?" Only the answer to the first question matters theologically, and that must be affirmative. To the second question one may freely give different answers, or, better, say "*transeat.*"

Bread and wine are not homogeneous entities for the chemist, true; but neither are they mere names or a mere relation to man. They have an objective and recognizable consistency. Theologically, there is no need to speak of the microcosmic phenomena detected by scientific experiment (although of course the same metempirical substance truly underlies them). It is sufficient that under the macrocosmic phenomena, this portion of bread or this measure of wine is designated and contained what the Church calls substance.

THE DECISIVE ISSUE

What then is the decisive issue that emerges from the recent controversy? It is that transubstantiation is not an event in the purely spiritual, or ideal, or moral order, which leaves the created nature of the terrestrial things unchanged in itself; but it is an intervention of divine power in the world of material creation in which we are incorporated, radically transmuting not only the meaning and purpose of those lowly elements but also their very constitutive being—into Christ's physical humanity. This is not "physicism," in the pejorative sense, but necessary Catholic realism. A firm faith does not shrink from this. For here is the point, I submit, at which Eucharistic realism stands or falls. No appeal, however lyrical or esoteric, to "the existential anthropology of the sign" can really succeed in blurring this issue.

We need have no quarrel with existential phenomenology if it keeps to its own professed sphere; but some supporters of the new Eucharistic opinions have tacitly exalted it into a metaphysic of ultimate reality. Judged as such, it is found wanting. New sign-function is not of itself new being. True, even in Thomist metaphysics, *ens et verum convertuntur*—that is, the ontological truth or intelligible significance of a thing is rooted in and coincides with its natural constitutive being; and if the natural being is changed, the ontological significance is necessarily changed, and vice versa. But if a further significance, even supernatural, accrues to a thing while leaving it unchanged in its natural constitutive being, that cannot suppress the original ontological significance, since this is identical with the natural being. In the last analysis, the new theory of transignification is found to be a misnomer: it is really one of *con*signification.

In the water of Baptism, indeed, or the chrism of Confirmation, there is a new supernatural significance of Christ's salutary action, superimposed on the natural significance of those unchanged substances. They remain water and oil. To say of bread, although unchanged in its natural being, that what was there before remains no longer, but has now been changed into a wholly different reality because of the higher significance that has accrued to it in the Lord's Supper—that is mere nominalism.

Nor will the appeal of Leenhardt's disciples to "the Hebrew mentality" or to "biblical categories" serve here. The Hebrew mind well knew how to think realistically as well as symbolically. The People of Israel looked to Yahweh not only to signify new finalities to their faith, but to intervene even in the physical world by his all-powerful word to *do* things in their favor. In the Scriptures the divine word sometimes endows things with a new sacred dignity and function while leaving them unchanged in themselves—for example, the loaves of proposition; sometimes it physically changes, multiplies, or destroys them. At Cana Christ used a material reality to signify his power and interpersonal concern; but he did so by changing that water into wine—an analogy the Fathers use to illustrate the realism of the Eucharistic transmutation.[6]

"Transubstantiation," it was said long ago and echoed recently, "overthroweth the nature of a sacrament." *Sacramentum est in genere signi*—yes; but sacramental signification has different modes. The consecrated species are the causal sign of Christ's corporal presence, not just in the same sense that they are the causal sign of spiritual nourishment, or of the Eucharistic sacrifice, but because they designate and render present his physical reality, invisibly but most really contained beneath them.

Here and there one hears it murmured that the Encyclical *Mysterium fidei* has not affected the theological state of this question, that it was merely an expedient warning against unguarded language and possible practical excesses. No, it was an authoritative answer to a theological doubt—an answer that theologians who do not teach in their own name or on the authority of their own insights will loyally accept. Paul VI expressly and unambiguously intervened in the specific context of this recent controversy to pass judgment on a trend of opinion that seemed to some to be opening a possible new line of theological development.

Certainly, the Eucharistic mystery is open to ever deeper meditation and exploration, and this the Pope encourages; but one particular approach, the way of mere transignification and transfinalization as recently proposed, he has shown to be a false scent. No true doctrinal development is possible by that way. The truly progressive spirit that seeks the genuine renewal of Catholic theology is very different from that which embraces any novelty because it seems to be "the new line." To attempt to pursue those discredited Eucharistic theories for ecumenical reasons would be an example of that compromising false eirenism which the Council has described as wholly alien to true ecumenism.

In the present-day enthusiasm for restoring to favor truths and values that have been unduly neglected in the past, it is easy to fall into imbalance on the other side. It is excellent to bring out the dynamic, communal, liturgical, and personalist values of the Eucharistic meal-fellowship—but not at the expense of other equally vital aspects of the sacramental mystery. In the past there was a one-sided emphasis on the reserved Sacrament to the neglect of liturgical life and its fulfillment in Holy Communion; but today, in reaction, there is too often a one-sided prejudice against what is called the "static" theology and cult of the Real Presence. The time has come when it seems necessary to restore the doctrinal balance by stressing once more, and in a new light, the values of the permanent presence of Christ in the sacrament. The Holy Father gives many pointers in this direction in his encyclical; and here, I think, lies a most fruitful field for deeper theological penetration in the coming years.

WHY THE PERMANENT PRESENCE?

I will conclude, then, by recalling briefly some of the sovereign values of the permanent Real Presence of our Lord in the Eucharist.

First, and above all, it has a supreme excellence in itself, which is simply identical with that of the Incarnate Word. This presence is most really the perpetuation of the Incarnation in this world in which we live. "The Word was made flesh, and dwelt amongst us" (Jn 1:14). The whole incarnational theme of St. John's Gospel is resumed in the Eucharistic mystery. In this flesh the light of divine glory shines in this world; in it God is objectively manifest. And just as the Incarnation itself was indeed ordained "for us men and for our salvation," but nevertheless the manifestation of divine glory in the God-Man was prior to and independent of those salvific consequences, so the same must be said of the perpetuation of the mystery of Christ in the Eucharist. His Real Presence there is indeed ordained to salutary consequences, to the Eucharistic sacrifice and to Holy Communion, but still has its prior and absolute divine excellence.

This truth, of course, must be held in balance with others. On the one hand we give praise for the excellence of the Holy Eucharist in itself, on the other we give thanks for its benefit to us. If one asks what is foremost in dignity and sanctity in the Eucharist, evidently Christ's presence far excels the benefit we receive by participating. But if one asks what was foremost in Christ's *purpose* in instituting the Eucharist, the answer is that it was to perpetuate sacramentally for all generations his saving sacrifice, and at the same time to unify his Church by the memorial banquet by which he gives himself as our food unto ever-lasting life. Although his real substantial presence does not depend for its excellence on those salutary purposes, it is in fact essential to both.

Moreover, the cult of the reserved Sacrament, which was implicit in Christ's intention when instituting the rite, does not detract from or overshadow those so-called "dynamic" values of sacrifice and commun-ion, but rather manifests and complements them. Since the permanent presence of our Lord in the Eucharist is one aspect of a total, undivided mystery, it necessarily links us both with the sacramental sacrifice and with the sacramental repast.

Every host reserved in the tabernacle or displayed in the monstrance is an oblation remaining from the altar of sacrifice. It was consecrated in that great action of the Mass, by which the one sacrifice of Christ is daily celebrated by Christ's priests and the work of our redemption rendered ever active.[7] Devotion to the divine victim in the reserved Sacrament prolongs, as it were, our sharing in the great liturgical action of the altar, and brings the spirit of the Eucharistic offering into all the hours of the day. So too, every reserved host is destined to be received in Holy Communion. The Eucharist in the tabernacle is a permanent invitation to the sacred meal and table-fellowship. Under the visible form of food, our Savior there invites us unceasingly to renew our sacramental and spiritual communion with himself and our community in his Mystical Body.

"From the fact that this most holy sacrament was instituted by Christ our Lord to be received by us," the Council of Trent teaches,[8] "it is not on that account any the less to be adored. For we believe that same God to be therein present, of whom the eternal Father, bringing him into this world, said: 'Let all the angels of God adore him.'" This presence of Emmanuel, God-with-us, fulfilling the long prophetic yearning of the People of Israel, is given to us as the permanent center of our adoration, love, devotion, and consolation; and not for the sake of individuals alone, but for the sake also of the whole community, as Paul VI further explains.[9]

In a manner it even hallows and protects the places and circumstances of our daily lives, as once the hidden corporal presence of Christ brought a blessing to the household of Zachary (Lk 1:40–56). In the cult of the reserved Sacrament, not indeed practiced in the earliest centuries, but later developed by the Holy Spirit through the life of the Catholic Church, these rich treasures latent in the divine gift have been brought into the light. And in some recent instances we have seen only too well the sad blight that can wither Catholic devotion when this sacred center of our religion is touched.

Another absolute value to be pondered is this: The real objective presence of Christ is a permanent sacramental sign, mysteriously operative even outside the times of liturgical celebration and communion, of the permanent unity of his Mystical Body.

Further, the confession of the truth of this Real Presence and of the real substantial change is the most insistent test and exercise of our faith; it is a constant, intransigent call to the all-important humility of faith, confronting all, priests and laity, in their daily lives. From the beginning, Christ made acceptance of this hard saying the decisive test of those who would follow him (Jn 6:60–69). If the intervention of divine power in our material world by the Eucharistic transmutation of substance scandalizes the preconceptions of human reason, so does that other astounding irruption of the divine into this physical world, which we call the Incarnation. The two mysteries of faith are closely linked. The real presence of Christ in the flesh under the sacramental veil draws its meaning from that primary sacrament of the Incarnation, God really present in human flesh.

And finally, the mystery of transubstantiation, by which lowly creatures of this material world are already transformed into Christ's glorious humanity, the noblest of all created realities, is an inkling and a pledge of that other, eschatological transformation of all things, several times foretold in the New Testament, for which "the whole creation waits with eager longing" (Rom 8: 19, 22), when there will be "a new heaven and a new earth" (Apoc 21:1; 2 Pet 3:13).

There, then, are some of the truths and absolute values of the Real Presence which should correct the one-sided emphasis of some recent speculations. These and other neglected truths must be restored to the doctrinal and devotional balance, if the renewal of Eucharistic and liturgical life in the Church, in the postconciliar era to which we are all committed, is to come to its hoped-for fulfillment.

NOTES

Francis Clark, S.J., is professor of dogmatic theology at both the Gregorian University in Rome and the recently constituted Pontifical Athenaeum of Heythrop, England, and author of the definitive *Eucharistic Sacrifice and the Reformation* (1960; reprinted in 1967). The present essay reproduces a public lecture given in Rome on December 1, 1965, under the presidency of Cardinal Heenan and before an audience of Council Fathers and others. It was published originally in *Emmanuel* in 1966.

1. "If anyone shall say that in the most holy sacrament of the Eucharist the substance of bread and wine remains together with the body and blood of our Lord Jesus Christ, and shall deny that wonderful and singular conversion of the whole substance of bread into body, and of the whole substance of wine into blood (the species of bread and wine alone remaining), a conversion that the Catholic Church most aptly calls transubstantiation, let him be anathema" (Canon 2 *de SS. Eucharistiae sacramento,* Denzinger-Schönmetzer 1652).

2. A fuller account of the whole controversy, with bibliographical particulars, is given by the author in his lecture course, *Adiumenta ad tractatum de*

SS. Eucharistiae sacramento (Rome, Gregorian University, 1966), pp. 108–184.

3. See *Adiumenta,* pp. 75–78.

4. AAS 57 (1965), p. 766. It seems opportune here to correct once again an extraordinary mis-statement which has been widely repeated both in America and in Europe. It has been asserted even in printed articles that no official Latin text of *Mysterium fidei* has yet been promulgated in the *Acta Apostolicae Sedis,* and that this delay presages possibly notable modifications to be made to the document. The fact is that the official Latin text was published in AAS at the earliest feasible date, in the issue of October 30, 1965, pp. 753–74.

5. Here, for example, is a typical passage, in which Colombo's words will be seen to be closely parallel to those I have just cited from the Encyclical: "Non è assolutamente possibile intendere la transustanziazione come un *puro* cambiamento di significato o valore religioso. La transustanziazione, secondo la dottrina cattolica, è anzitutto *una mutazione totale di realtá ontologica d'ordine corporeo* [a total change of ontological reality in the corporeal order]; che comporta poi senza dubbio, come sua conseguenza e suo scopo, una mutazione di significato e di valore religioso . . ." (*La Scuola Cattolica* 83 [1955] p. 93).

6. E.g., St. Cyril of Jerusalem's *Mystagogical Catecheses,* 4:7.

7. "Quoties sacrificium crucis, quo Pascha nostrum immolatus est Christus (I Cor 5:7), in altari celebratur, opus nostrae redemptionis exercetur" (Vatican II, *Constitution on the Church,* § 3). This truth, still a central issue in ecumenical dialogue today, is the main theme of the author's book, *Eucharistic Sacrifice and the Reformation.*

8. Denz.-Schön. 1643.

9. *Mysterium fidei,* AAS 57 (1965), pp. 771–72.

5 Transubstantiation
in Other Terms

The Eucharistic mystery is the heart of the Church, and, as Pope Leo XIII has said, "in it alone are contained, in a remarkable richness and variety of miracles, all supernatural realities" (*Mirae caritatis,* 1902). Precisely for this reason it is the mystery of faith par excellence, and as a consequence the great doctors of Scholasticism affirmed that, in Bonaventure's words, of all the mysteries it is "the most difficult to believe" (IV *Sent.,* d. IV, q.1, a.2). There should be no surprise, therefore, at the temptation that rationalism periodically brings forward to make it comprehensible, or at least less difficult for human reason. As a matter of fact, all Eucharistic heresies have pursued the same goal, from Berengarius of Tours (†1080) to Luther (†1546) and the Protestants. . . .

TRANSIGNIFICATION

As Father Clark has recounted above, in the climate of opinion known as the "new theology," which came into being for the purpose of adapting Catholic theology to contemporary thought and conscience, the doctrine of the Real Presence and of transubstantiation has been subjected once again to discussion. In *Humani generis* (1950) Pope Pius XII called attention to these points when he wrote that "there are not a few people who maintain that the doctrine of transubstantiation is founded upon an ancient notion of substance, and that in consequence it must be corrected in such a way that the Real Presence of Christ be reduced to a certain symbolism, inasmuch as the consecrated species are no more than efficacious signs of the spiritual presence of Christ and of his intimate union with the faithful, members of the Mystical Body."

Indeed some theologians have taught that transubstantiation must be interpreted as a profound mutation of the religious meaning of the bread and wine. For, they say, the bread and wine, like all other natural realities, possess, in addition to a scientific meaning and being, a religious meaning and being that is their authentic reality. But when, as a result of the offering of Christ, the bread and wine have become the efficacious sign of the sacrifice of Christ and of his spiritual presence, their religious being is transformed and through the creative will of God they acquire another religious being. Thus, they undergo the most profound of mutations; for even while retaining their scientific meaning and being, the order of being that constitutes their authentic reality has been changed.

There are a few who specifically reduce transubstantiation to this mutation of signification; and transubstantiation thus becomes a mutation of the religious meaning of the bread and wine, while their physical reality continues to subsist. But such a mutation can be understood in only a symbolic sense. In fact the religious signification, in as much as it is distinct from the physical order and even though it is said to constitute what is deepest in the reality of a thing, can exist only in the order of knowledge and in the logical order. Indeed, it is precisely in the order of knowledge that the signification of a thing exists; and this signification does not constitute, in an objective and transcendental conception of being, the very reality of the thing outside the subject. Hence, according to this opinion, the mutation of the bread and wine into the Eucharist belongs to the order of knowledge. In other words it is a symbolic conversion. As a result, even the presence of Christ in the Eucharist becomes symbolic.

The concept of *transignification* has recently been revived for pastoral reasons, in order to explain the Eucharistic conversion or transubstantiation in a manner better adapted to the modern mentality, which tends to be personalistic. . . . Such new opinions certainly claim to accept the dogma of the Real Presence of Christ in the Eucharist. They merely discuss the way by which Christ becomes present.

Thus, in the personalist theology of the present time, a distinction is made between the physico-chemical reality and the anthropological reality of the bread and wine. By reason of the fact that an object has meaning for man, it also takes on a signification that is the human reality of the object. As a result, the physico-chemical reality of the bread and wine acquires its signification and its human reality through the meaning given it by man.

In the Mass, according to this opinion, the physico-chemical reality of the bread and wine is not abolished and transformed, but their signification changes because the bread and wine have been chosen by Christ as the signs of the most profound gift of himself. For personalist theology the meaning and signification that an object has for man possess full reality, and it is precisely this reality that changes in the Eucharistic conversion. That is why this conversion is called "transignification" or "transfinalization." The term "transubstantiation," on the contrary, is unpopular because it calls to mind the concept of substance considered to be a medieval notion that prevents the proper understanding of Eucharistic conversion.

In order to understand correctly what is meant by the notion of transignification, it is important to know what is signified by the anthropological reality of the bread and wine—that is to say, what is the meaning and signification that bread and wine have for man. And in fact, a full reality is attributed to this anthropological reality, to this meaning and signification for man.

The discussion does not center upon the reality of the presence of Christ in the Eucharist that everyone claims to admit, but upon the way of conceiving the substance of the bread and wine, and, in consequence, the way by which Christ becomes present in the Sacrament.

First and above all, we must clarify what the Council of Trent teaches when it affirms that transubstantiation is the conversion of the entire substance of the bread into the body and of the entire substance of the wine into the blood of Christ, even though the species remain in existence.

We should note, therefore, that the conception of substance in the Tridentine definition must be understood not in Aristotle's philosophical sense, but as the natural and common-sense signification of the reality of the bread and wine as objective and concrete reality. Various philosophies may determine how they will understand this substance; but faith and dogma abstract from philosophical systems and refer to the natural and common-sense notion of the objective reality of the bread and wine indicated in the Tridentine dogma by the name of substance.

The encyclical *Mysterium fidei* affirms that dogmatic formulas

express concepts that are not tied to a certain form of human culture, or to a specific phase of scientific progress, or to one or another theological school. No, these formulas present that part of reality which necessary and universal experience permits the human mind to grasp and to manifest with apt and exact terms taken either from common or polished language. For this reason, these formulas are adapted to men of all times and all places. It must be admitted that these formulas can sometimes be more clearly and accurately explained. In fact, the achievement of this goal is highly beneficial. But it would be wrong to give these expressions a meaning other than the original. Thus, the understanding of the faith should be advanced without threat to its unchangeable truth.

Hence, according to the definition of the Council of Trent, it is the ontological and objective, concrete reality of the bread and of the wine that is transformed into the body and blood of Christ. The accidents or species remain, however, and become a sign in which the Lord gives himself so that he may be eaten by us.

After these considerations we can understand how these new opinions can "disturb the faithful and fill their minds with no little confusion about matters of faith," as *Mysterium fidei* declares.

What, indeed, is the ontological and objective reality that the Council of Trent calls by the name of "substance" and that is changed into the body and blood of Christ? It is said that the physico-chemical reality of the bread and wine is not destroyed and transformed, but that it becomes the sign by which Christ gives himself to be eaten. This fact of becoming the sign of the gift of Christ is said to be the veritable Eucharistic conversion. Hence it is a conversion of the signification of a reality that continues to exist in its physical sense. This signification of the physical thing for man possesses full reality; whence the full reality of the Eucharistic conversion.

In order to be in agreement with the Council of Trent, this change of signification must be a change in the reality which is substance, the objective reality of the bread and wine. Now, it is hard to see how the substance of the bread and wine indicated by the Council of Trent can be the very meaning or human signification of the bread and wine, about which the new opinions speak. The anthropological signification or reality of the bread and wine are understood immediately as a sign, a symbol, as profound a symbol as one may wish, but still a symbol, a sign; hence, in the order of knowledge; a symbol known by the human person, of total interest to this person, but superimposed upon the objective and concrete reality of the thing. Hence, if in the Eucharistic conversion only the sign or signification for man of the bread and wine changes, we have a mutation that is merely symbolic. In consequence, the presence of Christ in the Eucharist remains merely symbolic.

In other words, personalist theology claims that in the Eucharist the physico-chemical reality of the bread and wine remains, whereas the meaning and signification of the bread and wine change, so that we no longer have ordinary bread and wine. If this opinion is to be true, it must agree with the formula of the Council of Trent affirming that the substance of the bread and of the wine is changed into the body and blood of Christ. Therefore, this substance of bread and wine of which the Council of Trent speaks, when interpreted by the personalist theology, must agree with the meaning and signification of bread and wine. This identification, however, is very difficult to make, for the signification that a thing has for man, profound as it may be, cannot coincide with the objective, ontological, and concrete reality of the thing itself.

TRANSFINALIZATION

Following the same line of thought as the considerations on the change in the meaning and signification of the Eucharistic bread and wine, another conception has been affirmed which is similar to the preceding one and closely related to it.

All created reality, according to this argument, has its own specific end, which God himself—the Creator and watchful guardian of all things—has assigned to it. It is an end, therefore, that depends essentially upon God and reaches to the very root of reality. Now, in the liturgical action of the Mass, the oblations offered to God undergo a mutation of such a nature that their final end is changed. This means that they undergo a *transfinalization*. They acquire a new religious end, i.e., the end of making Christ present and of realizing an offering to God as an act of religious worship. The claim is made that it is precisely in this mutation of the end that transubstantiation consists. Hence, although the bread and wine retain their physical reality, nevertheless their religious meaning and their finality change. It is in this sense that Christ is said to become present by means of a transfinalization.

It is easy to understand that transfinalization itself, understood in the sense proposed here, and with reference to what we have already said about transignification, amounts to denying the "true, real, and substantial" presence of the body and blood of Christ in the Eucharist, by substituting a merely symbolic presence.

It was precisely because of these new opinions, which can lead to the errors of Berengarius of Tours and Protestantism, that Paul VI, in the encyclical *Mysterium fidei* (1965), affirmed once again the dogma of the Real Presence and of transubstantiation:

It is not allowable . . . [he stated] to exaggerate the element of sacramental sign as if the symbolism, which all certainly admit in the Eucharist, expresses fully and exhausts completely the mode of Christ's presence in this Sacrament. Nor is it allowable to discuss the mystery of transubstantiation without mentioning what the Council of Trent stated about the marvelous conversion of the whole substance of the bread into the Body and of the whole substance of the wine into the Blood of Christ, speaking rather only of what is called "transignification" and "transfinalization."

Moreover, the encyclical points out that the Catholic Church rightly calls the Eucharistic conversion "transubstantiation" (see Council of Trent, "Decree on the Eucharist," Chap. 4, can. 2). And the Church warns that if the integrity of faith is to be preserved it is necessary to use very exact terms, for the use of inaccurate words might suggest false opinions concerning faith in the sublimest mysteries—which God forbid. And the encyclical adds that it is intolerable that any private individual should, on his own initiative, attack the formulas used by the Council of Trent in presenting the Eucharistic mystery to the faithful.

TRANSUBSTANTIATION

It is clear, therefore, that these orientations can lead to the error of claiming a merely symbolic presence of Christ in the Sacrament. But as the encyclical itself points out, transignification and transfinalization can be understood in a sense acceptable to the Catholic Faith, that is to say, as simultaneous with transubstantiation and in conjunction with it, in the sense defined by tradition and clearly set forth by the Council of Trent.

The conversion of the substance of the bread and wine into the body and blood of Christ, taught by the dogma, likewise implies a transignification and a transfinalization of the bread and wine. In fact, the end and the fundamental signification of a reality are imbedded in its deepest metaphysical entity, and therefore the change in substance that comes about in transubstantiation likewise involves change in the ontological signification of the bread and wine, and change in their ontological finality.

Conversely, the transfinalization and transignification of the bread and wine can be understood as being produced by divine omnipotence in the very roots of their being. In this sense, transignification and transfinalization reach to the very root of the ontological and objective reality of the bread and wine—i.e., to the very substance of which the Council of Trent speaks. But then, transignification and transfinalization are seen to coincide with transubstantiation. And thus transubstantiation expresses the total conversion of the substance, understood in its reality. Transignification expresses the total conversion of the same substance in its ontological signification. Transfinalization likewise expresses the conversion of the same substance, understood in its ontological and essential finality.

In this sense the encyclical *Mysterium fidei* teaches that once the transubstantiation has been accomplished the species of the bread and wine undoubtedly acquire a new signification and a new end, since what exists is no longer ordinary bread and ordinary wine, but the sign of a sacred thing and the sign of a spiritual food. But they have this new signification and finality from the fact that they possess a new reality, one that we rightly call ontological.

NOTE

Monsignor Roberto Masi, professor of theology at the Lateran University in Rome, has published several monographs on the Eucharist. The present article, a condensation of these writings, appeared first in *Osservatore Romano* on November 12, 1965.

Jean Galot S.J.

6 Eucharistic Presence and the Christian Vision

It can be verified that recently there has been a certain loss of affection in regard to Eucharistic adoration.[1] In the doctrinal order two points seem to have contributed to this. First, the insistence placed on the liturgical and sacramental action, on the sacrifice of the Mass, has aroused in some a reaction against contemplating the consecrated host outside the time of the sacrifice. It often happens that in order to show the value of one aspect of the Eucharist, its other aspects are rejected to the shadows. The sacrament of the Eucharist is so rich that the very admiration experienced for one aspect of its mystery occasions the temptation to neglect a part of its richness and thereby to impoverish it.

The second reason leading to this elimination of Eucharistic adoration is the fact that the development of this worship came late. In the ancient Church the Eucharist was publicly adored but only during the time of the Mass and of Communion; and the Greek Church is still at this cultural level. In the West the desire to honor the Real Presence made itself felt in the Middle Ages by a new rite in the Mass: the elevation of the consecrated host at the moment of Consecration, a practice introduced in the twelfth century. Afterward in the thirteenth century the adoration of the host outside of Mass developed especially by the practice of processions of the Blessed Sacrament. The institution of the feast of Corpus Christi,[2] the Office for which was composed by St. Thomas,[3] was a sign that manifested this development. During the

86

fourteenth century there was begun the custom of exposition with the monstrance. At the time of the Renaissance the tabernacle was erected on the main altar. Private visits to the Blessed Sacrament were promoted everywhere in the eighteenth century by St. Alphonsus Liguori.

Those whose ideal is a return to the usages of the primitive Church and who refuse to admit an authentic progress in cult during the course of the later centuries would evidently be unfavorable to the development of Eucharistic adoration. They could even invoke the silence of Scripture on this point, observing that at the moment of the institution of the sacrament Christ told his disciples not to adore, but to eat his flesh and drink his blood.

Nevertheless, the development of Eucharistic adoration is not without its doctrinal guarantees. There has already been mention of St. Thomas with regard to the Office of the Blessed Sacrament. Is not the intervention of the greatest medieval theologian, who certainly could not be accused of an unenlightened piety, significant and does it not indicate an accord between the impulse to Eucharistic adoration and the profound doctrine of the Sacrament? Of even greater importance is the statement of the Council of Trent approving the public cult of adoration due to Christ present in the Eucharist. It also approved the special feast in its honor as well as processions and expositions of the Blessed Sacrament.[4] There is in this an infallible assurance of the conformity of this cult with the most authentic doctrine of the Church and with the most praiseworthy piety.

A fact of the present-day Church stands in sharp contrast to those who incline to think that this form of worship is to be relegated to the past. Religious congregations vowed to the perpetual adoration of the Eucharist continue to attract vocations; and new institutes now having a great influence (for example, those inspired by the spirituality of Charles de Foucauld) give a notable place in their life of prayer to the contemplation of the Eucharistic Christ.

Does not this constitute an invitation to attempt a better understanding of this cult, to seek its foundation in the intention of Christ himself, and to situate it more exactly in the total theology of the Eucharist?

AFFIRMATION OF THE REAL PRESENCE

What was the intention of Christ in the institution of the Sacrament? The fact that he did not expressly invite his disciples to adore the consecrated bread and wine does not imply that all Eucharistic adoration was outside his thought and his will. To determine the exact intention of the Master at this important moment, it is necessary to scrutinize his words.

Now the words of Jesus imply a will to give his presence to his disciples through the Eucharist, a presence destined for the sacramental repast but also of itself exceeding the exigencies and the limits of this repast. The Eucharistic presence is certainly established with reference to Communion, but this finality does not absorb it completely nor give it its total justification.

It could be conceived that the Eucharistic presence would be given only in the repast, in the actual act of eating; Christ would then be present under the appearances of bread only when it was being eaten. As is well known, it is in this sense that Lutherans have interpreted the words of institution.[5] For them the Eucharistic presence is measured by the use made of it in the sacramental repast. Hence, while they admit this presence, Lutherans condemn the cult of adoration given to the Eucharist, particularly in the tabernacle and in processions; for it is precisely such a cult that assumes the presence to be over and beyond the limits of the repast.

Nevertheless, the narration of the Institution is not of itself oriented toward the Lutheran interpretation. It does not limit the presence of the body and the blood of Christ merely to the requirements of the Communion repast.

This presence is put in relation to the sacrifice. In the consecration of the wine Jesus affirmed: "This is my blood of the new covenant, which is being shed for the multitude" (Mk 14:24). So also in the consecration of the bread he alluded to the sacrifice according to the fuller formula of Luke: "This is my body, which is being given for you." [6] This is an indication that the body and the blood pertain to a sacrifice before being given in a repast. Doubtless, Jesus is thinking of the sacrifice of Calvary, but he anticipates its realization in a mysterious, sacramental way; he makes his body and his blood present in their sacrificial state.[7]

In this body and this blood it is the presence of the immolation of the cross that he wished to give to his disciples. The same idea is to be found in the declaration stated by St. John: "The bread which I will give is my flesh for the life of the world" (Jn 6:51). The flesh of Christ will be given as nourishment insofar as it will be the object of an offering destined to profit all men. Consequently, the body and the blood must first be present in an immolation in order that afterward they might be given for eating and drinking. The presence is required for the sacrifice before being demanded by the sacramental repast.

It should be observed that in the sacrifice the presence of the body and blood has a universal effect: "for the multitude," "for the life of the world."[8] This effect is not limited to those who participate in the repast; it extends to all men. Thus it is that the sacrifice of the Mass possesses an efficaciousness for the entirety of mankind over and beyond the circle of those who communicate at it.

Moreover, in the way in which Christ expresses himself there can be perceived a sign that the presence of his body and his blood, while implicated in a sacrifice and destined for a repast, is not merely functional but has an absolute value. According to the version of St. Matthew, Jesus says: "Take and eat: this is my body."[9] He does not say: "Take and eat my body"—words that would have been suitable for the institution of the Eucharistic repast. From the words "Take and eat" He detaches the affirmation: "This is my body," thereby giving to it a more independent value. The reality of the presence of his body is affirmed in itself.[10]

This absolute value of the affirmation appears even more clearly in the versions of Paul and of Luke, where the invitation to eat is not even expressed and where the formula begins by simply saying: "This is my body. . . ." In the consecration of the wine there is no invitation to drink except in the text of Matthew; according to Mark 14:24, Jesus says: "This is my blood . . ."; and according to Paul (1 Cor 11:25) and

Luke 22:20 he says: "This chalice is the new covenant in my blood."
The first intention of Christ, then, is to throw light on the presence of
his body and of his blood, to draw the attention of the disciples to it. It
is not the repast that gives its meaning to this presence; it is rather this
presence that gives its sense to the repast.

Thenceforth, in order to participate in the sacramental repast the
disciples should first acknowledge this presence. St. Paul recalls to the
Corinthians this necessity of "recognizing the body of the Lord" to
avoid making an unworthy Communion (1 Cor 11:29). In order that
Communion may produce its sanctifying effect, it must be supported
on this discernment and acknowledgment of the Real Presence. Moreover, this presence dominates the repast, for it does not cease by the fact
that a Communion is unworthy. In such a case it persists to judge and
condemn the one whose dispositions of soul do not permit him to
receive profit from the Sacrament. By reason of the presence of the
body and the blood of Christ, the unworthy eat and drink their own
condemnation. The presence, then, is not measured simply by its
sanctifying effect in Communion, even though it is destined to produce
this effect.

From a first reading of the narration of the institution, then, it can be
concluded that Jesus has expressly emphasized the presence of his body
and of his blood. This presence is affirmed in an absolute manner. It is
the first reality of the sacrament of the Eucharist, the one that gives its
value to the sacrifice and to the repast, the one that the faithful must
recognize in order that Communion can contribute to their holiness.

PERSONAL PRESENCE

In affirming the presence of his body and of his blood, Christ affirms
the presence of his person. Theology has established this truth by a
reasoning process: since in Christ body and blood are indissolubly
united to the soul and divinity, it is the entire Christ who is present in
the Eucharist. But Christ had already suggested this total presence in
the very terms he used in the institution of the Sacrament.

As pointed out in Father Dupont's chapter, in all probability He used the Aramaic word for "flesh" and said: "This is my flesh." [11] This is actually the word expressly conserved by St. John (Jn 6:56–7), although the liturgical usage of the primitive Church had adopted the word "body." If the Evangelist did not here follow the ordinary vocabulary of the liturgy it was doubtless because he wished to remain faithful to the word pronounced by Jesus.

But in Hebrew and in Aramaic the word "flesh" tends to designate the whole person. In contrast to the Greek term "body," it does not manifest any opposition to the soul or to the spirit, for "the Semites do not have the Greek dichotomized conception of the human being." [12] Thus, the Psalmist says to God: "My spirit thirsts for you; my flesh yearns for you" (Ps 63:1). This flesh that yearns for the Lord is the person who, while having a body, experiences a spiritual aspiration. It is the entirety of the individual that is denoted by its material part.

So also when Christ says, "This is my flesh," he wishes to indicate that in his corporal presence his entire personal being becomes present. The body implies the presence of the person. In the Eucharistic discourse of St. John this meaning appears through the equivalation of the two statements: "The one who eats my flesh and drinks my blood has eternal life" and "The one who eats me will live by me" (Jn 6:56–7). To eat the flesh of Christ is to eat Christ himself.

Now the presence of a person has an entirely different value from the presence of a mere material body. The presence of a material body will be respected by a person only to the extent that it is useful to him. The presence of a person, however, always wants to be appreciated for itself; and it cannot be judged merely by its usefulness. A person calls for respect and love by the fact of his presence; it would be a denial of the reality of a person to welcome him only by reason of the enrichment that he brings.

Hence to envisage the Eucharistic presence of Christ only by reason of the enrichment it brings to the world in the sacrifice of the Mass and to the faithful in the Communion repast would be to neglect, at least in a way, that which is personal in this presence; it would be to receive it more as the presence of an object and not enough as the presence of a subject. It can be welcomed as it should only if there is a recognition of the absolute value that the presence of a person possesses.

In the intention of Christ this personal note of the Eucharistic presence does not have just a secondary importance. It was in the foreground of his preoccupations, as is shown by the context of the institution of the sacrament. At the moment that Christ prepares to leave his group of faithful ones to go to the sacrifice, he institutes, when anticipating the sacrifice, a new presence. At the time of the last moments he passes with his own, he wishes to prolong forever this intimacy, to assure to his disciples a presence at once corporal and personal that will perpetuate the presence of his Incarnation.

It is this that explains the emphasis given to the promise of "remaining" in the discourse after the Last Supper: Christ wishes to remain among his own and he invites his disciples to remain in him (Jn 15:4-7, 9-10). The Eucharist, on the effects of which he is apparently commenting, should contribute to the realization of this "remaining." Thanks to it, the instant of the farewell is the beginning of a new personal presence of Christ in the midst of his community.

To comprehend the importance of the Eucharistic presence, it is necessary to place it in the circumstances of the Institution, to see it with the eyes of Christ at the Last Supper. Overcome by emotion at the thought of leaving his disciples, he wills to remain with them; and he accomplishes this by means of the Sacrament. At the instant of its institution the Sacrament shows that the presence of the Savior, at the point of his departure, is definitively achieved for the disciples.

THE DIVINE PRESENCE AND FAITH

The personal presence of Christ is necessarily a divine presence, since it is the presence of the divine Person of the Word. The Eucharist attests the divine power hidden in the presence of the body and of the blood: Jesus can give his flesh to be eaten and his blood to be drunk only because he is God.

From the viewpoint of the natural order of things, the Eucharistic presence would be incomprehensible, inadmissible. It makes sense only on the level of the supernatural, on the level of the personal relations that God has begun with men by the Incarnation. The affirmation, "This is my body," implies a domination over the being of things and has for its foundation that other affirmation of Christ, "I am."

Christ can realize the consecration of the bread and the wine only in virtue of the power he possesses over being; and he holds this power because he is the absolute being, the fullness of being, the omnipotent being.

In applying to himself at various times the name of God as it was revealed at Sinai (see Jn 8:24, 28, 58; 13:19), Jesus has identified himself not only as the absolute Being but as the absolute Presence. He is the presence definitively established in the midst of humanity. By declaring his name as that of "I am," the God of Exodus had already wished to affirm not only his absolute existence and his complete independence and sovereignty but also his active and faithful presence together with the aid he will give to Moses. The "I am" guarantees the promise "I am with you." [13]

In the same way Christ affirms the indefectible presence of his "I am" in order to guarantee to his Apostles his perpetual assistance: "I will be with you." [14] He is the presence that will never abandon men. It is as the absolute presence that He has the power to institute the Eucharistic presence; it is as the absolute presence that He has actually instituted it.

It must be emphasized that "divine presence" says much more than "divine being." It signifies that the divine being is turned toward men, comes forward to meet them, and desires to enter into communion with them. It implies a personal contact. It is, of course, absolute presence, but engaged at the same time in relations with mankind. So it is that the Eucharist attests the "I am" of Christ only to express more completely the "communing" orientation of this "I am": "Behold I am with you all days until the end of the world."

The absolute presence will survive death. By the Ascension, of which the elevation on the cross is a sign and a prefigurement, Jesus will manifest this fact: "When you will have lifted up the Son of Man, then you will recognize that I am" (Jn 8:28). The glorification of Christ, consummation of his sacrifice, will throw light on the "I am" and will extend its influence throughout the world.

To justify his promise of the Eucharist, Jesus himself invoked his being lifted up. To the disciples in their shock at this promise, he says: "Does this shock you? What then if you should see the Son of Man ascending where he was before?" (Jn 6:62). If Christ can be present in the Eucharist, this is because in the Ascension he rises up to the divine level which was always his, but to which he rises now in the human nature of the Son of Man. Henceforth, he possesses in his human nature a divine power which through the Eucharist permits him to be "spirit and life" for his disciples (Jn 6:63). If it were not a divine presence the Eucharist would lose its value.

This is why the Master so vigorously expresses the importance of faith for the acceptance of the Eucharist. The discourse in which Jesus promises the Sacrament is partly devoted to this attitude of faith, so much so that some exegetes have assigned two distinct objects to the discourse: faith and the Eucharist. Actually, however, the entire discourse concerns the Eucharist; but that which is primary in this sacrament is the divine presence that demands to be recognized by faith. One cannot be nourished by the bread come down from heaven unless he believes in the divine presence that this bread brings to mankind. The promise of the Eucharist forces the hearers to a choice for or against faith; their attitude toward the discourse separates the believers and the nonbelievers (Jn 6:64).

What does this divine presence require as soon as it is acknowledged by faith? When God manifests himself, he demands our adoration; adoration is the religious attitude that results from faith. Certainly, in the Eucharist Christ offers himself in sacrifice and gives himself as nourishment. He asks his faithful to unite themselves to his offering and to receive him lovingly within themselves. But in making himself present on the altar of sacrifice, he also demands that he be adored. The gesture of elevation which in the rite of the Roman Mass involves the faithful in this adoration responds to a fundamental intention of the Savior himself.

Without this adoration the sacrifice could not be recognized in its sublimity, and the repast of Communion could not have all its value.

The greatness of the Mass consists in the fact that it is the sacrifice of the Son of God; the humanity is there offered but in its incorporation into Christ. So it is that the sacrifice is not seen in its true meaning unless there is adoration of the Victim, of the consecrated host.

The repast of the Communion should be preceded by adoration of the Eucharistic Christ. "No one eats this flesh, if he has not first adored it," says St. Augustine. The great doctor is commenting on Psalm 99, verse 5: "Adore the footstool of his feet, for it is holy." He adds that according to Isaiah (66:7) it is the earth that is this footstool. But how can the earth be adored without idolatry? It is the Eucharist that furnishes the answer:

> In my confusion I turn to Christ, because I seek Him at this point; and I find out how earth and the footstool of His feet can be adored without impiety. For He took to Himself earth from this earth, since flesh is from the earth and He took flesh from the flesh of Mary. Because He walked about in this flesh and because He gave us this flesh to be eaten for salvation and because no one eats this flesh unless he has previously adored it, I found out how the footstool of the Lord could be adored and how not only do we not sin by adoring it but how we sin by not adoring it. (*Enarrationes in Psalmos 98, 9; PL 37:1264*)

While ordinarily, as St. Augustine declares, matter cannot be adored without idolatry, here it must be adored under pain of sin. Evidently, matter cannot merit such an honor for itself; only one who "turns toward Christ" and seeks him adores the Eucharistic flesh. In the matter adoration reaches to the person of the Lord; it is itself a personal encounter that prepares for sacramental Communion. It is not a thing that is being adored, but a Person; adoration is love recognizing this person as divine.

EUCHARISTIC PRESENCE AND SACRIFICE

The Eucharistic presence cannot be detached from the sacrifice. It is possible that the cult of this presence by certain kinds of excessive manifestations and interpretations could give the impression of a worship alien to that of the Mass, of being without relation to the sacrifice of the altar. Eucharistic adoration would then appear to veil or relegate to a secondary position the important offering of the Mass; it would appear to be in competition with the Mass. This constitutes the motive that has inspired many of the criticisms of this adoration as well as some of the movements of disaffection with regard to it.

But the true worship of the Eucharistic presence cannot be conceived except in intimate relation to the Mass.

It is significant that this presence is given in the sacrifice. Christ becomes present on the altar only in the act of offering in which by the ministry of the priest he renews the immolation of the cross. As a single and indivisible reality, the Consecration is the accomplishment of the sacrifice and the gift of the presence. By this fact alone the Eucharistic presence already appears as inseparable from the Mass.

But there is more than this. Why does this presence prolong itself in an absolute manner beyond the act of offering? It is not because by overflowing the Mass it wishes to place itself outside the offering; neither is it that after having been established by the sacrifice, it becomes a stranger to the sacrifice by prolonging itself indefinitely. It perseveres precisely as the fruit of the consummation of the sacrificial offering.

To comprehend the prolonging of the presence beyond the act of offering, it is necessary to have recourse to the epistle to the Hebrews. According to this epistle the priestly function of our High Priest is not achieved by the offering Christ made of himself on the cross. By reason of his sacrifice the Son of God entered heaven as the Jewish high priest entered the sanctuary with the blood of the victims. It is in the heavenly sanctuary that he exercises his office of priest, interceding for us with the Father (Heb 9:11-24). There is, then, an act of offering done "once for all" (Heb 9:12), an entry of Christ into the sanctuary "once for all" (Heb 9:12), but also and as a consequence an unlimited presence of Christ before the Father as Priest and Victim of a sacrifice which has taken place in the past but the fruits of which are accumulated by a perpetual intercession. The result of the sacrifice of Calvary is eternalized in heaven.

The Eucharistic sacrifice that renews the immolation of the cross implies an analogous reality. It is accomplished in an act of offering that is completely achieved at the moment of consecration. By this offering, immediately accepted by the Father, Christ comes upon the altar as the glorious Victim. Thereafter he remains, Priest and Victim before the Father, to intercede for men and to bestow on them the fruits of his sacrifice.

The Eucharistic presence, indefinitely prolonged as a result of the sacrifice of the altar, is the sacramental sign of the unlimited heavenly presence of the Savior which followed on the sacrifice of the cross and which constitutes its perpetual consummation. In the tabernacle Jesus does not sacramentally offer sacrifice as he does at Mass; but after the act of offering he remains in the state of offering, in a victimal presence that gathers divine favors for men.

So it is that the presence of the tabernacle is the issue of the Mass, a result of the liturgical action prolonging its efficaciousness. Far from being beyond the liturgy, it is its mysterious summit (as Father Roguet calls it farther on), just as the celestial presence of the risen Christ constitutes the summit of the Redemption. From the earth where he remains, our High Priest continually presents to the Father his Eucharistic sacrifice, as above in heaven he ceaselessly presents to him the sacrifice of Calvary.

Instead of challenging and competing with the Mass, the Eucharistic presence assures that the influence of the Mass is always and continuously radiated out. It invites the faithful to join themselves to Christ's state of victimhood and thereby to live out more fully the Eucharistic sacrifice. It tends to implant among Christians in a more durable way the activity of intercession by which the sacrificed Christ obtains the forgiveness of sin and the abundance of the graces of salvation and holiness.

EUCHARISTIC PRESENCE AND COMMUNION

Just as it cannot be detached from the sacrifice, so also the Eucharistic presence cannot be separated from Communion. By giving his presence under the appearances of bread and wine, Christ evidently shows his intention that it should lead to repast; and this express purpose is an essential element.

But why does this presence, destined as it is for the repast, prolong itself beyond the repast? It is necessary here to have a clear understanding of the meaning and import of the Eucharistic repast.

The repast implies a vital assimilation. Food is assimilated by the one who takes it; it is incorporated into his being, it becomes his life. By giving himself as food, Christ makes his life pass into that of the faithful in such a way that they live the divine life more profoundly.

This life communicated by Christ is a spiritual life; the Eucharist itself is, according to the expression of Christ repeated by St. John, "spirit and life" (Jn 6:63), and, according to St. Paul, "spiritual food" (1 Cor 10:3-4). The reception of the body of Christ into the body of the communicant has, then, for its purpose the effecting of a fusion of spiritual life.

In an intimate union of a spiritual nature there is an aspect that has nothing corresponding or analogous to it in a material repast: this is the matter of personal encounter. A spiritual fusion can be realized only by virtue of a communion of persons. What the Eucharistic repast seeks to promote is the complete adhesion of the person of the recipient to the person of Christ in faith and love.

It can be seen at once that such an adhesion should be prolonged as much as possible. It should not be limited to the instant when the Christian receives the host. It is expressed, certainly, by the thanksgiving, the prayer in which the person's contact with the Savior seeks to express itself. But the intimate dialogue of the thanksgiving is not sufficient; it has to be continued and renewed throughout the day.

The presence of Christ in the tabernacle is precisely the thing that will help the faithful to renew this contact. It fosters what is called "spiritual Communion"—that is, the purely spiritual renewal of sacramental Communion. The Christian who comes to the sanctuary to seek the presence of the Lord renews his adherence to this presence by his acts of faith and love, just as he has already done at the Eucharistic repast. Since the essential effect of this repast consists in a spiritual communion, it is precisely this effect that is prolonged and takes on a new actuality. By placing themselves in the presence of Christ, the faithful commune spiritually with him.

Thus it is seen how the sacramental repast demands a Eucharistic presence that does not end with the repast. In the tabernacle Christ continues to present himself to his followers as their spiritual nourishment, as an appeal for their adoration and love, as an invitation to spiritual communion. Just as he achieves the consummation of the sacrifice of the altar by presenting himself to the Father as the glorious intercessor, so he achieves what was begun by the sacramental repast and completes the effect of Communion.

The Eucharistic presence, then, permits Communion as well as the Mass to impregnate Christian existence completely.

EUCHARISTIC PRESENCE AND THE MYSTICAL BODY

But let us enlarge our perspective still more. The establishing of a more profound spiritual communion with each Christian is not the only reason Christ perpetuates his presence beyond the Eucharistic repast. He wishes as well to strengthen this communion with the entire Church as well as with individuals. His presence is destined to nourish the life of the Mystical Body in its totality.

The entire Christian community has the presence of Christ as its foundation. It is constituted only by this presence; its members are united one to the other only by the more fundamental bond that links them to the Savior: "I am the vine, you are the branches" (Jn 15:5).

When Christ called himself the vine, the stalk that sends life into the branches, he was apparently thinking of the Eucharist; for the discourse after the Last Supper appears in great part to be a commentary on the institution of the Sacrament. The image of the vine makes for a better comprehension of the entire background of the mystery hidden in the consecrated wine; and the exhortation to "remain in me as I in you" (Jn 15:4) is connected with the announcement of the Eucharist permitting the disciples to remain in Christ as he does in them.

Without doubt, it is precisely by the Eucharistic repast that Christ nourishes the life of his Church. It is the repast that establishes a reciprocal dwelling of the disciples in the Lord and of the Lord in them: "Who eats my flesh and drinks my blood remains in me and I in him" (Jn 6:65). And St. Paul attributes to Communion the effecting of the unity between Christians, the formation of a single body: "Since there is but one bread, we form but one body" (1 Cor 11:17).

Nevertheless, there is an aspect of the influence of Christ on the Mystical Body that the Communion repast cannot express as sacramental sign: the continuity of a presence that at every instant influences the Christian community and communicates to it the power of charity.

Only the perpetual Eucharistic presence in the tabernacle can translate this continuity sacramentally.

So it is that by a sacramental reality Christ manifests and incarnates his incessant presence in the Mystical Body. In the tabernacle he remains as the source of love of the community he founded. The Eucharistic presence vividly shows how Christ resides at the center wherever is found a particular community of Christians. The sacramental mode of this presence permits a multiplication of this presence in many places; this makes it more concrete, more accessible, more demonstrative of a love wishing to be in all places in order to extend the bonds of communitarian charity.

Significantly, it is the sacramental presence that gives all its value to one of the last words of Jesus, words to which we have already alluded: "Behold I am with you all days, even to the end of the world." The Eucharistic presence is not especially envisaged in these words; they rather have a more general sense of the spiritual presence of Christ in the Mystical Body. But the statement attests the importance Jesus attaches to his presence. And in the sacramental order it is the Eucharist that is the means par excellence of spreading this presence. When he instituted the Sacrament, the Savior could not have been uninterested in the presence implied in it; on the contrary, he must have wanted the fullest expansion of this presence as a sensible sign of his spiritual presence and as a stimulus to a greater intimacy with his disciples. Without this sacramental reality his presence would have been possible, but it would have been less involved in our sensible world.

WORSHIP OF THE EUCHARISTIC PRESENCE

Can one neglect the worship of the Eucharistic presence by invoking the silence of Scripture on the matter, the absence of any statement by Jesus concerning the institution of such a worship?

Let us recall first of all that the interpretation of the intention of the Master pertains to the Church. The decisive criterion is to be found in the piety of the Church, which through the light of the Holy Spirit recognizes the amplitude of the divine appeal included in the Eucharist and responds to it by worship. The Church, however, has favored or organized the veneration of the Eucharistic presence outside of Mass and Communion: conservation of the host in the tabernacle, exposition, processions, visits to the Blessed Sacrament. We saw above that the Council of Trent by its infallible authority confirmed and approved the development of this cult of adoration. Hence, such a cult appears as an authoritative prolonging of the will of Christ.

Certainly, when reading the texts of Scripture, we must admit that the institution of the Eucharist does not include a recommendation of the cult of adoration. But it should also be noted that at the Last Supper the sacrificial aspect of the Eucharist is reduced to its simplest expression. The repast is given the emphasis. The sacrifice as it was offered at that moment by Christ scarcely seems to disengage itself from the repast; it does not permit us to foresee the considerable development the liturgy of the Eucharistic sacrifice will make. Only the principle of this sacrifice is established by Christ. The same is true for the presence: the principle of the Eucharistic presence is affirmed absolutely. It pertains to the Church to recognize it and to develop such consequences as are not enunciated by Jesus himself.

It is sufficient if in the intention of Christ there was a certain though implicit foundation for the cult of adoration of the Eucharist. We have shown that such a foundation exists by the fact that the Eucharistic presence was affirmed in an absolute way, that is, as perduring after the offering and without being limited to the use of the Sacrament in Communion. Such a permanence assures a prolonging of the effect of the sacrifice and of the repast as well as a more continued influence on the Mystical Body. Hence, the faithful who desire to associate themselves more completely in their total existence with the offering of the Mass, who wish to renew the personal contact produced by Communion, and who want to rekindle their charity at the permanent source that provides the unity of the Church are invited to turn toward the presence in the tabernacle. This presence, by claiming their personal adhesion, will tend to become the center of their individual lives as it is the center of the life of the Church.

Let us remark that the cult of the Eucharistic presence has its own characteristic features, even while being a complement of Mass and Communion. In the Mass the accent is placed on the personal offering uniting us to that of Christ; in Communion the dominant aspect is that of the transformation of our lives into that of the Savior. But the sacramental presence requires above all adoration and contemplation.

This specific characteristic of the worship of the presence is what we shall now attempt to grasp more thoroughly.

TEMPLE AND TABERNACLE

The intention of giving a presence destined to be acknowledged for its own value as presence and to be the object of a particular cult is to be more surely attributed to the thought of Christ when it is remembered that the Old Testament had already attached a great value to the presence of Yahweh in the midst of his people: the presence in the Dwelling Tent that accompanied the journeyings of the Hebrews and then the presence in the Temple of Jerusalem.

In speaking of the "meeting tent," Yahweh declared: "I will live in the midst of the children of Israel and I will be their God" (Ex 29:45).

There was a chosen place where God wished to be present in a "tent" or a dwelling analogous to the tents of nomads and to the dwellings of humans. To be sure, Yahweh was present in a more general manner in the life and history of the Hebrews by the love he had for them, by the assistance he gave them, and by the marvels he brought to realization in them. But in order to come still closer to them and to adapt himself to their terrestrial existence, the omnipresent Being decided to localize his presence on earth in a special way. This localization was the beginning of the incarnation of the divine presence.

The expression, "the meeting tent," clearly indicates the purpose of this localized presence, of this habitation of God on earth. It is in this enclosure that men had their meetings with God; it is, as Yahweh told Moses, "the place fixed for my meetings with you" (Ex 30:6). In this consecrated dwelling are made the most intimate contacts between men and God. Was it not there, according to the expression of Exodus, that "Yahweh conversed with Moses face to face as a man converses with his friend" (Ex 33:11)?

So also the presence of Yahweh in the Temple of Jerusalem was the center of Jewish cult. The Israelites went to the Temple to "see the face" of God.[15] The Levite in exile sighed and dreamt of the time when he would go to the "house of God" amid cries of joy and praise of a festive crowd: "My soul thirsts for God, the living God; when shall I go and behold the face of God?" (Ps 42:3). To be far from the sanctuary and not to be able to go to it was to be deprived of God himself, of the contemplation of his visage. If the happiness of heaven is defined by the vision of God face to face, the presence of God in the Temple is an image of the presence bestowed on the elect in heaven; and the act of worship that consists in going to "see the face" of God is the prelude of eternal life.

The incarnation of the Son of God was the accomplishment of the promise establishing the presence of God in the Temple. "The Word was made flesh and lived among us" (Jn 1:14). It is well known that the word used by John for "lived" is one meaning "to live in a tent." The purpose of this was precisely to evoke the "tent" where Yahweh lived in the midst of his people. If in the ancient covenant God offered his presence in a perpetual way and in a determined place, Christ, who came to realize fully the habitation of the Lord in our world,[16] could not give his disciples a presence that was less concrete and less continuous. Since in becoming flesh the Word established his dwelling among us, the words, "This is my flesh," must be an affirmation of a mysterious dwelling of a sacramental nature in the midst of men.

When the institution of the Eucharist is analyzed, we should not abstract from the vital experience of the Jewish people of the divine presence in the Temple nor of the disciples' experience of this same presence in their contact with the Word made flesh. We immediately recognize in the Eucharistic consecration formula "This is my flesh" the prolongation of the Incarnation, a new actuation of the coming down by which the Word in making himself flesh comes to live in the tent, comes to implant his presence in the midst of our human life.

Let us observe that "to live in the tent" could indicate a temporary dwelling; one could see there the suggestion of a transitory presence rather than a permanent one of the Word.[17] But the thought of John is that the Word has come with his eternity into the mobile compass of human life; He has identified himself with our fleeting existence in order to introduce into it his own eternal life. "To live in the tent" signifies the closest presence to us, exposed to the risks of earthly life, open to suffering and death, but always in view of a definitive permanence surmounting all change. It is especially the Eucharist that permits this presence to perdure after his death and assures to all generations the presence the disciples had enjoyed during his public life. The intention of the Incarnation "to live among us" is accomplished in the Eucharist.

We find this intention in the thought of Jesus when he compares his situation to that of the Temple of Jerusalem: "Amen, I say to you, there is here one who is greater than the temple" (Matt 12:6). What the Temple offered to the Jews, Christ wishes to offer to his own, but in a greater way. This he affirms in an episode that contains a discreet allusion to the Eucharist—the episode when he justified his disciples for having gathered and eaten grain on the Sabbath day. He did this by recalling the act of David, who entered the house of God and took the loaves of proposition to eat them with his companions.[18] Type of the Messiah, David had given his followers sacred food in the Temple; Christ can give his followers a greater food, for there is in him something greater than the Temple, since he is the divine presence in person. Being the perpetual Eucharistic presence, He could dispense the Eucharistic nourishment without ceasing.

Christ also identified himself as the true Temple when he prophesied: "Destroy this Temple and in three days I shall raise it up again" (Jn 2:19). Thereby he announced his resurrection, considered here as the reconstruction of the Temple because of the Resurrection's permanent significance for worship. The risen body of Christ is destined to play the role that had been the Temple's; it is to assure a permanent divine presence at the center of the Christian cult. This divine presence of the glorious Body of Christ at the center of worship is realized by the Eucharist.

Since we have now seen the Eucharistic presence in the perspective of the Temple as the conclusion of the Incarnation, let us also note that it is likewise the issue of the Resurrection: the glorious body of Christ establishes the new Temple. The tabernacle of our churches, then, seems to respond to a fundamental intention of the Master, that of living indefinitely in his resurrected flesh among us and of thus being at the center of the Christian cult.

EUCHARISTIC ADORATION

Because it is an incarnated spiritual presence, the Eucharistic presence demands a spiritual but incarnated cult. Because it is a presence in a given place, it looks for a clinging to this place. The Dwelling of God in the Old Testament needed to receive the visit of men; the tabernacle, multiplied in the universe, invites Christians to visits that are frequent and regular. The visit to the Blessed Sacrament is a response to the visit of God. (See Father Rahner's chapter for extended discussion of this topic.—*Ed.*)

Here again it is worthwhile to put before our eyes the scriptural background. The entire destiny of the Jewish people was begun by a visit of God to Abraham; this visit, according to the story as told in Genesis, was the origin of the posterity of the patriarchs (Gn 18:1-15). Told in an anthropomorphic way, this divine visit shows the desire of God to bind himself to men in intimate relation. Like the divine presence in the "Meeting Tent," it is a beginning of the Incarnation, a step by which God puts himself on the level of men.

The journey of the people toward the Promised Land is similarly announced by Joseph at the moment of his death as the fruit of a visit of God: "I am about to die, but God will visit you and will bring you from this country into the country which he promised on oath to Abraham, Isaac, and Jacob" (Gn 50:24; see also Ex 3:16). Accordingly, the visit denotes the great intervention of God in the history of Israel, an intervention that is to be concretized in the establishment of the messianic kingdom.

At the time of the exile the Jews sighed for the visit of God, for this visit would be the signal of national restoration (Jer 29:10). This visit that was hoped for by the entire nation was also besought as an individual favor:

Remember me, O Lord, as you favor your people; visit me with your saving help that I may see the prosperity of your chosen ones, rejoice in the joy of your people, and glory with your inheritance (*Ps 106:4-5*).

Let us note that the visit is analogous to the presence but its accent is not on permanence. It is a presence offered at a determined moment in order to communicate a grace, a blessing. The visit implies the nuance of a greater activity; it is the time of a divine gift that is more intense and more efficacious.

At the beginning of the New Testament the canticle of Zechariah blesses "the Lord, the God of Israel, because he has visited and delivered his people" (Lk 1:68; see also 1:78). Later the crowd at one of the resurrections performed by Jesus will praise God in the same way: "A great prophet has arisen among us and God has visited his people" (Lk 7:16). The crowd, however, was not able to appreciate the full sense of this visit. In order to comprehend it they would have had to take into account that the "great prophet" arisen among the people was God himself making a visit.

An episode in the infancy gospel clarifies the reality signified by the word "visit" even more than do these cries of thanksgiving for the "visit." The first action of Mary after the accomplishment of the mystery of the Incarnation is a visit. This first visit of the Messiah is the inaugural sign of his visit to mankind. For in Mary who goes to see her cousin it is the Savior who is drawing near to men. He comes to fill Elizabeth with the Holy Spirit and to thrill her child. Christ is the one who is active on this visit.

Let us observe that this inaugural visit implies an effect of profound spiritual transformation. It could already be noted in the Old Testament that when Moses left his meetings with Yahweh his face was transfigured: "The children of Israel saw that the face of Moses was radiant" (Ex 34:35). In the Visitation the transformation was more intimate. Elizabeth had not only a radiant visage, but her soul was filled with a new grace, filled with light and joy.

It is necessary that the divine visit be received by a well-disposed soul. When Jesus weeps over Jerusalem, he announces the total destruction of the city, giving as the reason that "you did not know the time of your visitation" (Lk 19:44).

At the Last Supper Jesus reaches the last moment of this great visit of God to his people. At the time when this visit is drawing to a close, the institution of the Eucharist has as its objective the renewal and multiplication of it endlessly. It is to ensure a permanent presence, ceaselessly nourished by repeated comings.

The human visit should be the response to the divine visit. The visit to the Blessed Sacrament renews in a special way the dialogue with Christ present in the tabernacle. Certainly there should be in Christian life a dialogue with Christ present in the soul. But while the habitation of the Lord in the secrecy of the soul arouses one form of intimacy with him, another form of intimacy has need of the visit to the sanctuary.

It is not sufficient for the Christian to address himself to Christ as he is found within himself. After becoming aware that the Lord is closer to him than the depths of his own being, he must also regard the Lord as he is outside of himself, present himself before him, and speak to him in the way of a man who speaks to another man. The visit, which is a manifestation of friendship among men and which God has made a manifestation of love toward mankind, should also be a manifestation of the love of men toward Christ. The visit to the Blessed Sacrament helps to incarnate the relations of love.

The incarnation of the relations of love—this is the profound meaning of the visit. This, let us emphasize, is justified not merely by psychological considerations, by the stimulus it gives to prayer; neither is it motivated only by the desire not to leave Christ in the tabernacle in solitude. (See Father Robilliard's chapter, on the "prisoner of the tabernacle" motif.—*Ed.*) Certainly, it is desirable that the Christian, moved by the coming of the Son of God who willed to take the trouble of coming to him, should be acutely aware of being invited to take the trouble of going to the Lord. But the visit is founded much more fundamentally on the nature of the love relations between God and man resulting from the mystery of the redemptive Incarnation.

By reason of the Incarnation, intimacy with the Lord is linked to visible manifestations, to material signs. This is the principle of sacramentalism and of everything that is visible in the growth of the Mystical Body. The personal dialogue with God must find its source in the sacramental mystery, for it is by sensible signs that Christ meets men and communicates himself to them. However interior it may be, union with God retains an essential rapport with the visible reality of the Church and with her sacramental structure. The more this rapport is lived, the more divine intimacy can be established in the soul.

By a more intense participation in the sacramental reality of the Eucharist, the visit gives further incarnation to Christian prayer and enroots it in the mystery of the Word made flesh. It reanimates faith and places it in the most complete perspective; for the faith of the New Testament is, if we may say so, summed up in faith in the Eucharist. We have seen above that in the gospel Christ attached a decisive importance to this option of faith (Jn 6:60–70). Likewise, the visit expands charity since the bonds of love uniting the members of the

Mystical Body are sustained by the eucharistic presence of the Savior.

Hence, it is easier to understand that if in the Old Testament the visit of God is a moment rich in blessing, the Eucharistic visit is destined to favor the unfolding of grace. It favors this by anticipating in an obscure and distant way the ultimate goal of this grace. It is an opportunity given to the Christian to "see the face" of God; it is an opening toward the beatific vision. The eyes of faith contemplate for an instant in a face-to-face context the nearness of Christ that will later reveal the eternal light.

This face-to-face encounter is destined to make the visage of Christians radiant like that of Moses long ago. It enables them "with faces unveiled to reflect as in a mirror the glory of the Lord" so that they become "transformed into his very image" (2 Cor 3:18). In other words, after contemplating the Lord in his Eucharistic presence, the faithful are commissioned to carry a reflection of him to men. This reflection should be apparent in all their conduct; they are thereby stimulated to be witnesses of Christ.

The transformation brought about by the visit is not a superficial one. It reaches the depths of the soul; for, as with Elizabeth, its tendency is to bestow the fullness of the Holy Spirit. The visit can thus contribute to the metamorphosis of human life into a fully Christian life.

CONCLUSION

The worship of the Eucharistic presence is not an aberration. The Church gives us this certainty in a decisive way. Scripture, even though it is highly concise in the narration of the Institution, permits us to surmise that the intention of Christ was to establish a permanent sacramental presence at the center of the Christian cult. This desire for a presence offered to be adored is confirmed by certain declarations of the Master; and it had been prepared for in the Old Testament by the cult of the divine presence in the Temple.

In order that the Eucharistic presence be truly venerated according to its total value, it is necessary that it be done outside of Mass and

Communion as a prolongation of their mystery. It must be emphasized again that there can be no question of forms of rival pieties: Eucharistic adoration is closely linked to assistance at Mass and to frequentation of the Holy Table. The worship of Christ present in the tabernacle is the best continuation of the Mass. It can do nothing but strengthen the fervor of Communion and its thanksgiving.

It would, then, be an error to pretend to ban or restrict Eucharistic adoration on the pretext of better assuring the celebration of the sacrifice of the Mass. In the single but complex sacrament that is the Eucharist, the different aspects are intimately linked together and mutually involve each other: presence, sacrifice, repast. Without the presence of Christ the sacrifice and the repast would lose their most precious substance. Hence the worship given to the Eucharistic presence is of such a nature that it develops participation in the sacrifice and the repast.

Through the primary importance of the Eucharistic presence, the sacramental order reflects and manifests the structure of the Christian religion, which is first of all a religion of a person, a religion of the presence of the incarnate Son of God who was dead but who rose again. Adherence to Christianity is attachment to the person of Christ become glorious by the consummation of his sacrifice. Hence Christians are invited to adhere to this person in his sacramental presence. In this way they will enter more profoundly with Christ into the redemptive sacrifice and draw fruits from it more abundantly in Communion.

NOTES

Jean Galot, S.J., who teaches theology at the Collège St. Albert, Louvain, is the author of several works, most recent being *Les Religieux dans l'Église* and *Renouveau de la vie consacrée*. Of his two chapters in this volume the preceding one appeared first in *Nouvelle Revue Théologique* in 1963 (v. 85, pp. 19–39), and was translated for *Review for Religious* (with whose permission it is used here). The second, which we have retitled "Eucharistic Presence and the Christian Community," appeared in *Civiltà Cattolica* on March 20, 1965, and was published in translation in *Emmanuel*.

1. A recent (February 5, 1962) pastoral letter of the bishops of Holland urges the faithful to react against this movement of disinterest.

2. See F. Callaey, "Origine e sviluppo della festa del 'Corpus Domini,'" *Euntes Docete,* 10 (1957), pp. 3 and 33.

3. The attribution of this Office to St. Thomas was relatively late, even in the Dominican tradition, since it was made only after 1322. The tradition, however, is reliable, for in the final analysis it rests on the testimony of Tolomeo of Lucca, disciple and the confessor of the saint (C. Lambot, "L'office de la Fête-Dieu. Aperçus nouveaux sur ses origines," *Revue Bénédictine,* 54 [1942], pp. 62–6). Nevertheless, it should be noted that the office was considerably altered at the time of the reform of the Breviary by St. Pius V; moreover, in its original form it derived from another Office (see C. Lambot, "L'office," pp. 83–94). Actually a number of Offices had been previously composed, the oldest of which was made at Liège by an Augustinian of Mont Cornillon (see F. Callaey, "Origine," pp. 18 f., and C. Lambot and I. Fransen, *L'office de la Fête-Dieu primitive, textes et mélodies retrouvés* [Maredsous, 1946]).

4. DB 888. The Council anathematizes those who maintain "that Christ, the only-begotten Son of God, is not to be adored in the holy sacrament of the Eucharist with the worship of latria, including the external worship, and that the Sacrament, therefore, is not to be honored with extraordinary festive celebrations, nor solemnly carried from place to place in processions according to the praiseworthy universal rite and custom of the holy Church; or that the Sacrament is not to be publicly exposed for the people's adoration, and that those who adore it are idolators . . ."

5. Luther's own position was more nuanced. The Reformer affirmed that the Eucharistic presence was limited to the "use" of the Sacrament, and he formally excluded the Real Presence in the ciborium or in processions. But he understood the "use" in a wide sense and did not simply identify it with the moment of Communion: he distinguished between *usus* and *sumptio.* Specifically, he admitted the Real Presence from the Consecration to the Communion, even when the Communion took place several hours afterward as in the case when it was carried to a sick person (see H. Grass, *Abendmahlslehre bei Luther und Calvin* [Gütersloh, 1954], pp. 212–21). Lutherans abandoned this wide conception of the "use" and reduced the real presence to the *sumptio,* the reception of the Sacrament.

6. Lk 22:20. Paul gives a briefer but analogous formula: "This is my body which is given for you" (1 Cor 11:24).

7. The phrases "which is being shed" and "which is being given" are in the Greek present participles which by reason of an Aramaic influence can signify an immediate future and hence are related to the sacrifice of the morrow. Nevertheless, the present tense also keeps its value as designating an already actual experience of this imminent sacrifice. This is noted by H.

Schürmann, *Der Abendmahlsbericht Lukas 22:7–38* (Münster, 1955), p. 42; see also in the same sense J. Betz, *Die Eucharistie in der Zeit der griechischen Väter, II,* 1 (Freiburg, 1961), p. 42.

8. It is clear that while Paul and Luke use the expression "for you" in place of "for the multitude," this is probably due to a liturgical application, a particular adaptation, of the general formula pronounced by Christ.

9. Matt 26:26; and see also Mk 14:22: "Take."

10. This is the truth so well perceived by St. Thomas when in discussing the permanence of the Real Presence he opposed the opinion of St. Bonaventure, who subordinated this permanence to the possibility of its use in Communion. St. Thomas forcefully affirmed the permanence of the Real Presence even when the Host accidentally becomes unfit for Communion, insisting on the principle that the Presence persists as long as the "species" of bread and wine persist. Father de Montcheuil (*Mélanges théologiques* [Paris, 1946], p. 81 f.) sees in this a manifestation of the role which St. Thomas, in his theology of the Sacrament, attributes to philosophical views on the constitution of matter, while St. Bonaventure bases his thought exclusively on the religious notion of the sacramental sign. But one can well ask if St. Thomas does not rather owe his position to a greater fidelity to revealed data and specifically to Scripture which contains the absolute affirmation of the Real Presence. The Angelic Doctor appeals to the "truth of the Sacrament" and invokes a passage of St. Augustine, who in turn cites St. Paul: "Iudicium sibi manducat et bibit" (ST III, q.80, a.3).

11. One can see an exposition of this in J. Bonsirven, "Hoc est corpus meum," *Biblica,* 29 (1948), pp. 205–19. See also J. Jeremias, *Die Abendmahlsworte Jesu* (Göttingen, 1960), pp. 191–3, and J. Betz, *Die Eucharistie,* II, 1, pp. 37 and 178, and I, 1, p. 39 f.

12. J. Bonsirven, "Hoc est corpus meum," p. 207.

13. Ex 3:12, 14. In his interpretation of the "I am" Father Allard has given special emphasis to its openness to others: "to be with," "to be for" ("Note sur la formule 'Ehyeh aser 'eyeh," *Recherches de science religieuse,* 45 [1957], pp. 142 f.).

14. Matt 28:20; see my article " 'Je suis,' nom de Dieu et identité de Jésus," *Revue du clergé africain,* 14 (1959), pp. 142 f.

15. For example, Is 1:12; and see Ex 23:15–7; 34:20, 23–24; Dt 16:16; 31:11.

16. In St. John's Prologue this mission of Christ to realize the presence of God in the midst of men does not result merely from the phrase "he pitched his tent amongst us" but from the entirety of verses 14 to 18, which are related to the theophany of Sinai narrated in Exodus; and this scene of Exodus is entirely dominated by the idea of the divine presence among the

Jewish people (see M.-E. Boismard, *Le Prologue de saint Jean* [Paris, 1953], p. 169).

17. As Lagrange notes: "The nomad carries his shelter from one place to another—an image of the transitory character of human life." But he also adds: "But those who live in tents, though they seem to count less on permanence than those who live in stone houses, travel about together and have more solidarity with each other" (*Evangile selon saint Jean* Paris, 1925], p. 20).

18. In comparing the text of Mk 2:26 and Lk 6:4 with 1 Kgs 21:7, H. Riesenfeld concludes "that the synoptic narration of the episode is completely independent of the text of the Old Testament, while the evangelists use the terminology of the Eucharist, as a simple comparison with Mk 14:22 is sufficient to prove." This is also the case of the terminology of the multiplication of loaves. Consequently "Jesus attributes to David, prototype of the Messiah, an act that prefigures the Christian Communion" (*Jésus transfiguré* [Copenhagen, 1947], p. 321).

II. The Real Presence in Liturgy and Life

The Eucharist contains the Church's entire spiritual wealth. . . . The other sacraments, as well as every ministry of Church and every work of the apostolate, are linked with . . . and directed toward it.

Decree on the Ministry and Life of Priests, § 5

A. M. Roguet, O.P.

7   The Eucharist
and the Liturgy

My theme could not be stated more authoritatively than Pope Paul VI has stated it at the very beginning of the encyclical *Mysterium fidei:* "If the sacred liturgy holds the first place in the life of the Church, the Eucharistic mystery stands at the heart and center of the liturgy, since it is the font of life by which we are cleansed and strengthened to live not for ourselves but for God, and to be united in love among ourselves" (§ 3).

Such a declaration stands on its own. I should, however, like to make it more explicit and to stress the profound doctrinal truths it takes for granted. I shall then try to deduce the consequences of that declaration, first on a somewhat theoretical level, and then from various viewpoints of a more practical nature.

I. THE SUMMIT AND THE SOURCE
OF THE LITURGY

Let us enter at once into the heart of the matter: the Eucharist is the summit and the source of the liturgy because it contains our Lord after the manner of a "substantial presence" (*Mysterium fidei*).

Article 7 of the Vatican Council II Constitution on the Liturgy indicates several modes of the presence of Christ in the liturgy: in the priest who consecrates, in the proclamation of the Word of God, in the sacramental actions, in the prayer of the assembly of the baptized gathered in his name. The Constitution points out all these presences in order to determine the definition of the liturgy as the integral worship offered by the Mystical Body, both head and members. On this mystical realism it establishes the superiority of any liturgical celebrations over all the other works of the Church, whereas formerly—before *Mediator Dei*—the superiority of the liturgy was generally based on juridical arguments that were much less convincing because depending more on the will of the Church than on the nature of things.

All these presences of Christ in the liturgy deserve to be recognized as *real* presences. *Mysterium fidei* states that the expression "Real Presence" is not to be reserved to the Eucharist exclusively (§ 39), as too often happens among Catholics. They are real presences in the sense that they are not metaphorical presences, creations of the imagination or theological assertions; they are not purely spiritual presences, depending for instance on the state of grace or on the actual attention of the participants. They are real presences because they are the normal effect of objective causes. Let us suppose that by any remote chance the Word of God were proclaimed in a liturgical assembly without its being listened to or understood by anyone, or that all the members of that assembly were in the state of mortal sin, or that some unexpected incident were to monopolize their attention. Christ would not be the less effectively present for all that in the proclamation of the Word and in the prayer of the Assembly of the baptized.

But the same article 7 of the Constitution states that Christ is "especially" (*maxime*) present under the Eucharistic species. That *maxime* is an absolute superlative. Between this presence and those we have enumerated, there is not only a disparity of level or of intensity but a difference of nature.

However real the other presences may be, they are dynamic and transitory. The priest who consecrates is Christ sacramentally, but only at the moment he consecrates as Christ puts his own words in the mouth of the priest. It is really Christ who baptizes and absolves through the priest who baptizes and absolves, but at that particular moment only. He is present with a presence that is real and active but momentary in the proclamation of the Word; and that is why we must treat with reverence the book that contains it. But we would not think of adoring that book. It does not contain Christ, whereas Christ is present under the consecrated species in a substantial manner. That is what the word "transubstantiation" means, and that is a good reason for retaining that word: the Eucharistic consecration effects the passing of the substance of the bread into the substance of Christ. And, what is perhaps more important, Christ is present after the manner of a substance—which should deter our imagination from trying to form an image of how the whole Christ can be present under the tiny particle of a host and how that host can be broken without Christ's being divided in himself, as also from wondering how Christ can be present simultaneously in the heaven of his glory and beneath the species of millions of hosts consecrated daily on our altars. (See ST IIIa, q.76: "On the Way in Which Christ Is in This Sacrament.")

Some are of the opinion that the progress of science in the analysis of matter has made the words "substance" and "transubstantiation" obsolete. (See the chapters by Father Clark and Monsignor Masi on this point.—Ed.) All they prove thereby is that they do not quite understand the point at issue. For no matter what depths science may reach in the exploration of matter, it will never penetrate beyond the level of physics and of phenomena. Substance and transubstantiation lay far beyond that, on a level accessible to the intuition of the intellect alone and unattainable by any analytical process or standard of measurement.

Moreover, we may for a moment lay aside this terminology, which smacks of Scholasticism. For we can prove the same truth on the authority of biblical theology, which is more favorably received today. Jesus offered in sacrifice and gave us as a food his body and his blood or, to put it better perhaps as in the sixth chapter of St. John, his flesh and his blood. We should not deal with these expressions analytically, wondering what the one means separately from the other. We should deal with them synthetically, cumulatively, as with so many other biblical expressions—"enter" and "leave," which cover every intervening move, or "bind" and "loose," which include every intervening act of authority. Flesh and blood denote a complete human being as such; they denote a person. Christ is present under the species of bread and of wine with his flesh and blood, that is, in his substance, or better, in his person since he is a human and living being.

Such an approach would have disposed of many problems of the past, especially concerning Communion under both species, which should be considered not analytically but synthetically. We thus manage to rediscover what the Scholastic theologians achieved with the theory of concomitance, a theory which, as an explanation, is not an article of faith but which accounts for a truth of faith accepted as evident by Christian intuition: the personal and integral presence of Christ under both Eucharistic species, reunited as it were under each of the two species, or under every one of their fractional parts.

A personal and integral presence. . . . The person of the Christ-man is the Word of God. The substantial presence of Christ in the Eucharist is therefore the presence of the God-man—that is, the presence of Christ as priest, since the formal cause of the priesthood of Christ is the personal union of his humanity and divinity. As man he can offer sacrifice, but as man-God he can offer a sacrifice in the name of all mankind, and a sacrifice that is acceptable to his Father and reconciles us with him.

If the liturgy is defined as the sacerdotal work of Christ performed by the Church, it is quite evident that by this substantial and personal presence of Christ under the species, the Eucharist stands at the heart of the liturgy.

Let us now return to the other presences of Christ in the liturgy. We have just seen that the Eucharistic presence surpasses them to the highest degree: *maxime*. This, however, does not mean that these presences are not related to the Eucharistic presence. They are infinitely inferior to it, granted; but they are derived from it and owe their reality to it. If the presence of Christ is real in the priest as he consecrates, in the Word of God, in the assembly at prayer, the reason is that all these presences are directed to the Eucharistic presence. If you lessen the reality of the Eucharistic presence by reducing it to a dynamic, instrumental and transitory presence, you actually deprive the other presences of all reality, you modify them into purely spiritual and virtual presences. It seems to me that the history of dogma is proof enough of that. Wherever the real, substantial presence of the Eucharist was minimized, the other sacraments became hardly more than sacramentals or ecclesiastical practices, the essentiality of the Apostolic succession and of a ministering priesthood faded away, and the Church became nothing more than the invisible assembly of the elect.

After having indicated the different presences of Christ at work in the liturgy, the same article 7 of the Constitution *Sacrosanctum concilium* defines the liturgy as the "exercise of the priestly office of Christ" by the Church. Now, every priestly function is twofold in purpose: it is cultual, giving glory to God; and it is salvific and sanctifying for the benefit of man. We are reminded of this twofold function of the liturgy throughout the Constitution (§§ 5, 7, 10, 33, 59, 83).

It is clear that if Christ is personally present in the Eucharist, he exercises therein the cultual function of praise. He took the bread and then the cup, "and when he had given thanks," according to Paul and Luke, or "when he had said the blessing," according to Matthew and Mark—two different expressions but with the same meaning. Hence the name Eucharist, the thanksgiving par excellence, given to our sacrament. We could reach the same conclusion by seeing in the Eucharist a representation of the cross, and therefore a sacrificial act. The first purpose of every sacrifice—especially of the unique sacrifice, the sacrifice par excellence that is the cross—consists in giving to God the glory due to him.

As to the salvific and sanctifying function that is also essential to the liturgy, it is eminently fulfilled by the Eucharist. Jesus presented to his Apostles the bread as his body "given for you," according to Paul and Luke. According to John, after the multiplication of the loaves Jesus said: "The bread that I shall give is my flesh, for the life of the world" (6:51). The cup was that of his blood "poured out for you" (Luke) and "for many" (Mark and Matthew) "for the forgiveness of sins" (Matthew). It is the cup of the covenant—that is, of the union of men among themselves to form a people united in God. The redemptive and sanctifying value of the sacrifice of the cross is a fundamental principle of the mystery of the redemption: "On him lies a punishment that brings us peace, and through his wounds we are healed" (Is 53:5).

The water and the blood gushing from the pierced heart of Christ on the cross are symbols of the graces his sacrifice pours unceasingly upon mankind. "For it is from the side of Christ as he slept the sleep of death upon the cross that there came forth the wondrous sacrament which is the whole Church," as the Constitution of the Liturgy declares in article 5, which points to the liturgy as the continuation and representation of the economy of salvation. The historical and sacramental complex of this economy, which takes in both the Old and the New Testament, is summed up and centered in the paschal mystery. In fact, Baptism associates us with the death and resurrection of Christ. But the Eucharist goes still further. It gives us the dead and risen Christ. It gives us the dead Christ because we re-enact the action of the Last Supper, wherein Christ offered himself in sacrifice and committed himself to his sacrifice.

But even as a memorial the Eucharist recalls the risen Christ and the meals which, after his resurrection, he took with his Apostles—the appointed witnesses of his resurrection who ate and drank with him (Acts 10:41). Moreover, if we consider the Eucharist as a sign not only of the past but of the present as well, it contains Christ as he actually is—that is, risen and living in the glory of heaven. Lastly, it gives us the pledge of our future resurrection by depositing in our very bodies a leaven of resurrection.

"It is from the side of Christ as he slept the sleep of death upon the cross that there came forth the wondrous sacrament which is the whole Church." That is the last thought I should like to dwell upon concerning the primacy of the Eucharist vis-à-vis the whole liturgy. The liturgy is, in fact, the work of the entire Church. Etymologically it is the *leiton ergon,* the work of the people, of the People of God as such. In any liturgy, even if celebrated by the smallest and poorest of local communities, especially when a parish community is concerned, that community "represents the visible Church as it is established throughout the world" (Const. on Lit., § 42). More still, it is "with all the warriors of the heavenly army" that "we sing a hymn to the Lord's glory" (*ibid.,* § 8).

The liturgy derives this Catholic, universal, and indeed cosmic characteristic from the Eucharist; for the Eucharist contains really and substantially the personal Christ, that is, the *res et sacramentum* is really contained in the Eucharist. But of what is this *res* the *sacramentum,* of what is *Christ* the *sign?* Of the whole Church, of all mankind gathered in charity, for Christ is the "eldest of many brothers" (Rom 8:29); he has immolated himself not only for his people but "to gather together in unity the scattered children of God" (Jn 11:52) and to reconcile them with God (Col 1:20).

Such is the ultimate *res* of the Eucharist, a *res* not contained but signified and designated by the *res et sacramentum,* Christ immolated for all mankind. The Catholic and (at least as a hope and a trend) ecumenical and missionary character of the liturgy is one of its distinctive features because the Eucharist is its center, its source, and its summit.

II. DOCTRINAL CONSEQUENCES

I should now like to examine briefly the consequences of these principles for a correct understanding of the three fundamental elements of the liturgy: the sacraments, the celebration of the Word of God, and the Divine Office.

1. *The Sacraments*

We have for too long a time distinguished between liturgy and sacraments, to the point of separating them and teaching them in different courses. The harm done was twofold. Overlooking the cultual value of the sacraments, we were led to "administer" them with greater or lesser speed, satisfied with the minimum required for validity. We were exposed consequently to deprive them of any value as a sign or a witness. And we risked confusing the *opus operatum,* their objective efficacy, with an automatism that practically ignored the virtue of religion.

As to the liturgy, by separating it from the sacraments we necessarily reduced it to a ceremonial adornment of little or no vital importance. *Mediator Dei* reacted strongly against that by rejecting any juridical and esthetic definition of the liturgy and listing the sacraments with the Eucharistic sacrifice and the Divine Office as the three great realities that integrate the liturgy. The Constitution on the Liturgy devotes the entire Chapter III to the sacraments and it affirms (§ 59) that their purpose is "to sanctify men, to build up the body of Christ"—which is their communal aspect, too often overlooked—"and finally to give worship to God."

Certainly the word "sacrament" connotes first of all the sanctification of man, and the word "liturgy" the worship of God. But they are not really opposed to each other; the distinction is merely a nicety of language. The sacraments are part of the liturgy and, like the liturgy, exercise a twofold function: cultual, in reference to God; and salvific, in reference to man.

All the sacraments are closely linked to the Eucharist. That is a standard thesis of theology. They are directed to, and derived from, the Eucharist. For them also the Eucharist is the source and the summit, and this not only because they are always directed to its celebration; for that is but an exterior sign, indicative of a much deeper reality—namely, that they owe their efficacy to the Eucharist. Baptism justifies only because it includes ontologically the desire for the Eucharist. According to a common theological opinion, if a catechumen were to exclude the Eucharist when receiving Baptism he would be invalidly baptized, for he would be rejecting the profound reality of Baptism, which is incorporation into Christ.

Confirmation is subordinate to the Eucharist for the same reasons. Indeed the name "confirmation" signifies that this sacrament confirms and completes Baptism by leading to the fullness of the supernatural life those newly born to it. And we may add that it confers the strength to make before an unbelieving world the splendid profession of faith that is participation in the Eucharistic sacrifice.

Penance is directed to the Eucharist not after the fashion of a blank check or a juridical permit but as a reconciliation of love that not only ratifies but in a certain way anticipates the gift of self—essentially a disavowal of sin—and the union of charity through the reception of the

Eucharist, the sacrament of Christ and of the unity of the Church, which sin had either impaired or destroyed.

The Anointing of the Sick perfects Penance somewhat the way Confirmation perfects Baptism: it battles with the forces of death and contributes to the work of the Resurrection, of which the Eucharist gives us a pledge and a beginning. And we can only be delighted that the Council has re-established the normal order of the sacraments by having the Anointing take place before Viaticum (§ 74).

Marriage reproduces the union of Christ and the Church, which is realized much more fully through the Eucharist.

As to Holy Orders, there is no sacrament more entirely directed to the Eucharist, since it confers the power and the mandate to celebrate the Eucharist as also to preside over the work of evangelization and of all the activities of the Church that culminate in the Eucharist.

Forgive me for recalling such familiar notions. We might, however, draw greater inspiration from them in our catechesis, which too often treats the sacraments as separate, consecutive, and quasi-independent realities, whereas they constitute an organism of which the Eucharist is the heart, a system of which the Eucharist is the sun.

2. Sacred Celebrations
of the Word of God

The liturgical renewal, approved by the Constitution on the Liturgy, has stressed the prominent place of the Word of God in the liturgy. "In sacred celebrations there is to be more reading from holy Scripture, and it is to be more varied and suitable" (§ 35); and "the treasures of the Bible are to be opened up more lavishly, so that richer fare may be provided for the faithful at the table of God's Word. In this way a more representative portion of the holy Scriptures will be read to the people [at Mass] over a set cycle of years" (§ 51). And these beautiful promises are to be realized much sooner than we think.

Much emphasis has been laid on the homily to be drawn "from the sacred text" (§ 52)—that is, it should enlarge on and apply the biblical readings or, in any case, "should draw its content" (§ 35) from them and develop them much more according to the economy of salvation than according to their moralizing or apologetic perspectives.

Finally, the reform of the Mass, already effected, assigns the readings to different ministers, even to laymen, and arranges for them to be proclaimed away from the altar in the "place of the Word."

As is pointed out in the next chapter, nothing of all this should be considered as competing with the Eucharistic action properly so-called. The two tables, that of the Word of God and that of the consecrated bread, do not interfere with each other. They integrate the same communal meal; the first prepares the second. For a participation in the "mystery of faith," it is fitting that faith be awakened and nourished with the Word. The Word is read away from the altar so that the altar may recover its unique dignity as the place set apart for the sacrifice.

If the homily takes the sacred text as a starting point, it should be more than a simple exposition of the text; it should lead the listeners to participate in the Eucharist by offering it, by offering themselves with it, and by receiving it with a strong and enlightened faith. The Constitution therefore reminds us (§ 56) that "the two parts which, in a certain sense, go to make up the Mass, namely, the liturgy of the Word and the Eucharistic liturgy, are so closely connected with each other that they form but one single act of worship." We could add, "and a single sanctifying act," the unity of which comes from its culminating in the Eucharist proper.

Moreover, the Constitution (§ 35) and the Instruction for its implementation (nos. 37–39) recommend strongly the Bible services or the "sacred celebrations of the Word of God," fashioned with a certain liberty of adaptation after the pattern of the first part of the Mass. But in this case we are dealing with celebrations of the Word that do not end externally with the Eucharistic celebration.

I have just said "externally" because in reality such celebrations are profoundly linked to the Eucharist, as we shall now see by examining briefly the three major categories in which they may be classified.

A. The first category consists of sacred celebrations organized with the approval of the Ordinary as substitutes for Sunday Mass that is unavailable, because of the lack of a priest. It is evident that if, in such a case, the *sacramentum* of the Eucharist and the sacramental sacrifice are wanting, that celebration is nevertheless directed entirely to the Eucharist. It cannot really take the place of the Mass, but it should make the lack of it less deeply felt, while retaining of the Mass the elements that are still possible and that draw their full value only from their being related to the Eucharist: the gathering of the community, the reading of the Word, the chanting of psalms, the homily, the prayer of the faithful, and the Our Father.

B. The second category includes the sacred celebrations of the Word that encase, as it were, and enhance the value of actions referable to a sacrament or to a sacramental but without involving the Mass for reasons of a practical, pastoral, or pedagogical nature: for instance, the different steps of the catechumenate, a wedding or a funeral without Mass, and even the conferring of Confirmation. It is clear that in all these cases the Eucharist is not absent from the over-all perspective, since we are dealing with sacraments all directed to the Eucharist as to their end.

And if there is question, let us say, of weddings or of funerals celebrated without the Mass because of an unbelieving community, the omission of the Mass is not meant for all that as an approval of this lack of faith or as an infliction of a "privation of Mass" to penalize these remiss Christians, but as an attempt to draw them more effectively to the Eucharist—a mystery temporarily beyond them—through a celebration better suited to their condition and considered not as an *Ersatz* of the Eucharist but as an instructional means of leading them to the Eucharist.

C. Finally, we may place in a third category the sacred celebrations of the Word of God that should be classed as celebrations *de luxe* rather than as a sort of liturgical *dole*. Such are, for instance, the preparations for the great feasts during Advent and Lent, or the prolonging, with evening services, of the most important Eucharistic celebrations of the year. It is as clear as daylight that these celebrations of the Word of God are closely linked to the Eucharist, since they either prepare for it or are derived from it and are, so to speak, its overflow. That is what should inspire us to organize these celebrations not as evening study sessions or as more or less interesting literary and musical gatherings, but as real assemblies of prayer where fervor prevails, where silence is given a place of honor, and where we may learn to listen to the Lord and give ourselves to him.

3. The Divine Office

The Eucharistic sacrifice is a "sacrifice of praise." It applies that biblical expression to itself in the Canon of the Mass at the Remembrance of the Living. Certainly it is much more than that: it is the memorial of a sacrifice, that is, a sacramental sacrifice, at once commemorative and effective. But this expiatory and propitiatory sacrifice is offered in praise to God; it is literally wrapped up in thanksgiving. The Divine Office, however, is nothing more than a sacrifice of praise; and as such it constitutes most fittingly a preparation, a continuation, and a joyous closing of the Eucharistic action.

The Office is in a way a thanksgiving after thanksgiving. It brings out the theocentric and magnanimous aspect of the Eucharist which, in its very celebration and reception, we are apt to forget somewhat by concentrating more on the presence and gift of Christ than on our own gift and sacrifice of self to God. Are not the almost complete lack of participation of the faithful in the divine praise of the Office and the little esteem of some priests for it responsible for a certain want of balance in Eucharistic piety—a piety that has become too anthropocentric? But this brings us to the last part of this report, which we shall devote to the practical consequences of the doctrine we have tried to expose.

III. PRACTICAL CONSIDERATIONS

We have specified adequately, I hope, how the Eucharist is the source and the summit of all liturgy. This implies the logical inference that the liturgy is not confined to the Eucharist—or rather to the Mass, which is the Eucharistic action, the confection of the Eucharist, the Eucharist *in fieri* (in the making), but which is not all the Eucharist. We can well ask ourselves whether all the effort spent in the last twenty years to make the faithful appreciate the Mass, to make them participate actively in the Mass, has not had, along with unquestionably worthwhile and fundamental results, that of depreciating and scuttling other forms of prayer in general and Eucharistic devotion in particular. In the life of the majority of today's Catholics the Mass rises like a magnificent monument, but one lost in the midst of a devotional desert.

It is true that previous generations have to some extent made too much of processions and benedictions of the Blessed Sacrament. Parading the Blessed Sacrament in the midst of an indifferent populace or in a private enclosure does not, obviously, correspond to the great triumph that the Procession of Corpus Christi, when instituted, was meant to be. Almost daily benediction of the Blessed Sacrament, gone through hurriedly and amounting to the most stereotyped performance imaginable, conformed neither to the spirit of the liturgy nor even to the legislation of the Church, which considers exposition in the monstrance as a solemn manifestation and therefore of relatively rare occurrence. We had come to making of "Benediction" a sort of evening Mass. It is not then surprising that the real evening Mass should have resulted in the discontinuance of "Benediction."

But on the other hand, this suppression has gone too far. We do not have to apologize for this manifestation of Eucharistic piety under the lame pretext, for example, that it was unknown to antiquity and still is to the Orient. (See also Father Galot's chapters on this point.—*Ed.*) The Oriental liturgies are more prolonged, contemplative, and even redundant than the Roman liturgy, which is short, juridical, and a bit arid. Nevertheless, even the Roman liturgy lingers somewhat between the Consecration and Communion. It is normal for a Eucharistically formed person to want to tarry awhile on the occasion of exposition of the Blessed Sacrament, which is clearly linked to the Mass. The host we adore has been consecrated at Mass and is destined to be consumed in Communion. Its adoration is not therefore to be dismissed as superfluous simply because we possess Christ under presences other than that of the Eucharist. True enough, "Christ lives in our hearts through faith" (Eph. 3:17), but our faith needs to be sustained and vivified with sensible signs.

If we argue that Christian antiquity was not familiar with exposition
of the host, we err precisely by archeologism: we forget that the piety
of the Church evolves and grows, and that we have no right to frown
on the accretions of a relatively recent past in the name of a more
remote past. As Father Karl Rahner observes very well in his chapter
below, and also in excellent book *L'Eucharistie et les Hommes
d'Aujourd'hui,* if we want to return to antiquity, we should go the
whole way. Let us practice its strict fasts, its long ceremonies often
during the night, its public and prolonged penances. Let us not be
content to select from antiquity only what is easy.

Without reverting to the hurried and over-frequent "Benediction" of
yesterday, we should form the faithful, and us priests as well, in the
habit of making prolonged visits before the Blessed Sacrament exposed.
Let us organize solemn expositions that strengthen the faith, that
include biblical readings evocative of the mystery of the two Tables,
litanies of invocations for the needs of the Church and of mankind, and
especially periods of silence. Some complain that our communal celebrations are wanting in silence. That complaint is often justified by the
indiscretion of certain commentators, but it is also accounted for by the
very nature of the Mass, which is an action and in which the Word of
God plays an indispensable role. Let at least adoration of the Blessed
Sacrament exposed offer us the possibility of practicing the silence and
the profound prayer that are a necessary antidote to the feverish and
noisy agitation of modern life.

I have spoken of the celebrations of the Word and of their essential
relation to the Eucharist. This relation could be stressed by arranging
for these celebrations to take place before the Blessed Sacrament exposed, or in any case by bringing them to a close with exposition of the
Blessed Sacrament, thus underscoring their sacred character and allow-
ing the Word to bear lasting fruit in the silence of adoration. It is easy
to apply what I have just said to private Eucharistic devotion, whether
it has to do with a visit to the Blessed Sacrament during the day or
with thanksgiving duly prolonged after Communion. Can we say that
we truly love the Lord in his Eucharist if we cannot remain with him a
few minutes when he comes to give himself so totally to us, and when

he is substantially present in a sacrament that permits us to keep him among us in his sacrifice and in the gift he makes of his flesh and blood to be our food, our strength, our sanctification, and our joy?

The visits to the Blessed Sacrament I have called to mind bring up the question of the tabernacle. Placing the sacred Reservation outside the main altar is certainly in conformity with the best tradition— which, for that matter, had remained the rule for cathedral and collegial churches. It is an excellent piece of Eucharistic pedagogy. The altar recovers its proper function, its identity as the table of sacrifice. The Council's recommendation that Communion be received with hosts consecrated in the course of the same sacrifice will be more easily followed. On the other hand, in a large church the altar for the Sunday Mass is often isolated in a wilderness of pews and, for good reason, is removed from the faithful by a rather large sanctuary.

But that is not a sufficient reason to separate systematically the tabernacle of the sacred Reservation from any altar, to reduce it to a wall cupboard, or to relegate it to an isolated chapel. Today, of course, that is allowed with the permission of the Ordinary. Nevertheless, it seems to me that the best solution, the most commendable and practical, the one that fosters Eucharistic piety the most, consists in placing the tabernacle of the sacred Reservation on an altar, the altar on which Mass is offered on weekdays. In any case, if there are serious reasons for placing it outside any altar, we should see to it that the place be dignified and well adorned, as directed in the Instruction *Inter Oecumenici* (§ 95). Moreover—and these two requisites are not always easy to reconcile—it should be located in a very accessible place, easy to identify as soon as one enters the church, and should at the same time lend itself to recollection in order to foster and facilitate visits to the Blessed Sacrament.

By way of both summarizing and enlarging on the preceding considerations, I should say that at present the faithful hardly come to church anymore except to participate in the Mass. So much so that in order to get them to hear a sermon or attend a celebration of the Word, we consider it almost always necessary to announce that it will close with a Mass. That may well be due to excessive sacramentalism. We ought to

be able to come to church even when we have nothing to receive for
our trouble and, I would almost say, nothing to do except to remain
silent and just be there close to the Lord in order to love him and sing
his praises. Alas, parish Vespers and Compline were already on their
way out. We can say that the evening Masses, which we have no
intention of either deploring or blaming, gave the finishing stroke to
the participation of the faithful in the Divine Office. We like to hope
that the perspectives opened by the Conciliar Constitution on the
restoration of the major hours of the Office, better adapted to the
participation of the faithful, will be more than a beautiful dream.

CONCLUSION

The generations that preceded us have perhaps slightly misunderstood, to the benefit of secondary and marginal devotions, the center of
all liturgical and ecclesial life that is participation in the Mass. But
today let us make sure that Eucharistic piety is complete and well
balanced. There is more to it than having rediscovered the center, the
axis, the source and the summit. All these words repudiate monopoliz-
ing and exclusiveness. They necessarily call for an environment, for
approaches and extensions. Liturgical piety would not be truly Christian if it were to mean the disappearance of every form of piety—
Eucharistic, sacramental, contemplative, laudative—which, far from
being foreign to the Mass, provide it with its framework, its subsoil, its
atmosphere.

Without that, the Eucharist is exposed to becoming a *center* without
a circumference, a *source* without a river, an isolated *summit* without
any slopes or shoulders to link it with the surrounding plain below.
Eucharistic piety must remain rich in all the harmonics that Christian
tradition has progressively developed under the action of the Holy
Spirit if we wish participation in the liturgy to be not only active and
intelligent but also, as again required by the Conciliar Constitution,
complete—that is, profound, all-inclusive, and *fruitful*—that is, sanctifying and radiating.

NOTE

A. M. Roguet, O.P., editorial director of *La Maison-Dieu,* was a founder of the Centre de Pastorale Liturgique (France's liturgical conference) and a member of the Council's preparatory Commission on the Liturgy. He is also the author of several well-known works, among them *Christ Acts Through the Sacraments* and *Holy Mass: Approaches to the Mystery.* The above chapter was given first as a conference of the Bordeaux National Eucharistic Congress in 1966 and was published in *Parole et Pain,* Nos. 14 and 15, 1966. His second chapter, "The Eucharist and Contemplative Prayer," was written for *La Vie Spirituelle,* issue of May, 1954, and the translation appeared in *Emmanuel* in November of that year.

Jean Galot, S.J.

8 The Eucharistic Presence and the Christian Community

As we recounted in another context in Chapter 6, in recent years the cult or worship of the Eucharistic Presence has come under attack, with a notable drop in devotion toward it. And this we ascribed to its apparent lack of biblical foundation and its having been unknown in the practice of the primitive Church. Indeed, it has been looked upon as a later outgrowth that may interfere with the Sacrifice of the Mass and tend to supplant it. Some writers stress the fact that Jesus did not tell his disciples to adore his body but to take it and eat it.

A TREASURE OF THE CHURCH

In some churches and chapels the Blessed Sacrament is no longer reserved in a place of honor for all to see it and venerate it, but it is relegated in a corner or to the side as something of a leftover that does not require special worship. Some would want to suppress exposition and benediction of the Blessed Sacrament; they shy away from any visit to a church for the purpose of honoring the presence of the Lord.

If the liturgical movement were to aim solely at a return to the primitive customs of the Church, it would be moving toward an archeological restoration, not toward an outpouring of the riches of the faith and of worship according to a plan adapted to the present day. This movement is, in reality, the fruit of a tradition that should endeavor not to lose anything of the legitimate growth attained in the course of centuries.

Genuine worship is not limited to the days of the primitive Church; it is the worship of a Church that has never ceased to live and to manifest herself ever more perfectly. It is a life that, for its being in continuity with the past, moves ever onward to a better tomorrow. Worship is forever in a state of progress. That is what the Constitution on the Liturgy demonstrates.

In the progress achieved over the centuries, we note the development of Eucharistic adoration, which took shape especially at the time when medieval theology was busy defining the essential points of Eucharistic doctrine and delving into the full significance of faith in the Real Presence. We should like merely to emphasize the fact that this Eucharistic worship has been productive of fruits of sanctity. The witness of the saints proves that this worship is part of the living Church and an important element in her mission of sanctification of the world.

That is the witness Pope John XXIII invoked in his message of July 5, 1959, to the 18th National Eucharistic Congress of France, held at Lyons. The declaration of principle made by the Pope on that occasion, with an appeal to the example of Curé of Ars, is worth quoting.

Besides the more solemn celebration of Holy Mass and the general Communion of the faithful, what is, in final analysis, a Eucharistic Congress if not a prolonged and fervent visit to the Blessed Sacrament? You have observed as We have that many in our day are neglecting this touching practice of Christian life, so dear to devout souls, which consists in recollecting oneself before the tabernacle to fill one's soul with the gifts of God. Worse still, it seems that, under the influence of ideas foreign to traditional piety, some deliberately hold this practice in disfavor.

We would wish all the Congressists of Lyons to return to their homes persuaded of the excellence of this practice and eager to have it appreciated and loved by all those around them. You have only to think of the long hours spent by St. John Vianney, at the beginning of his pastoral ministry, alone in his church before the Blessed Sacrament; of the outpouring of faith and love of this great soul at the feet of his Master, of the marvelous fruits of holiness he reaped for himself and for so many others from these fervent Eucharistic prayers. There is no doubt that a flood of grace would stream down upon your families and your country if, enlightened and sustained by the example of their priests, an ever greater number of souls were to learn a lesson on this point from the saintly Curé of Ars.

It is in adoration of the Blessed Sacrament that are enkindled and fostered the dynamics of the apostolate. (*AAS, 1959, 537–538*)

Eucharistic worship therefore constitutes a treasure that the Church cannot justifiably abandon. And in the present chapter we should like to show not only that it should be preserved as a legacy of the past but also that it harmonizes with certain profound trends perceptible in the contemporary Church and, in fact, satisfies the needs of the mentality of today. Let us confront this worship with the liturgy of the Word, with the return to biblical sources, and with the requirements of a communal spirituality.

LITURGY OF THE WORD

The contemporary liturgical movement has aimed at giving broader scope to the cult of the Word of God. In the celebration of the Mass the liturgy of the Word plays more actively the role proper to it through a more vital and effective adaptation to the assembly of the faithful. The insistence laid on the homily is part of this renewal. In extraliturgical ceremonies, an important place is usually given to the divine Word by a reading of, or commentary on, extracts from Holy Scripture. In certain churches the Missal or the Bible remains permanently exposed so that the faithful may return in the course of the day to nourish their souls with the sacred words.

We should be restricting the cult of the Word unduly were we to picture it as opposed to, or competing with, the cult of the Eucharistic Presence. (See also the preceding chapter by Father Roguet on this point.—*Ed.*) What, in fact, is the real scope of the liturgy of the Word if not that it necessarily leads, at its summit, to the veneration of Christ? Otherwise it would cease to be what it ought to be and would completely fail of its goal. "In the beginning was the Word," declared St. John at the opening of his Gospel. That Word is the Person of the Son of God, and the Christian religion is the religion of the Word not precisely because it is the religion of a book, but because it is the religion of a Person. In the Christian perspective the fundamental Word is Christ, and all the words found in the sacred books are the proclamation or the expression of that one Word.

"The Word was made flesh." The great book opened before us by God is his Incarnate Son. The eternal Word, who was "in the beginning," has come to earth in time and has willed "to dwell among us." The Evangelist declares that this incarnate Person has made us penetrate into the mystery of God: "No one has at any time seen God. The only-begotten Son, who is in the bosom of the Father, He has revealed Him" (Jn 1: 18). The Incarnate Word has told us who God is and, by his existence here below, has revealed to us the secrets of the divine Being.

St. John stresses the greatness of this gift by comparing the Law, the Word par excellence of the Old Testament, with the truth revealed by Christ: "The Law was given through Moses; grace and truth came through Jesus Christ" (Jn 1:18). The final revelation of God came no longer through the action of a purely human intermediary but through the Son of God made man. The difference between the two is the difference between one who, like Moses, speaks about God, and one who, being God, speaks to us about himself. The revelation is direct. God makes himself known no more by means of words that others speak, but by means of a divine Person present among us. The liturgy of the Word should never lose sight of the fact that, by virtue of the nature of Christianity, it must be a liturgy of Christ. The Old Testament is only a preparation of the Presence of the Word made flesh, as the New Testament is only the expression of it. The sacred books must therefore make room for the Person of the Son of God.

It is here that the profound link between the liturgy of the Word and the veneration of the Eucharistic presence becomes evident. If revelation consists essentially in the coming of the Son of God and if the presence of Christ among men is the ultimate truth about God, the permanent presence of Christ in the tabernacle remains then the revelation par excellence of the truth of God. That presence is God, who gives himself out of love in perpetuity. It is the principle truth that imposes itself upon us: "God is love" (1 Jn 4:8). The Word made flesh, who abides in the sanctuary, deserves a worship that perfects the cult with which we venerate and receive the Word contained in the books.

Thus it becomes apparent how wrong is the perspective of those who may have been tempted to replace, in the churches, the veneration of the Eucharistic Christ with the veneration of a book. *The cultus of the book has meaning only if it leads to the veneration of Christ in the tabernacle as the one divine Word.*

It is true that by deferring to Eucharistic adoration the liturgy of the Word becomes silent. But does not the reception of the Word call for silence? It does happen that some liturgical celebrations are too replete with human words—so much so that they make it almost impossible for the Word of God to penetrate silently into souls. The Incarnate Word that dwells in the tabernacle possesses a silent splendor and is capable of helping the liturgy to appreciate better the value of silence.

The value of the personal presence of Christ as the supreme Word is still more susceptible of being appreciated in our day, since it harmonizes well with the tendency of the modern apostolate. We note, in fact, that this apostolate often places the accent more on a witness of presence than on preaching. The word that gathers hearts closer together is personal behavior, example, and a life of brotherhood in one's own little world. Such is the tendency that has manifested itself in certain forms of Christian presence in the world of labor and in the spirituality inspired by Charles de Foucauld. That form of presence merely prolongs the mystery of the Incarnation, of the divine Word that speaks by taking on flesh and dwelling among us. And it is particularly in accord with a worship of the presence of God among men, the worship of Eucharistic adoration, in which are revealed both the drawing power of that Presence and the response of faith in its devotion to a Person.

RETURN TO BIBLICAL SOURCES

The return to the Bible, so much to be admired in the Church of today, is most suited to help us explain better and to justify worship of the Eucharistic presence.

The researches of the exegetes concerning the words of the Consecration lead us to interpret these words in a sense that calls still more for adoration. In the Greek text of the gospels, we read: "This is my body." These words evoke only the thought of the body of Christ. But in the Hebrew or Aramaic language, the words "This is my flesh" had a broader meaning. The word "flesh" usually designated the whole person. By stating that his flesh was present, Christ wished, therefore, to speak of the gift of his entire self through the gift of his body, as was brought out in Part I of this volume.

But the presence of the Person of the Lord calls for a personal response on the part of Christians. A person cannot be treated just like a thing, even if it is the holiest of things. A person has a right to respect and love; its very presence demands recognition as the presence of a person. It invites dialogue; and since we are dealing with a divine Person, that dialogue is carried out in faith and adoration. It is true that Jesus has not formulated an explicit wish that his Eucharistic presence be venerated. But then neither has He given specific directions concerning the organization of a liturgy of sacrifice. He limited himself to issuing a statement that was to serve as the foundation for the development of Eucharistic worship.

In the course of the paschal meal, he instituted a new spiritual meal that implied a sacrifice and drew its value from the presence of his flesh and blood. The words of the Consecration are the affirmation of this presence; and they suggest, by the absoluteness with which this presence was proclaimed, that it is a presence given for all time and not restricted to the moment of the sacrifice and of the meal. Jesus did not say "I give you my flesh to eat," or "This is my flesh for the duration of the sacrifice and of the meal," but "This is my flesh," without condition or limitation of time.

The one who pronounced these words is the Word who became flesh and dwells among us. By proclaiming himself present in his flesh, did he not imply that he meant to continue dwelling among us? The Eucharistic words connote an extension of the Incarnation and, at the Last Supper, Christ gave sufficient evidence of his intention to remain with his disciples: "Abide in Me, and I in you. . . . abide in my love"

(Jn 15:4, 9). Thus he manifested his intention of offering us not a passing presence but an eternal one.

The whole biblical background of the first Eucharistic Meal confirms this intention. When Jesus said to his disciples, "Do this in remembrance of me" (Lk 22:19), he replaced the paschal meal, which was being held in remembrance of Yahweh and of his favors, with a meal that was to be repeated in remembrance of himself. Thus he took the place of God himself, He set himself at the center of the new cult in the same way that Yahweh was at the center of the old cult. Now Yahweh was present to the old cult in a perpetual manner in the Temple of Jerusalem. God stood in the most sacred section of the Temple, the Holy of Holies, where the Ark of the Covenant had been placed of old. His presence was considered as an assurance of protection and as a source of blessings; it consecrated the covenant made with the Jewish people.

While he desired that the new cult be effected in remembrance of himself, Jesus also wanted to give his disciples a perpetual presence. The remembrance of himself, still more than that of Yahweh, had to be rendered always actual, because the Incarnation was meant to assure a greater closeness of God to humanity. If the divine presence was the great treasure of the Temple of Jerusalem, the presence of Christ had to become the great treasure of Christian churches. It would be inconceivable that the Savior should not have given his disciples what the God of the Old Covenant had given his people—a permanent presence.

Thus the recommendation, "Do this in remembrance of me," included the intention of establishing a living and perpetual remembrance of Christ in Christian worship. Every repetition of the words, "This is my flesh," would assure this remembrance by proclaiming a Presence which, of itself, had no limits as to duration. The person of Christ would multiply indefinitely the places and the moments of his presence among men to draw them to himself from everywhere and at all times.

By willing this personal Presence at the center of worship and by willing it to be unceasingly actual and active, Christ asks his followers for a homage full of faith and love, a personal devotion that appreciates the permanency of the gift.

SACRIFICE AND PRESENCE

Among the criticisms made against the worship of the Eucharistic presence is that it competes with the Mass, tends to make us lose sight of the sacrifice. If, however, we consider the biblical background of the sacrifice of Christ, as enunciated in the epistle to the Hebrews, we realize that sacrifice and permanent presence, far from conflicting with each other, complement each other. The cultus of the Presence stands out as the normal prolongation of the liturgy of the sacrifice.

The epistle to the Hebrews does not provide us with a doctrine of the Eucharistic sacrifice. What it treats of is the sacrifice of the cross. It dwells upon it as the one and supreme fulfillment of all the cultual sacrifices known to Judaism and insists on the fact that the sacrifice of Calvary was "offered once" (Heb 9:28), but it underscores still more the perpetual fruit of this transitory offering.

It describes the sacerdotal action as an entering into the sanctuary, recalling the act of the Jewish High Priest who, on the day of the Feast of Expiation, entered the sanctuary to sprinkle the tabernacle with the blood of the victims. By his immolation on the cross, Christ entered with his own blood into a sanctuary which is heaven itself (Heb 9:24). He entered there once for all in order to remain always in the presence of the Father and intercede for us. According to the epistle to the Hebrews, the sacerdotal function of Christ consists essentially in that intercession gathers the fruits of the Sacrifice. As a result of the offering there is a permanent presence of Christ before the Father, a presence that intercedes for, and obtains, graces of salvation for humanity.

Seen in this perspective, the sacrifice does not end with the act of the offering. It points to an eternal presence in which the offering is seen as perpetuated in its effects. If it is so for the sacrifice of the cross, we should not be surprised to find a similar pattern in the Eucharistic sacrifice, which commemorates it and renews it sacramentally. The offering, which takes place on the altar at the moment of the Consecration, results in a presence that is susceptible of being perpetuated indefinitely. Christ remains on the altar as Priest and Victim to intercede with his Father in behalf of men and to make them share in the fruits of the sacrifice.

If the sacrifice of the cross is expressed sacramentally in the sacrifice of the Mass, and more especially so at the Consecration, the presence of the glorious Christ in heaven, in a state of intercession after his sacrifice, finds sacramental expression in the presence beneath the sign of the host in the tabernacle. Remaining indefinitely present, the Savior no longer offers his sacrifice but continues to extend its benefits by interceding with the Father to grant us his graces.

The Eucharistic Presence stands out better in its relation to the whole work of salvation when it is viewed against the biblical background of the epistle to the Hebrews. Thanks to this presence, the Eucharist conveys more completely the total mystery of the Redemption, a mystery that does not merely consist in the offering of the Passion and in the triumph of the Resurrection and of the Ascension, but also includes the permanent presence of the glorious Christ near the Father for the dispensing of graces to humanity.

Thus, far from interfering with the Mass, the presence of Christ in the tabernacle serves to manifest its fruits and to assure still more its efficacy. The presence of the glorious Christ in heaven does not eclipse the value of the sacrifice of the cross; on the contrary, his unceasing intercession underscores its superabundant and inexhaustible value. In the same way, the Eucharistic presence neither veils nor obscures the value of the Mass but tends to perpetuate its effects.

The worship of the Eucharistic presence really becomes the complement of the liturgy of the Mass. It helps Christians to understand better that their participation in the Mass ought to have a lasting influence on their way of life and that it ought to be followed by a communion with the Passion of Christ in the joy of the Resurrection. By drawing close to him who dwells in the church in the glorious state of his offering, they are encouraged to live the Eucharistic sacrifice more deeply. By coming to visit him who intercedes unceasingly for them with the Father, they become more completely receptive of the graces they receive from him and are induced to unite themselves actively to this intercession, to the never-ending prayer of the eternal Priest for the sanctification and salvation of men.

CENTER OF THE COMMUNTIY

That the Mass and the Eucharistic presence complement each other is confirmed also in the life of the Christian community; for the worship of the Eucharistic presence satisfies the needs of a community.

The liturgical assembly gathers together around the sacrifice of the altar and seals its solidarity by partaking of the Eucharistic Meal. In Communion, Christ strengthens sacramentally the union of his faithful. Received equally by all, he tightens the bonds of their union with himself and of their union with one another. By renewing and deepening their charity, He adds solidity to the structure of the Church. It is not only each member that benefits by the Eucharistic food but the entire community, which thus strengthens its unity.

The gathering of the faithful for the Eucharistic meal, however, lasts only for a moment, whereas the Church needs a permanent center of charity. In the sacramental economy the permanency of this center is obvious. Just as Christ renews his Church in charity through the Eucharistic meal, so he counts on his Eucharistic presence to form a center that ever radiates the power of his love on the Christian community.

Under this aspect the presence of Christ in the tabernacle aims at prolonging indefinitely the effect of Communion, since it completes the meal as well as the sacrifice. In fact, the Eucharistic presence seeks to preserve and develop quietly throughout the day what the Eucharistic meal sought to realize in one moment of intense spiritual effectiveness. Continuing to offer his presence in the tabernacle, the Savior invites the faithful to come to him in order to recapture the intimacy enjoyed in Communion and drink from the living fountain of charity.

Certainly an order of things could be imagined in which Christ would not have been permanently present to the community in sacramental form. It would have been enough for him to be present in a purely spiritual manner. Such a spiritual presence was announced by the promise: "Behold, I am with you all days, even unto the consummation of the World" (Matt 28:20). This presence was brought about not only for purposes of assistance, but also as a permanent source of life for the Mystical Body: "I am the vine, you are the branches" (Jn 15:5). In point of fact, from that presence of Christ the Christian community receives at every moment what it needs for its existence: "Without me you can do nothing" (Jn 15:5). It would be surprising, however, if this permanent presence of Christ in the community he founded did not have its counterpart in the sacramental order. In any case, in the comparison analogy in which Jesus called himself the vine, he made allusion to the Eucharist he had just instituted. We must keep in mind that the image he drew of a community as branches receiving from the vine the sap that makes them live, was presented by him as an illustration of the Eucharist. After having given the Eucharistic food to his disciples, the Master spoke of a permanent communication of life. After having given them the consecrated wine, he spoke of the plant of the vine. He himself, therefore, implied that he wanted to be present in a perpetual manner by means of the Eucharist in the community of his disciples.

Thus, thanks to the Eucharistic presence, Christ has willed to remain in many places as a center of life and charity in the midst of each Christian community. The hidden Presence in the tabernacle is motionless but not inactive; it is the source of the togetherness, of the oneness of Christians. It cannot be denied that this sacramental giving of the presence of Christ to his Mystical Body renders his presence more real and more accessible to all men. Through the tabernacle found in every parish church is proclaimed more forcefully the place of the Lord in the midst of the parish, his watchful care of every moment, and his hidden influence on the community.

This sacramental presence is an invitation. The function of the sensible sign in the sacramental order is to bring spiritual realities closer to human life, to introduce them into our world in a more realistic fashion. The host present in the tabernacle helps us to understand the closeness of God and invites the Christians to get in touch with their Master. When they enter a church to make a visit, they are actually returning to the living center of the community.

Does not the Eucharistic presence tend to group the faithful around the Savior just as the disciples gathered around Jesus during his public life? The disciples had the privilege of living close to God, a God present in a particular place and made visible under the form of a man. The Christians have the advantage of also being able to reach a God present in a definite place, a God visible under the sign of bread. Their gathering together around the tabernacle tends to rebuild the ecclesial community under a sensible form, just as the primitive Church took shape around the presence of Christ. The community recognizes the one who is its center, adheres more intimately to the presence of the Savior and restores in him its unity.

CONCLUSION

The cult of the Eucharistic presence is not out of date. It is in perfect harmony with the tendencies of our day. In fact, it brings to the liturgy of the Word the indispensable complement or crowning-point without which this liturgy would miss the central mystery of the Christian religion, the "Word made flesh." It agrees with the biblical interpretation of the words of the Consecration as they were pronounced by Jesus, for that interpretation stresses the personal presence of the Savior and is an invitation to a personal union of faith and adoration. Moreover, it occupies the place that belongs to it in the biblical perspective of the Sacrifice, according to which the offering of Calvary climaxes in the heavenly presence of the glorious Christ who intercedes with the Father without ceasing; this teaching of the epistle to the Hebrews leads to the conclusion that the Eucharistic sacrifice also climaxes in a permanent presence where the fruits of the offering are gathered.

Finally, the communal doctrine of salvation throws light on the function of the Eucharistic presence: the community receives its life and its love from a permanent center that is the very person of Christ.

Union with this presence guarantees the preservation and the growth of the communal life of the Church.

Thus it is clear that the worship of the Eucharistic presence is still vital today for the Church; it completes the celebration of the sacrifice and of the Eucharistic meal.

(See biographical note on Father Galot after Chapter 6.—Editor)

J. A. Robilliard, O.P.

9 Eucharistic Worship in the Divine Economy

It is matter for rejoicing that the Mass is still held in high esteem by our contemporaries. It is the consummation of worship, the final synthesis prepared by every other religious act. The love of the Son of God culminates at the instant when, in giving us his flesh and quenching our thirst with his blood, he introduces us into God. It is the moment of intimacy, of the exchange of lives, of honor rendered to the Father. When, after the act of sacrifice, we prostrate ourselves before the Blessed Sacrament and adore the God-man, our Mediator and our King, who is totally concerned with us and totally devoted to our service, it seems like a retrogression into a less perfect religious act than sacrifice, for in the order of dignity or of perfection, adoration certainly takes second place.

But adoration is first in the order of genesis, in the ascent of the soul to God, as a preparation for Mass. In this light it is false to claim that adoration is consequent upon the Eucharistic celebration. It is ordered to the sacrificial banquet and is as it were the preamble. Before the use and reception of the Sacrament, i.e., Communion, even before the sacrifice is completed and accomplished by the consecration of the wine, Jesus is there. It sufficed for the bread to be transubstantiated into his body. The priest at the altar is the minister of the sacred Presence before being the minister of the consummated sacrifice, and he hastens to affirm it by raising up the host, by presenting the host for the adoration of the faithful. It matters little that this adoration, too

147

quickly absorbed in the profundity of the paschal banquet, is afterward resumed at leisure. Nor does the importance that is given it or the time devoted to it matter. In as much as it is a preparation of the soul, Eucharistic adoration is anterior to the sacrificial banquet and gives access to it.

This is surely what is implied in St. Augustine's oft-cited words: *"Nemo autem illam carnem manducat nisi prius adoraverit."* [1] This is likewise the conclusion to which we are led by St. Thomas Aquinas' admirable treatise on the virtue of religion, which classifies in rigorous system the order of genesis, the various activities stemming from the religious sentiment. Here they are, from the most hidden to the most outwardly expressive: devotion and prayer (which are altogether interior); adoration (which engages both soul and body); the rites of offering (and first of all, sacrifice); finally, the rites of reception, of participation in the divine (for example, the *Sacrament* of the Eucharist and its use, which is Communion). In this stately framework it is easy to situate the various parts of Eucharistic worship in their proper place.

I. THE INTERIOR ACTS

1. Devotion (*devotio*)

The most secret, fundamental religious act is the offering of a person that surrenders itself in all that is most personal to it—its will; and that consecrates itself totally to the service and worship of God. This is the ancient meaning of the Latin word *devotio*. Devotion is the consecration of divine goodness, of all the blessings that stake out the Christian's path, the consecration too of one's weaknesses, and the eagerness to subject oneself without reservation to God's good pleasure. "Behold, I come to do thy will, O God." These are the words that Holy Scripture (Ps 39:7-8) places on the lips of the Son of God as he comes into the world and says to his Father:

> Sacrifice and oblation thou wouldst not,
> but a body thou hast fitted to me:

In holocausts and sin-offerings thou hast had no pleasure.
Then said I, "Behold, I come . . ." *(Heb 10:5-7)*

Now at the beginning of Jesus' passion, when, after a long agony he had succeeded in subjecting his human will and the aspirations of his heart to the eternal and disconcerting will of the Father in heaven, when he had fixed his highest freedom in this submission, Jesus reaffirmed the proclamation that had marked his coming into the world: "Whom do you seek?"—"Jesus of Nazareth."—"I am he." He surrendered himself. He was handed over to sinners, chained.

Should we identify this state of captivity into which Jesus entered at the close of his agony with the state in which he finds himself under the Eucharistic species—a Victim, so to speak, of the sacrament that he instituted, handed over to the hands of priests, which are sinful hands, negligent hands, and sometimes sacrilegious hands? But it is scarcely fitting to speak of the "divine prisoner of the tabernacle." Others have already ridiculed this formula, and not without reason.

It is very true that the nineteenth century, which abounded in piety and was lacking in theology, has made the worst possible use of the beautiful theme of Jesus as captive of his love in the Eucharist.[2] We have before us a picture of that period, in which we see a prison grille replace the door of the tabernacle, and behind the grille a Jesus wearing chains and weeping day and night as he prays over our misery. These sentimental and clumsy expressions of devotion are unbearable, but it is useless to laugh at them. It would better to try to underline their fundamental purpose.

The historian would be the one to question on this. For while the nineteenth century compared Jesus-in-chains to Jesus present in the host, the seventeenth century freely used the same approach and honored Jesus "captive of the will of his priests." It would be very interesting to inquire at what period, in what climate of opinion, there was transferred to the Eucharist a little scriptural note that was called to mind whenever one thought of Jesus-in-chains: "I will not let thee go except thou bless me" (Gn 32:26). We can see this verse applied to the

Eucharist in a pseudo-Bonaventurian *Expositio missae* that dates at least from the fourteenth century.[3]

The nineteenth century compared Jesus-in-chains to Jesus in the host, identifying the two mysteries. We should be content to compare them without identifying them. We can visualize what Christ lived through, his death and resurrection, on our own level, as human facts experienced by Jesus in his frail humanity. From this point of view they are historical facts that have fallen back into the abyss of the past. Thus the crucifixion, considered as a crime planned by the Pharisees, does not go beyond the realm of history. It is something that did happen; it exists no longer. But there is another consideration. The principal cause of our salvation is God himself, it is the power of the Eternal, and the Eternal encompasses time and coexists at every moment of the evolution of the world. The reason the death and resurrection of Christ did not fall back into nothingness is that the power of God took possession of the sufferings and joys of Jesus to work our salvation. The weakness of Jesus, in as much as it is the instrument of salvation and becomes the power of God, is coextensive with all epochs of time. The reality that overflows the limits of history, the reality with which we remain in contact is the totality of the mysteries of the life of Christ insofar as they save us and bear fruit. To those who came to put him in chains, Jesus, who was sent by the Father and was fulfilling the Will of the Father, said: "Behold, I come." He had been sent by the Eternal and the Eternal spoke through his lips.

Even now, Jesus does not stop saying: "Here I am" and delivering himself up to sinners. The gesture is always there, not as being afflictive here and now, but as a salutary gesture seized by the power of the Eternal and producing the delectable fruit of the Eucharistic Presence.

The Eucharist in its entirety is the fruit of the Passion in its entirety. But each of the moments of the Passion possesses a fruitfulness of its own. The mystery of Jesus-in-chains bears fruit in this Eucharistic Presence of which we are so little aware. When we approach the consecrated bread we should kindle in our souls the fundamental religious act, the devotion, the total availability, the offering of our will to Christ present in the Eucharist. . . .

2. *Prayer*

After devotion, there is a second interior act stemming from the virtue of religion: prayer. In the presence of the tabernacle all forms of prayer are useful and highly to be recommended. There is, however, a form of prayer that seems particularly adapted to the Eucharistic Presence, that one expressed in Psalm 122:1: 'To thee I lift up my eyes, O thou who dwellest in heaven." This is the prayer that the good old man Chaffangeon used to make during his visits to the Blessed Sacrament,[4] as he described it to the holy Curé of Ars: "I look at the good God and the good God looks at me."

The theorists of prayer would speak of the prayer of simplicity, of the prayer of quiet, of loving attention to the present God. It is good to listen to the theorists. But it is more profitable to ask our Lord to grant us the understanding of the heart, indeed, to fascinate us. For he looks at us first, and looking at us with mercy, he causes us to look at him with the eyes of faith. He is there under the species of bread in the plenitude of his grace and of his mysteries. His gaze is at once the smiling glance of the Child God, the thoughtful look of the artisan of Nazareth, the look that made Peter weep, and that now rests upon us.

He is there as the prophet, the seer, whose face was veiled by the Sanhedrites, so rich was he in revelations from on high.

He is there as our God, as the Eternal to whose eyes every temporal thing (past, present, and future) is subject. What we have been is present to him. What we shall be is equally present to him.

In short, the two purely interior religious acts (devotion and prayer) help us understand correctly what God carries in his bosom from all eternity: His desire for our salvation and his vision of us. Jesus, the captive of his love in the Eucharist, is consecrated to the eternal will, and looking at us with a merciful glance, he espouses the eternal vision of his Father. To make a visit to the Blessed Sacrament is truly to respond to the Eternal. You will object that in this case the Will of God is concerned with a changing "exterior," subject to the flux of time, namely, our salvation, and that his gaze rests upon us in our contingent and temporal existence. But to will and to know are purely immanent activities, whose inwardness cannot be compromised, and which, when exercised by God, culminate in him. They follow the condition of the Eternal; they must be said to be eternal.

There are, however, two divine actions that come forth from God, so to speak, that pass into and are consummated in creatures and in time. These are the creation and the government of the world. As far as God is concerned, this universe is unquestionably something "outside" himself. A new religious attitude comes into being: adoration.

II. THE ACTS OF ADORATION

Adoration honors God as the One who, through creation, brought us forth from nothing into existence and who, by his government, preserves us in this same existence. We see at once that to adore Jesus in the Blessed Sacrament is to address ourselves to him as the Creator of the universe, and, even in his humanity, as the Re-Creator of a world that sin had degraded. It is something more: it is to stand before the divine King and Mediator-King, the conserver of our existence, the defender of the Kingdom of God and guardian of its unity. It stems from a logic immanent in created things that Eucharistic adoration presents itself in fact as worship rendered to Christ the King. Already St. Thomas Aquinas called to mind Christ the King in the first stanza of his *Pange lingua,* and he wanted the invitatory of Matins for the feast of Corpus Christi to celebrate the lordship of Christ the King over all nations: *"Christum Regem adoremus dominantem gentibus."*

Corpus Christi, however, does not repeat the feast of Christ the King. For even though Jesus reigns in heaven in all the dimensions and splendors of his glorified body, he does not reside under the Eucharistic species as if he had left the place of his glory and traveled after the manner of a satellite through the stars. He is there very simply by reason of the fact of the change of the bread into his body, and only the species of bread relate him to the ciborium and to the tabernacle as to his dwelling place. Such a unique mode of presence certainly deserves a special feast of its own. Besides, it calls to mind much less the glorified Christ in heaven (regardless of what too many spiritual writers seem to think) than the Mediator-King delivering himself up to the hands of sinners in order to save them, undergoing death and rising again.

Adoration is principally a matter of the soul. It is reverence and humility. Reverence, that is to say, a fear of making ourselves equal to God, a fear of comparing ourselves to him; and humility, that is to say, the retreat of the soul into its insignificance, moderation with regard to personal exaltation over foolish hopes.

If adoration limited itself to these interior sentiments of reverential fear, of modesty of heart, it would not be strictly religious, it would not have the quality of homage, it would not do something for the glory of God. But this reverence is completely dedicated, and puts into movement the body itself, that carnal universe created conjointly with the soul and governed by God as is the great physical universe. Adoration is simply a reverential fear and humility going to the point of externalizing themselves and finding their supreme expression in beautiful actions. . . .

III. THE SACRIFICIAL BANQUET

Religious devotion and the prayer of simplicity honor the eternal will and gaze of the Father in heaven.

Adoration is an homage of the creature, protesting its dependence in time upon "The One who is."

But now we consider the creature honoring God as the Master of life, re-integrated into him by rites of participation and of offering, whose loftiest expression is the sacrificial banquet that we humbly call the Mass.

The Mass honors God as Life and the source of all life whether the faithful welcome his divine life in themselves as the bread that restores, comforts, and consoles, or whether they offer up their own lives in sacrifice, so that they may be transmuted into God and transfigured into him. There has to be an exchange of life between God and men. For God wants men as his friends, and there is no friendship—that is to say, no reciprocal love—except on the basis of an exchange of life.

When two beings pledge their lives to one another, this pledge makes of them henceforth intimate friends and as it were penetrable to one another. The Eucharist is the bond of a reciprocal love. It is a sacrament in that the life of the Father in heaven passes into us through the body of his son. It is a sacrifice in that our life passes into God in the blood of the crucified. Sacrament, sacrifice, these two terms cannot be dissociated. They stem from one and the same friendship. Life is like a river that flows down the mountain and loses itself in the ocean. In its course through the plain the river takes into itself the water of the spring, and at that same instant it is drawn toward the immensity toward which it is flowing. God is, for us, both the spring and the ocean. As the source of divine life, he dispenses the Bread of Life to us in Communion. As the immensity of life, he carries us away, once we have been sacrificed, into the ocean of love. In the same instance the flower opens to the rays of the sun and offers the sun its beauty. Communion and sacrifice cannot be dissociated. They are to be distinguished.

1. *Communion*

To receive Communion is to receive Life from on high, the Bread of Heaven, the Living Bread. The soul is incapable of this receptiveness if it is inwardly separated from God and the Church by mortal sin. In this deplorable state it might use the Eucharist *sacramentally,* that is to say, without going beyond the visible sign. He alone eats the flesh of Christ *spiritually* and likewise drinks his blood who has been made a participant of the unity of the Church in the bond of charity and enjoys the benefits of the communion of saints.

In Communion the Blessed Virgin Mary plays an eminent role. Being more fervent than anyone else, her burning charity is poured into hearts and sets them afire. Hence it is natural that anyone who sees himself lacking in fervor should ask the Virgin Mary to take his place since he is such an awkward and uncouth child. She is the purveyor of the Eucharistic banquet. What the consecrating priest actually calls down upon the altar is what Jesus received from Mary—his body and blood; and what the cross returned to Mary in separated form but filled with divine energies. And yet Mary was not in the Cenacle, at table with the Apostles. The hero of the sacred banquet was St. John.

A newly ordained priest and first communicant, in the flush of youth, purity, and intellectual vigor, St. John allowed himself to be intoxicated as he rested on his Master's heart. He put all other things out of his mind. He tasted the sweetness of God in an immense repose. And Jesus found repose in John. He deigned to be comforted and consoled by him. He consented to be helped in his sorrow by his first communicant; he entrusted to him his most burdensome secret, the name of the traitor.

Compared to this First Communion, our own Communions are tepid. What is it that prevents the Sacrament of the Eucharist from bearing its fullest fruit in us? It is not our mortal sins. That is out of the question, in as much as they would prevent us from even approaching the Communion rail. It is our present venial sins; it is our state of relaxation, the distraction and dissipation of our souls, the thousand futilities that inhabit us.

2. Sacrifice

There is no point in belaboring the human and religious significance of meals. Christians are keenly aware of it. They more easily forget that the Eucharist is not only the sacrament by which we nourish ourselves, but also the sacrifice in which we must participate. The sacrifice offered to God holds precedence over the sacrament that man uses. We receive Communion only in order to have the strength to be a victim, and in the sacrificial act to be transformed and as it were consumed into God.

Such a perspective would arouse less repugnance and would even be readily accepted, if we had a more favorable notion of sacrifice. The spirituality of seventeenth-century France bears a heavy responsibility for this. It looked upon sacrifice as a "return to nothingness." It identified sacrifice and adoration, the latter being in fact an affirmation and protestation by creatures of their nothingness.

To sacrifice is not to destroy or to kill, and death is not pleasing to God. To sacrifice is to overcome death, to go beyond death in an effusion of blood. The blood, the life are poured out in the presence of

God to honor the one who is Life and the source of life, the one who transmutes our life into his in order to transfigure it. Never in the history of Israel has the killing of the victim been reserved for the priests. Sometimes laymen were placed in charge of killing (see Ex 24:5). What was reserved for the priests was the manipulation of the blood, the effusion of the blood on the altar, the life offered to God "out of respect for his majesty and love for his goodness" (St. Thomas).

The act of sacrifice is deeply penetrated with faith, hope, and charity. If anyone doubts it, he might draw light and certitude from an analysis of the act that is the contrary of the sacrificial act—namely, suicide.

The man who commits suicide in a lucid state (if that is possible) is a despairing person who is turning to the abyss. Life is devoid of meaning and interest. It is too hard. He thinks he can dispose of his own life, be the master of life. Conversely, he sometimes cuts himself off from society, and in every epoch society has held him in disgrace.

But there is no sacrifice outside the climate of hope and love, or without a burning desire to obtain a release as yet unhoped for, to be re-integrated in the plenitude of life, to be united to supreme Life. Within a community, it is the noblest member who is sacrificed, and the community supports him and finds itself elevated in him. The victim himself experiences a peace beyond death. Death no longer counts. Death has no importance any more. The apparently lost cause has been won back in a better universe. Listen to what a member of the Resistance in World War II wrote before being shot by the occupying forces:

. . . I go in peace. The future is assured. I am without regrets, without anxiety, without emotion. *I belong to tomorrow.* My executioners already belong to yesterday.

Noble words on the purely human plane, and yet they agree with the sacrificial mystique that all religions have professed.

But what paganism had outlined vaguely has found its eminent realization among Christians. The sacrifice of Christ is continuous with the sacrifices of all times. And yet it is so perfectly original, so impossible to reiterate, so lacking in identity with other sacrifices, that it gives them all signification and value. As the intermediary between the Father of heaven and humanity, Christ receives from the community of the just the capacity to be a victim like them. He receives from his Father, to whom all life returns, his mastery over his own life, and the power to give it at the moment of his choice without committing suicide. He is the only one to be at once sacrificer and victim, sacrificing and sacrificed. His sacrifice is unique for time and eternity.

Jesus has said: "I am in the Father and the Father is in me" (Jn 14:10). This beautiful mystery of living and reciprocal immanence, this integration of the Father and Son is a living unity is the mystery that is honored in every Mass, every celebration of the sacrificial banquet, in which God comes down into the hearts of Christians so that they may enter and dwell in him. There is nothing to seek beyond that. Everything is consummated in the bond of love. But we do not eat the flesh of the Lord until after we have adored it.

NOTES

J. A. Robilliard, O.P., teaches on the faculty of the famous Dominican *studium,* the Saulchoir, near Paris. The present article appeared in *Revue Eucharistique du Clergé* (Montreal, P.Q.) from May through August of 1960, and in translation in *Emmanuel.*

1. St. Augustine, *Enarratio in Ps. 98,* PL 37:1264, no. 9. And he comments on his affirmation with these words: "Not only do we not sin by adoring it, but we sin in not adoring it."

2. On this point, see *La Maison-Dieu,* 11 (1947), pp. 179–184.

3. Here is the text: "Elevat ergo sacerdos corpus Christi in altari, quasi dicat: Ecce quem totus mundus capere non potest captivus noster est; ergo Eum non dimittamus, nisi quod petimus prius obtineamus." *Opera omnia S. Bonaventurae,* Ed. Peltier, v. 12, p. 268. On this *Expositio missae,* see A. Franz, *Die Messe im deutschen Mittelalter* (Freiburg, 1902), p. 463.

4. To *visit* signifies "to see often."

10 Eucharistic Piety

An imposing building remains the same though it may look different according to the side from which one views it. The same is true of the Holy Eucharist. It is a sacrifice, a memorial, a thanksgiving, a sign of the new and eternal covenant, an epiphany and presence of Christ, a sacred meal. The human mind is too limited to grasp all these aspects simultaneously. Thus at different periods in the history of the Church, different facets of the Eucharist have been emphasized, as they corresponded to the need and atmosphere af each successive age.

The veneration of the Holy Eucharist has gone through diverse phases that may even seem to be almost contradictory, if viewed only from the outside. Yet it remains essentially the same piety, the same faith and the same reverence, though the expression varies. In the fourth century the communicant received the Lord's body in his hands and was careful that no crumb should fall to the ground since, according to the *Mystagogical Catecheses* of Jerusalem, he bore in his hands something more precious than gold and jewels. The same faith and the same reverence are shown when the Sisters of Perpetual Adoration kneel for hours and turn their eyes in prayer toward the monstrance, placed at the center of the blazing candles.

The fact is that for centuries—one can say, for the first thousand years—the Eucharist, although forming the innermost kernel of Christian piety, remained so much in the background that one cannot speak of a distinct Eucharistic devotion. The main lines of the great Eucharistic liturgies were of course already laid down, in their classical forms, and they conveyed the eternally valid mystery. The Eucharist was celebrated and received, but none of the hagiographers before the twelfth century thought of mentioning how often the saint received Communion or other similar details which would reveal his attitude to the Eucharist. The fact that priests said Mass often or even daily is sometimes noted in passing, but nothing analogous is expressly mentioned in the lives of holy layfolk. The Eucharist was an organic part of their spiritual lives and it was taken for granted. The Eucharist was indeed for them the central act in Christian life, but this central act was not clearly singled out and illuminated. The Eucharist was a kind of radiance around the central point, and other lights gleamed in this halo of light.

For many years the central point in Christian life was Baptism. Baptism is an illumination, a rebirth to divine life, the paschal resurrection with Christ, an incorporation into Christ and the Church. The Eucharist appeared as the obvious continuation of the life grounded and begun in Baptism. This is why we find on the tombstones of the catacombs various pictures which refer to Baptism: Noah in the ark, Moses striking the rock, the Samaritan woman by the well. We tend to say of a dead person that he was "fortified by the rites of the Church," and we have in mind the Eucharist; but in the early period they were inclined to think of Baptism. For this reason, the faithful who have died and whom we pray for at Mass, are still described today as those "who have gone before us in the sign of faith." They have gone before us marked with the seal of faith, Baptism; their faith was confirmed and sealed by Baptism. In the early creeds, then, where we do not expect an enumeration of the sacraments, Baptism is mentioned, but not the Eucharist.

The early Christians turned their minds principally to the starting point of Christian life, but also to its conclusion. Christianity is an invitation to the great marriage feast. It is the proclamation of the kingdom of God, to be realized at the end of time. It is the beginning of the marriage feast of the Lamb, spoken of in the Apocalypse.

In the last hundred years archeologists have discovered in the Roman catacombs and elsewhere representations of meals. A few scholars have thought that they depict the Eucharist or at least the Last Supper or the multiplication of loaves or a love-feast. None of these interpretations is wholly satisfactory. They are certainly not historical representations of the multiplication of loaves or the Last Supper. The guests sit at a semicircular table called *sigma;* bread and fish are on the table, jugs of wine stand nearby. It is certainly not an historical feast: the Eucharist is only its earthly beginning, and the *agape,* in particular the *agape* of the dead, is only a foreshadowing of it. It is the feast at the end of time. It is the great gift of divine grace alluded to in the Postcommunions of the Missal where, even after Communion has been received, we further pray that we may receive even greater gifts. It is glory, which is why the antiphon *O Sacrum Convivium* describes the Eucharist as an earnest of glory to come. It is the *Marana tha* ("Come, Lord Jesus") of the early Church, conveyed in the language of images.

The early Church had a much stronger sense than we have of the eschatological fulfillment, even when it no longer counted on the imminent return of the Lord. It prayed "thy Kingdom come" with much more fervor than we usually do, and in the light of this hope the brightness of the Eucharist was almost overlooked.

Yet the early Church lived out the life of grace and the sacraments in the present, too. And from this point of view the Eucharist occupied a central place. Since the Eucharistic movement began, and especially since Pius X, the example of the early Church has often been proposed—their daily Communions, their devout celebration of the sacred mysteries. The appeal to the example of the early Church is justified. Though there has undoubtedly been some idealization born of over-enthusiasm, the facts we know are important and sufficiently eloquent.

It is true that they did not in general celebrate the Eucharist daily—for technical reasons this was scarcely practicable—but the Eucharist could be taken home after the Sunday celebration. There is evidence of a widespread custom of receiving daily the holy bread, "before any other food." The practice was taken for granted to such an extent that the prayer for daily bread in the Our Father was understood, in the earliest patristic exegesis, to refer primarily to the bread of the Eucharist.

There was no precept of the Church imposing Sunday celebration.

But participation seems to have been so general that, as Justin reports, all came together on Sunday, townspeople and country folk; deacons bore the Eucharist to those who were prevented from coming. Further, there was great reluctance to forego the Sunday liturgy when persecution broke out again and participation spelled mortal danger. For what caused the Christians to be persecuted and threatened with death was not their faith—anyone could believe what he liked—but their particular form of divine worship, so early on Sunday morning, and so independent of the official pagan cult. Persecution was directed against the form of worship. Yet the Christians held firmly to their Eucharistic meetings. And when we read in the *Acts of the Martyrs* the defense of those who were accused during the Diocletian persecution, it expresses the feeling of many others: without the *dominicum* we could not exist. One can perhaps say that the majority of the martyrs of that period died because they held fast to the Eucharist.

And yet relatively little is said about the Sacrament or about the presence of the body of Christ. But there is much about what should result from them. The sacred Communion of the Sacrament is the force which binds into unity the communion of saints. The *communio* is repeatedly mentioned, but in a way which makes it impossible to know whether the Sacrament or the community is meant.

St. Augustine should be mentioned in this connection. He has often been reproached with stressing so much the symbolic side of the Sacrament that its particular content, the real presence of Christ's body and blood, was no longer properly expressed. Less has been heard of this complaint in the last few years, as new sermons of the great doctor have been discovered in which he makes his position clear. Nevertheless, it remains true that he scarcely ever speaks of the Eucharist without immediately indicating its social meaning, its power of uniting the community of the faithful. "The meaning of the sacrament," he says in Sermo 55,7 "is unity, so that we who are taken up in his body as his limbs, should be what we receive." Christians receive the body of Christ that they may become the body of Christ.

The Eucharist was not considered in isolation as an object of veneration or as a particular form of Christian piety, but rather as an essential part of Christian living. Moreover, this view can be seen in the New Testament, where Christians are invited to unite themselves with Christ: "Draw near to him, the living stone . . . you too must be built up on him, stones that live and breathe, into a living temple, to offer up these spiritual offerings which God accepts through Jesus Christ" (1 Pet. 2:4). What are these spiritual offerings? Are they merely good works and a genuine Christian life? Or is the Eucharist meant? Plainly, both are referred to. The offering of the Christian life, that is the day to day work, endurance and suffering, is constantly gathered up and offered to God in the Eucharist, so that it is not so much the individual who achieves something remarkable, but rather that all together form a spiritual temple in which God is glorified.

The Eucharist was the celebration of the community. That is why the plural is used in the official prayers of the priest, and the dialogue between priest and people takes the form of invitation and acclamation. That is why until the late Middle Ages, at least on Sundays and holydays, the liturgy was the common celebration of all, and the clergy, gathered round a common altar, concelebrated and communicated together.[1]

Even so, there are traces in the early Christian period of a piety that is directed, immediately and expressly, toward the Sacrament itself. This is true of Chrysostom, who has been described as the *Doctor Eucharistiae*. He praises the greatness and dignity of the Sacrament. It is striking that in him (as already in some earlier Christian writings) the Sacrament is described as the "awful" mystery and the altar as the "fearsome" table. Although he concentrates his attention on the Sacrament and loosens it to some extent from its context in the economy of salvation, he makes his hearers aware of the greatness of the divine mystery in its totality, and this is in fact given in the Sacrament.[2]

In the Western Church a similar development came to dominate; and it was much stronger than in the East. The reverence due to the Sacrament was increasingly emphasized—the early Church may perhaps have treated it too nonchalantly. But now more and more precepts and rubrics were laid down for the reception of Communion; the prescriptions of ritual purity in the Old Testament were invoked;

reverence grew, Communion became more infrequent. Theological discussion sought to elucidate the nature of the Eucharistic presence, and the question of the precise moment at which transubstantiation took place aroused interest.

It is most instructive to trace the development of one small ceremony. In the early Middle Ages the part of the Mass from the beginning of the Preface to the Our Father was still thought of as a whole, as the Eucharistic prayer, as thanksgiving to the divine Majesty to whom the sacrifice is offered. This was expressed in the rubric instructing the congregation, at pontifical Mass, to bow when the celebrating bishop sang *adorant dominationes, tremunt potestates*. From that point onward they were to remain bowed down throughout the whole Canon until the concluding Doxology.[9] When the *Sanctus* began, they had all to kneel down and remain on their knees, praying before God's majesty.

Then the attitude changed imperceptibly. The change of posture was delayed. It was no longer placed before but after the *Sanctus*. Thus the feeling grew that it is only with the *Te Igitur* that the prayer of consecration begins; and the homage now goes to the Sacrament. What precedes, so it is thought, is only an introduction, a "preface"; only after it do we enter the realm of the sacred mystery. And so people begin to kneel down after the *Sanctus* in honour of the Blessed Sacrament. It is certainly a possible and meaningful approach; but it differs from that of early ages.

A second development completes and reinforces the first. Germanic sensibility sought everywhere something visible and tangible. People wanted, for example, to see and venerate holy relics. Thus the desire to see the Sacrament grew, and it was all the greater since people so seldom dared to receive it. So, within the Canon, the moment of consecration is singled out by raising the Sacred Host and letting the people see it. This undoubtedly significant custom began in Paris about the year 1200 and spread to the Rhineland. But toward the end of the Middle Ages the practice of being present only for the actual moment of consecration had become an abuse; people came in to look at the Host and then left the church immediately.

The tendency to emphasize the holy Sacrament and make it an object of special veneration remains, even after the reforms of the Council of Trent. The development is certainly justified and is an enrichment of the life of the Church, unless something more important is thereby disturbed and destroyed. The feast of Corpus Christi and the Corpus Christi processions begin. The monstrance is introduced to display the Blessed Sacrament to the faithful in a worthy setting. Exposition during Vespers and during Mass is introduced. Holy Hour and Benediction start. *Quarant' ore,* which from the earliest period had been used during Holy Week to recall the forty hours spent by our Lord in the tomb, is now transformed into forty hours of prayer before the Blessed Sacrament. In church the tabernacle takes the central place and outweighs the altar in importance. The idea spreads that a church is primarily the house of God, and only requires reverence when the lamp burns within it. A sacramental piety develops which, even within the Mass, values and understands only the Consecration, because at that moment Christ becomes present.

Not all these developments can be approved. For the result of much far-reaching emphasis was to isolate the Blessed Sacrament from the original context of its foundation. A static view of the Sacrament became all too often predominant; the main interest centered on the abiding Presence. The dynamic understanding of the mystery as thanksgiving, sacrifice, and communion, as the taking up of human wretchedness into the transforming power of Christ's mystery, was considerably weakened.

Yet the Mass was maintained and continued in its inherited form with great fidelity; the texts and rites were preserved in their entirety. But the remarkable thing is that this admirably preserved liturgy, which harmonizes all the important aspects of the Eucharistic mystery, had little effect on the piety of the clergy. To the people the liturgy became remote and alien; but clerics, too, in spite of their fidelity to the rubrics, failed to grasp its meaning.

Early Christianity, which had laid the foundations of the Eucharistic liturgy still visible today in all liturgies of East and of West, sought to enshrine two leading ideas: the Mass is the memorial of the Lord, and it is the offering of the Church. These two thoughts are expressed, clearly, at a decisive point of the Mass as we know it today: *Unde et memores . . . tam beatae passionis . . . offerimus praeclarae majestati tuae hostiam puram. . . .* This twofold prayer is found in the earliest Eucharistic prayer that has come down to us, in the liturgy of Hippolytus of Rome. Dating from about 215, the text reads, after the words of consecration: *Memores igitur mortis et resurrectionis eius offerimus tibi panem et calicem.* The idea expressed is this: what we have just done is a memorial of the Lord, in accordance with his command at the Last Supper. He handed over to us, as a memorial, the offering of his body and the outpouring of his blood, so that we might never forget who is our hope and our salvation. There is a further idea: that we too should present to the heavenly Father the offering of his body and the outpouring of his blood, as an expression of our own Christian self-giving and worship of the divine Majesty.

This primitive form of Eucharistic celebration expresses with clarity —heightened in the course of the celebration—that we are dealing with the body and blood of the God-man, and that the body and blood of the Lord are really here present. The mind did not, however, linger on the fact of presence, but pressed onward dynamically to the reception of the holy food and the prayer of thanksgiving that concludes the feast.

As the Eucharistic cult was self-explanatory and was itself the main form of Eucharistic piety, it not unnaturally happened that the memorial and offering receded into the background; they were taken for granted as an inherited possession. In the explanations of the Mass given to the faithful and committed to writing, the memorial of the Lord is strongly emphasized. From the end of the eighth century the Mass was conceived as a dramatic representation of the history of salvation from the fall of Adam to the coming of the Redeemer and beyond that to his second coming at the last day. Later, the scope of the representation was gradually restricted to the sufferings of the Lord. So one can understand how Corpus Christi mystery plays, which flourished at the start of the modern period, could incorporate extracts from the older Passion mysteries. In the Bozen Corpus Christi play, tableaux of the sufferings of Christ were carried in procession, both in the form of Old Testament types and scenes from the New Testament. In this way the thought of the *anamnesis* was kept alive.

Neither did the idea of sacrifice disappear. It was kept alive in the minds of the faithful chiefly through the Offertory procession. For many years, every Sunday, there was the widespread custom of an Offertory procession in which the whole community took part. In the late Middle Ages the Offertory procession took place at least on great feast days: on the four feast days that corresponded to the "four seasons"—such was the general rule. There were also Offertory processions on special occasions like funerals, weddings, guild and confraternity celebrations. One must admit that this practice, in which money had a certain part to play, was exposed to dangers of misunderstanding and formalism. People thought not so much of sharing in Christ's sacrifice as of sharing in the Offertory gifts, about which some highly dubious theories were prevalent.

The Offertory practices of the Middle Ages in decline roused the wrath of the Reformers. Not only did they exclude the Offertory procession from the Church's traditional liturgy, but they removed all traces of sacrifice from the Mass and left only the commemoration of the Last Supper; for they held that the Church cannot offer sacrifice; there is only one sacrifice, that made by Christ on the cross.

The Council of Trent and the theology derived from it insisted, in answer to the Reformers' positions, that the Mass is not an independent sacrifice, but the re-presentation of Christ's sacrifice. They stress that Christ is the priest of this sacrifice as he was in the sacrifice of the cross, and yet that there is a true offering in the Mass and a true and enduring presence of the body of Christ, not simply *in usu,* at the moment of reception. The Eucharistic interest of the last few centuries has thus been directed to the offering of Christ; the fact that the Church and the faithful have a part to play has been obscured. This is a reaction against the medieval view.

Interest has also been concentrated on the Real Presence of the Lord in the Sacrament. The defense of the traditional, inherited, inalienable doctrine led to such an emphasis. It was at this time that the various forms of Eucharistic cult we know so well were introduced. Eucharistic piety comes to mean veneration of the Eucharist, prayer before the Blessed Sacrament exposed, Benediction, Mass processions, Holy Communion—but with all the stress laid on the fervor needed in preparation for Communion and thanksgiving after it. For the isolation of the Sacrament and the concentration on the Real Presence affected the view of Communion. The idea of participation in the sacrifice, in the sacrificial food, loses ground—in the eighteenth and nineteenth centuries Communion was distributed chiefly outside Mass—and Communion is regarded as the visit of the Savior who comes out of the tabernacle. Even when Communion was received during Mass, devotion to Communion was an independent thing having hardly anything to do with the Mass.

Perhaps no age showed so much fervor and devotion in preparing children for Communion as the nineteenth century. Tension was great among the children and their teachers. Excitement reigned for weeks and months. First Communion became the most beautiful day of one's life, for it was the child's first encounter with the Savior.

But is it really the first meeting with the Savior? Some must have raised this question. For the first meeting, the great transforming encounter, has already taken place in Baptism where the child is incorporated into the body of Christ, is received into the Resurrection of Christ, becomes a Christian. But the Eucharist, in which Christ is present, and Communion, in which he is personally received, so overshadowed all the other sacraments that almost nothing more remained of them, even of Baptism, than a prescribed rite through which certain effects of grace were mediated. Communion was an isolated peak, and therefore the devotion of Communion became a separated thing.

The stimulus to frequent Communion provided by Pius X did little to change this attitude, however much good it may have done in other respects. If the nineteenth century had stressed the veneration of the Blessed Sacrament, the emphasis was now shifted to its reception, and this was indeed a great step forward. But even in catechisms of our own day, Eucharistic doctrine is frequently presented under the following heads: Sacrament, Mass, Communion. Sometimes the order of

presentation is: Sacrament, Communion, Mass. It is therefore legitimate to speak of the disintegration that has taken place in the conception of the Eucharist. All the elements are there. All the dogmas of
faith are maintained and zealously confessed; but unity between them,
a sense of the harmony of the whole doctrine has been lost.

Yet we must admit that even with this form of piety, the Blessed
Sacrament has been the source of countless blessings—and great
strength. The Sacrament is rich enough for people to live on a part of
the great mystery: on, so to speak, a fragment of the Host. It would not
be difficult to draw up a long list of saints whose piety centered on the
tabernacle: from St. Paschal Baylon whose relics were specially brought
from Spain to the Munich Eucharistic Congress, to Damien de Veuster
who said that he would have been unable to bear life among the lepers
if the Savior had not been present in the tabernacle of his chapel. These
outstanding figures represent millions of devout faithful and zealous
Christians who followed the same path and became holy in the same
way. We should not dare to criticize their piety or claim to be superior
to them. Their devotional forms were good and, in their situation,
inevitable and right, even if they were not the best possible.

Yet we can and must grant that the time had come to overcome the
separation of the parts. In an age when life is increasingly secularized,
when to many people God seems more and more remote, the Church
must place before men the full power of her teaching and mysteries.

The liturgical renewal of this century is simply the attempt to restore
the parts to the whole, and particularly to bring out the full, integrating
meaning of the Eucharist. The historical studies of the preceding
generation have enabled us to see more clearly the development of the
liturgy and to grasp the process by which the partial aspects of the
Eucharist were gradually divorced from each other. They likewise have
enabled us to understand the ideal present at the beginning and so
badly needed in our time.

The Eucharistic Congress held in Munich in 1960 was perhaps the
first great opportunity of making the newly discovered ideal known
publicly. It was no longer simply the cult of the Eucharist on a vast
scale; the celebration of the Eucharist was set in the context of the

whole economy of salvation. For there we witnessed the Church, we saw how she celebrates and receives the Eucharist—and thereby we honored the Eucharist. We witnessed the power the Eucharist has of uniting and holding together the People of God. The *Corpus mysticum* was seen in the full, ancient, and complete meaning of the term.

It is not by chance that this expression was first used of the Lord's sacramental body. We receive in Communion the mysteriously hidden body of the Lord, the *Corpus mysticum*—such was the way writers spoke in the Carolingian period. But the mysteriously hidden body can effect a fresh realization, a new embodiment of itself in the visible human world; it can express itself in the multiple limbs that make up the body of Christ, the Church. The Church is indeed the body of the Lord, it is the earthly revelation of what is contained in the Sacrament and what will one day be perfected and fulfilled in heaven.

The discovery of the Church, the reawakening of the sense of the Church, is one of the most welcome aspects of the contemporary religious renewal. The strength that the sense of the Church has already attained appears most clearly in church architecture. The ecclesiastical architecture of the last decade may not be comparable to Baroque architecture or to the great Gothic cathedrals in its appeal to the aesthetic sense or its artistic richness; but it can be compared in meaningfulness and depth of religious feeling. In Baroque the primary concern was to draw down to this earth the glory of heaven and the rejoicing of the Church triumphant; Baroque sought to make the house of God reflect the glory of heaven. Human beings, here on earth, were only marginal figures in the plan, whatever the scale of the building.

Modern church architecture has begun, rightly, to express the reality of the *ecclesia,* the sacred assembly, gathered together here on earth, its mind raised toward God and the coming of his kingdom, knowing that though it is called by him, favored by him and nourished by the Holy Bread from the altar, yet it remains firmly in this world and gives glory to God in this precise place.

The new-found sense of the Church, one of the most welcome aspects of the contemporary religious revival, carries with it the recognition that the Church, gathered together and held together by the Eucharist, is not a vague, shadowy reality beyond time (though one often gets this impression when people speak of the excellence and divine qualities of the Church), but is the empirical Church here and now, drawn from this world, grouped around this altar, made up of men and women of all classes and ages. And this multitude of people, assembled to celebrate the Eucharist, is not raised above the earthly world into a sphere that has nothing to do with everyday cares; on the contrary, everyday life and the harsh realities of earthly existence are borne to the altar Sunday by Sunday, represented in the gifts of bread and wine, bread from our earthly fields, wine from our earthly vineyards.

These gifts, offered in gratitude, are taken up in the all-embracing offering of Christ, spiritualized in him and transformed into a hymn of praise to the divine Majesty. That is precisely what we found at the outset, in the first epistle of St. Peter: the faithful are living stones built up into a holy temple, so as to offer their whole now transformed lives through Christ to God.

The liturgical movement, it has been said, has reduced the honor paid to the Savior in the Eucharist. That may be so. The main emphasis is now placed not on a partial aspect, a single truth in the wide range of doctrine, but rather on the specific and central focus of the whole doctrine. Our attention is directed to the central point, and this center begins to shine with clearer light; but the surrounding areas, hitherto perhaps dull and obscure, are also illuminated. We understand the Church better, the Church that celebrates the Eucharist, and the unity of the Church that the Sacrament calls for; we understand better Baptism from which the Church is born; and Scripture, the other table of God nourishing us at the start of every Eucharistic celebration, has acquired a new and richer relevance.

Enlightened thinking on the Eucharist knows well that salvation cannot lie simply in the frequency of Eucharistic celebration, that the total of Communions is not the best way to measure the spiritual state of a parish, that sacramental life must not be separated from the personal, spiritual, abiding encounter of the person with his God. A high esteem for the Eucharist suggests that it requires gradual preparation, that prayer in common outside Mass should also have a place in the devotional life of a parish: that there should be a place for the Word of God and awareness of the good news that has been proclaimed; that preaching of the Word and worthy divine service go hand in hand.

In fact, we need not worry about a special devotion to the Eucharist. If only it could be integrated into the whole of Christian life, as it was in the early Church! We must see to it that the faithful understand the full richness of God's love, conveyed to us in Christ and answered by faith, hope, and charity. Then they will of their own accord enter into the *Gratias agamus Domino Deo nostro,* the great *Eucharistia* that our Lord himself taught us. That is the healthiest and most durable form of Eucharistic piety.

NOTES

Josef A. Jungmann, S.J., is a member of the theology faculty at the Canisianum, Innsbruck, Austria, and has published numerous works on the liturgy, most notable being the classic *The Mass of the Roman Rite.* The present chapter appeared first as an article in *Way* (London) for April of 1963.

1. M. Andrieu, *Les Ordines Romani III* (Louvain, 1951), p. 178.
2. G. Fittkau, *Der Begriff des Mysteriums bei Johannes Chrysostomus* (Bonn, 1953), pp. 122 ff.
3. J. A. Jungmann, *Gewordene Liturgie* (Innsbruck, 1941), pp. 120–136.

11 The Eucharist
and the Prayer of Christ

In the course of illustrating how the sacrifice of Christ fulfilled the typical sacrifice of expiation described in Chapter 16 of Leviticus, St. Paul shows our Lord entering the Holy of Holies after this sacrifice, bearing his own blood so as "to appear now before the face of God on our behalf" (Heb 9:24).

We must conclude that Christ lives in a state of intercession analogous to the intercession of the high priest who, after the sacrifice of expiation, entered the Holy of Holies each year bearing the blood of the victim. The sacrifice of Calvary, as a sacrifice of expiation prefigured by the sacrifices of the Old Law, inaugurated the reparative intercession that will remain until the Parousia an aspect of Christ's heavenly life in which we all share through faith.

The picture of the heavenly liturgy that St. John outlines for us in the Apocalypse leads us to the same conclusion. The Lord is described as "a Lamb standing, as if slain" (Apoc 5:6). In his glorious life in heaven Christ preserves, in a way we cannot pinpoint, something that is an immediate reminder of the immolation that opened the door of heaven to him. In his encyclical *Mystici corporis,* Pope Pius XII calls him *hostia clarificata in caelis* and affirms that it is as a victim that he exercises his eternal priesthood, "since he lives always to make intercession" (Heb 7:25) for us.[1]

The conclusion is that there is only one prayer: the prayer of Christ, a prayer that is coextensive with his life. If our prayer is to be heard by the Father, it must be part of Christ's prayer. Hence "to pray in his name" is to pattern our prayer on the prayer of Christ. The invitation to pray without ceasing calls upon us to make us cleave ever more consciously to the *élan vital* of the total Christ, in which we have shared since our admission into the Church.

SHARING IN CHRIST'S PRAYER

At each Eucharistic assembly the Church celebrates and enters into all the aspects of the mysteries of Christ's life, under the sacramental signs. At the times of each celebration the entire Church militant wedges an opening into eternity, as it were, by the fact that each of her members becomes aware, in the measure that he participates actively in the celebration, of his part in the life of the Church triumphant united to her Head.

The sanctity of the Church guarantees that she always has members consciously living their life of union with Christ, and consequently this opening into eternity is a permanent fact for the Church militant, continually in adoration before the *infinita et divina Majestas Christi* [2] and joining herself to him in the total gift that he makes of himself to the Father.

But this does not hold true for each of her members. Outside the sacramental celebrations in which we participate, each one returns to his daily life on the natural level, with the attendant danger of blunting if not losing the dispositions that kept him united to his Head in the bond of the Spirit.

Thus our participation in Christ's life of prayer, from one Mass to the next, remains rather passive. We continue to take part in it absolutely as long as we do not place any formal obstacle to it. But we have a tendency to allow ourselves to be carried along by it, without contributing to it in a personal manner. And this does not constitute a proper response to the Apostle's appeal for prayer.

The community celebrations of the Eucharist thus appear as the vital moments of this life of prayer that we share with Christ but lived afterward with far less intensity during the course of our day. Our life of union offers the aspect of a series of disconnected spurts followed by periods of lesser intensity, in which there is inevitably a loss of spiritual energy.

But for Christ, life does not consist of disconnected spurts, and in the measure that we consciously live our union with him, our life should not consist of spurts either. In inviting us to strive to attain a life of prayer by intensifying our conscious union with Christ, St. Paul reminds us that through our incorporation with him we are in a state of intercession and that the attitude we have concretized in the ritual act at the time of the sacramental celebration should continue unceasingly to quicken us and to guide our behavior.

We must admit that in order to accomplish its full effect in our life and to maintain this effect, the Eucharistic celebration in which we have participated actively demands renewed efforts on our part to rise again and again to the level of participation that it had enabled us to achieve.

In order to succeed in living a life of prayer, we need exercises in mental prayer. We must set aside certain times when we turn our minds and hearts to the Lord, moments that will be the mainspring of our efforts to be united to his will in every aspect of our life. These will be the times of vital action, of communion with the mystery, and also of spiritual Communions that will produce their effect *ex opere operantis* only, but always in relation to the Eucharistic celebration. The more numerous they become, the more they will tend to generate the intermittent spiritual contact that will be our answer to the Apostle's invitation.

It is easy to see how, in the mind of the Church, the successive hours of the Divine Office were intended to perform this function. The call to continually renewed conscious participation is patterned on the rhythms of human life. It brings together spiritually the members of a community living their life of union in an atmosphere of sacramental celebration.

Can Eucharistic piety play an analogous role among the many Christians of our own time who do not have the close bond of monastic observance and do not always possess the scriptural and liturgical training to find an efficacious stimulant in the Canonical Office?

In order to answer this question we shall have to make a short historical inquiry into the matter of devotion to the sacramental Presence outside the Mass. It will enable us to bring out an aspect that we consider to be its essential element, although popular devotion has long neglected it because circumstances have led the Church to give greater emphasis to another complementary point of view.

THE SACRAMENTAL PRESENCE IN HISTORY

The First Eucharistic Expositions

The first permanent expositions of the Blessed Sacrament of which we have authentic proof date from the last years of the fourteenth century. We learn that in 1395 in a Bavarian province "a monstrance was placed behind the main altar, whose transparent crystal allowed everyone to see the Blessed Sacrament." [3] John of Marienwerder also represents the Venerable Dorothy, who lived in Danzig during the last years of the fourteenth century, as hastening toward the church before dawn *ut videret ibi Eucharistiae sacramentum, quod aperte in una monstrantia ibi servabatur, et sic fervorem sui desiderii in aliquo refrigeret.*[4]

This custom was sufficiently widespread throughout Germany in the fifteenth century to arouse the reaction of ecclesiastical authorities on several occasions.[5] And we believe that the many *Sakramenthause* of this period equipped with grilled doors were so constructed with a view to the exposition of the Blessed Sacrament.

The very terms of the decree of the Council of Cologne (1452), which defended exposition at other times than the Octave of Corpus Christi, "so as to render greater honor to the Blessed Sacrament," show quite convincingly that these expositions were without solemnity, and very different in spirit from that which inspired the institution of perpetual adoration in France during the nineteenth century. In order to understand the meaning of these primitive expositions we must consider them in the context of certain more ancient practices that were quite widespread at the time of their introduction.

Without taking a stand here on the origin of the Elevation and the modifications initiated by the decree of Eudes de Sully,[6] it is undeniable that in the thought of the faithful of the fourteenth and fifteenth centuries, the sight of the consecrated host was the occasion for spiritual Communion, to take the place of sacramental Communion, which had become quite a rare event. The words of the motet *O salutaris,* composed to be sung *"in elevatione, inter pleni sunt caeli et benedictus qui venit"* [7] give evidence to support this view, and many contemporary preachers condemned the habit on the part of the faithful of leaving the church after the Elevation in the thought that the essential part of their participation was then at an end.

While the Church showed her disapproval of such abuses, she never condemned the teaching of the thirteenth-century theologians for whom the sight of the host was a stimulant to faith.[8] During this same epoch we see the Church incorporate a short exposition of the Sacrament in the rite of the Communion of the Sick. The pastor was supposed to show the host to the sick person, and to exhort him in the vernacular to make a profession of faith in the One he was about to receive under the veils of the Sacrament.[9]

Before the ritual of Paul V (1614) forbade the bringing of the Eucharist to sick persons who were known to be unable to receive Communion,[10] many rituals of the first half of the sixteenth century made provision for such cases. They agreed with Nicolas de Blony, who wrote in his *Tractatus sacerdotalis* (Lyons, 1553): *"Tantum ostendat sibi corpus Christi, et suadeat sibi pie credendum et sentiendum de ipso: et sufficit tibi pro communione sacramentali, quia nihilominus ipse spiritaliter et non sacramentaliter, si est sine peccato mortali, communicaverit."*

In the text of the *Incunable* ritual of Rheims (late fifteenth century), after the description of the exposition at the Communion of the Sick, we find a special classification: *"De infirmis qui pre nimia infirmitate non possunt sacramentum eucaristiae recipere,"* where we read the following:

Talibus insinuatur fides ut supra [i.e., by showing them the host] *et eam confiteatur infirmus petatque veniam et indulgentiam ac indulgeat omnibus. Et presbyter tenens hostiam dicat:* "If it were possible for you to receive this most Blessed Sacrament, you would eagerly do so. Therefore if you pray to our Lord in this most Blessed Sacrament to forgive you all your sins and faults, it is his good pleasure that you receive him spiritually and have in your soul the effect and power of the Sacrament."

Now this exaggeration in practice, which had long existed in the Church, was to be officially condemned. The best refutation of it is the one attributed to St. Juliana of Mont Cornillon. On her deathbed in 1258 she said to her abbess, who was urging her to look at the host that she could not receive: *"Non necesse est, domina mea, videre in praesenti vita quem visura sum in aeterna"* (*Acta Sanctorum,* April 1). But even though the practice should be examined with caution, the meaning attributed to it in authorized texts does not allow us to doubt of the interpretation given to the exposition that preceded the Communion of the Sick, and it gives a clear idea of the meaning to be attributed to all Eucharistic expositions in the context of the period.

A consideration of these usages would indicate that the permanent expositions whose existence we have seen in Germany and elsewhere at the same period *were not instituted to affirm faith in the Real Presence, which no one felt the need to defend at that time.*

These expositions were devoid of external solemnity, and it does not seem to have occurred to anyone, even in the Conciliar decrees that condemned the custom, to suggest that it would be fitting to respond to the permanent sacramental presence with a permanent human presence. As far as we can see, the need to assure uninterrupted adoration was not felt. Rather, the purpose was to place the Sacrament directly before the eyes of the faithful, to be a stimulant to their faith and an invitation to a spiritual Communion that each one would be free to prolong as long as he chose and resume as often during the day as he pleased.

It can be declared that these expositions constituted a silent invitation to individual prayer in the line of the community celebration, and that the sacramental presence of Christ was sought in order to benefit from it rather than to honor it. Perhaps it would be better to say that it was thought greater honor was being paid to it in the measure that greater benefit was derived from these visits.

The Forty Hours

The highest point in this evolution of Eucharistic exposition, as an invitation to prolonged spiritual Communion, was the institution of the Forty Hours Devotion.

Although the examples we have cited so far come mostly from France and Germany, we should not conclude that the attitude of Italians was any different. The rite of the exposition during the Communion of the Sick is described in the *Liber sacerdotalis secundum ritus sanctae romanae et apostolicae Ecclesiae* published in Venice in 1512, and the report of the Inquisitors on the violation of the pontifical interdict on the city of Todi in 1328 gave evidence of an exposition of the Blessed Sacrament.[11]

Consequently when, during the war between Francis I and Charles V, the Capuchin Father Joseph Ferno decided to invite the people of Milan to take turns offering up uninterrupted solemn supplication to God during the Forty Hours, it was soon decided to expose the Blessed Sacrament with a view to making this new form of prayer easier.[12]

What was really new about St. Charles Borromeo's institution of the Forty Hours was neither the uninterrupted exposition nor the official announcement of the exposition, but the fact that everyone had the maximum opportunity to heed this call since the Forty Hours were celebrated successively in all the parishes and collegiate churches of his episcopal city.

A study of the texts shows that there is a perfect continuity between the medieval tradition and the thought of St. Charles. As a matter of fact, we must avoid judging the solemnity of this exposition in the light of present-day practices of perpetual adoration or attribute the same purpose to it.

We smile nowadays when we read of the regulations regarding the darkening of the windows,[13] and the interdiction against the poor entering the church and disturbing those at prayer by their begging.[14] The fact remains that these texts bear faithful witness to a spirit, and this spirit is still basically that of the Clementine Instruction that regulates the Forty Hours expositions of our own day.[15]

Everything has been meticulously regulated with a view to facilitate silent prayer. We have no basis for considering exterior décor as an homage rendered to the presence of Christ.[16] The implicit teaching of St. Charles' *Avvertenza* and of the diverse pontifical instructions that repeated it and adapted it to the city of Rome is that the sacramental Presence was recognized and honored outside of Mass in the measure that it was made use of spiritually.

Therefore, we are still within the medieval context. *The exposition of the Body of Christ invites us to spiritual Communion.* This principle was first applied to a rapid communion of desire that might replace a sacramental Communion deemed to be impossible. We have seen it extend to the spiritual Communions that consist of the frequent renewal of mental prayer during the day, and culminating in the solemn appeal to the faithful to give a place in their lives to this mental prayer in which the Church is incessantly engaged in union with her Head. Through his *Avvertenza* St. Charles Borromeo brought Eucharistic exposition to a maturity of form where everything is studied and regulated with a view to rendering the invitation to prayer more efficacious.

A Change of Perspective

This conclusion may well surprise us, for perpetual adoration was instituted in France during the last century with a very different end in view. The dominant idea of the Eucharistic renewal of the nineteenth century, with which the names of St. Peter Julian Eymard, Father Hermann, and Mlle. Tamisier are associated, was the notion of the "guard of honor." The thought of Christ abandoned in the tabernacle haunted fervent souls, and they felt obliged to compensate by their faithfulness for the neglect his sacramental Presence suffered from the multitude. God's presence called for the answering presence of man. We see that the very meaning of reparation underwent an inflection. The intention was not so much to join in Christ's reparative prayer, as to make reparation to Christ himself.

To what must this change of attitude be attributed?

The point of departure, as we see it, appears to have been a reaction

in Rome itself against the weakening of the religious spirit induced by
the rebirth of paganism. Pope Paul III gives us a picture of it in his bull
Dominus noster Jesus Christus of November 30, 1539, in which we read
that "The Bread of heaven was kept in abject places, without any sign
of veneration to reveal the presence of the great God who deigns to
become our food. When the most Blessed Sacrament was carried
through the streets of the city as Viaticum to the sick, one could see
that it passed amid general indifference."

When the same bull approved the first Roman confraternities of the
Blessed Sacrament founded at the Minerva by a Dominican, Father
Thomas Stella, the Pope defined the general purpose of these groups as
follows: "To provide our Lord present in the Eucharist the homage
and worship that are his due, and to make reparation for the outrages
committed against him." This was an entirely new orientation, and one
that was to put its stamp on the Eucharistic devotion of the following
centuries.

We know about the rapid development of parish confraternities of
the Blessed Sacrament throughout Christendom,[17] and the immense
influence that they had in France on all forms of popular devotion. To
it we owe in great part the institution and the multiplication of
Benediction of the Blessed Sacrament during the seventeenth century.
Going beyond the idea of appealing to the people to establish on a
permanent basis a form of prayer that would remain personal and
silent, they were invited to make short manifestations, considered above
all as a public affirmation of faith and a means of honoring the presence
of Christ.

The new devotion was not established without very strong opposition, which did not come solely from the Jansenists.[18] But it had solid
psychological foundations, and these favored its establishment. Beyond
doubt the attacks of Reformation preachers made Catholics feel the
need of defending their faith in the Real Presence, and they sought to
affirm it on the level of ritual action as a natural defense
mechanism.[19]

The idea of personal adoration certainly did not disappear. The
opposite is abundantly proven by the great number of confraternities of

the Blessed Sacrament whose rules require adoration, with or without exposition, as a personal duty. We believe, however, that in the minds of the faithful this adoration itself had already changed meaning. In order to understand it we must remember that exposition of long duration was introduced in France in a very special form that was foreign to the spirit of the *Oratio sine intermissione* of St. Charles Borromeo and Pope Clement VIII.

We know how the opportunistic attitude of the Jesuit Fathers of Macerata, near Loretto, won us the privilege of celebrating the Prayer of the Forty Hours under certain special circumstances on days of feasting. At the time of its inception in 1556, it was a countermanifestation [20] intended to draw to the churches crowds tempted by the pleasures of the carnival, and it spread because of its successful use of the same spirit. Every effort was made "to focus all eyes upon the magnificence of the decorations, to charm the ears by the sweet and inspiring tones of voices and instruments, and to captivate the whole man by the pomp of the ceremonies and the eloquence of the preachers. All of these things, during the ordinary Forty Hours Devotion, are not and cannot be tolerated, except in a very limited way." [21]

Now this was the practice followed for the Forty Hours of Quinquagesima, which was introduced in Paris in 1616 in the church of Saint-Nicholas-du-Chardonnet and spread rapidly afterward with the magnificence proper to it. Accustomed by frequent Benedictions to interpret the exposition of the Blessed Sacrament as an homage rendered to Christ, the faithful naturally came to consider the sumptuous décor as a means of honoring the sacramental presence. [22]

We can see that there had been a radical change in perspective. Instead of stressing the *raison d'être* of the Presence, everything henceforth stressed the presence itself, to which we must "render the honor and respect due to it, and especially the homage of our own personal presence." [23] The Eucharist was now looked upon as the sacrament of the Presence that must henceforth be affirmed and defended in a world without faith. It was no longer felt that the meaning of what Pius XII would later call the *sacramentum permanens* went far beyond this simple affirmation.

The "Sacramentum Permanens"

We do not want to suggest that this new orientation characterizing the Eucharistic renewal of the nineteenth century is erroneous. We merely say that if it monopolizes the attention of the faithful to the exclusion of everything else, it remains incomplete. The two aspects are complementary and we must consider them inseparable, while attributing to them their respective value.

Before inviting St. Peter to take a specific part in his work, our Lord asked him to make a profession of faith in his person and in his mission. Such a profession is the ineluctable point of departure of any participation in the work of Christ, and it could not have been lacking in the expositions of the fourteenth and fifteenth centuries. In a homogenous world, however, where even sin was committed in an atmosphere of faith, it was not found necessary to pause to give it public expression. It was enough that each person translated it by his own internal movement.[24]

Recent pontifical texts invite us, without taking anything away from the affirmation of faith in the Presence (which is more necessary than ever in our own day), to make of our Eucharistic adorations a participation in Christ's prayer. In this way all the richness of the Eucharistic spirituality prior to the Reformation is recaptured, and the Presence in the tabernacle once more becomes an invitation to incessant prayer.

In explaining that in the tabernacle we do not have the sacrifice of the Lord because the tabernacle is not an *altare permanens,* Pius XII assures us that we have in the tabernacle a permanent presence of the Lord which is a sign for us.[25] He clarifies the point by showing that Christ first makes himself present by the sacrifice, and that he is in the tabernacle as a *memoria sacrificii et passionis suae.*

Thus he is in the tabernacle in a state subsequent to the sacramental sacrifice, and the very modalities of this presence are an immediate reminder to us of this sacrifice. Now we know that his presence in heaven is the sequel to his bloody sacrifice, that it constantly calls the sacrifice to the minds of those who surround him in the vision, and that his reparative intercession in our favor, in which his triumphant Church continually participates, is constituted precisely by the fact that it also calls this sacrifice to the mind of his Father. For us, therefore, who gather around him through our faith, the Eucharistic presence of Christ after the Mass is the "sacrament" of his heavenly life, which calls to mind in particular the intercessory aspect of this life, and invites each one to take part consciously in it in union with the Church.

In defining the visit to the Blessed Sacrament as "recollecting ourselves in silence at the foot of the tabernacle in order to fill our souls with the gifts of God," [26] Pope John XXIII taught us that Eucharistic prayer is a spiritual communion with the fruits of the sacrifice of Christ, and consequently presupposes our participation in his action. In his encyclical *Sacerdotii nostri primordia,* he stated this explicitly when he affirmed that the Curé of Ars "by his adoration of the Word Incarnate . . . raised his simple and pure soul up toward the Blessed Trinity, the supreme object of his love." There is no clearer way of making us understand how much our cleaving to Christ through Eucharistic faith makes us share in the upsurge of his life toward the Father, invites us to share in this upsurge which is his incessant prayer and thus benefit from the fruits of this prayer.

We are tempted to say that the presence in the tabernacle is the *sacramentum orationis,* because it reminds us on the one hand that any communal Eucharistic life lived in its most intense degree [27] demands a life of mental prayer as its complement and fulfillment; and on the other hand, that all mental prayer is essentially a communion with Christ in the prolongation of the sacramental Communion received during the public celebration of the Mass, and in consequence is subject to similar requirements.

This point would call for a separate development going beyond the limits set for our study [and treated elsewhere in the present volume.—*Ed.*]. We shall merely suggest here that if we consider the Eucharist under all its aspects we shall find it in the focal point of the harmonious synthesis between individual piety and communal piety in the single context of the liturgy.

PRESENT-DAY EUCHARISTIC WORSHIP

The permanence of prayer is the life of Christ. Thus we do not have to make incessant prayer a reality. It already exists, and the permanence of the sacramental presence brings it within our reach. The problem is to know how to make use of this presence in order to realize in each of us a maximum participation in the prayer of our Lord Jesus Christ.

The problem will not be solved by the mere fact of establishing permanent Eucharistic adoration in a church by an uninterrupted succession of adorers. True, the sacramental presence of Christ in the tabernacle invites us to respond by our own presence before him. And since his presence is a permanent one, our presence should be perma nent also. But the invitation is addressed to each one of us individually, and we know we cannot answer it merely by a physical presence on our part. To Christ's sacramental presence must correspond, on the part of His members, the spiritual presence consisting essentially in a conscious participation in His prayer.

A Sign

But if the uninterrupted chain of adorers does not realize in fact either the maximum participation of each of his members in his own incessant prayer, or incessant prayer as such, it nonetheless plays an irreplaceable role in the Church as a witness.

Every monastery is a microcosm of the Church, a sign of her life in the totality of its aspects. And yet it is perhaps inevitable that attention turn first of all to the independence of the monastery from the surrounding world, and to the harmonious interdependence of its members under the direction of the abbot. The monastery's life of prayer is also seen as finding its nourishment and expression in the conventual celebration of the Eucharist and in the succession of the Canonical Hours. But the continuity of this life of union, lived silently everywhere within the monastery's precincts, escapes the eye.

This helps us to understand the role of the religious congregations dedicated to perpetual adoration.[28] It is their mission in the Church to be a sign of the continuity of her life of prayer around her Head. There is an analogy here with the practice adopted at one period in the life of Cluny of chanting the Canonical Hours without interruption, as a sign of this continuity. But the community of adorers goes further. It does not merely signify. It invites. For, like the *oratio sine intermissione* of St. Charles Borromeo, the exposition of the Blessed Sacrament that the community of adorers makes possible invites not only the members of the community but all passers-by to unite themselves to the prayer of Christ.

A permanent Eucharistic prayer, solemnly organized in the name of the Church, can be carried out only by communities that have received the mandate to do it. We know, however, that in certain parishes in Flanders and the United States families assure the permanence of adoration before the tabernacle. These efforts remind us that this continuity need not be realized with solemnity or in a religious community in order to be a valid sign.[29] What is necessary to the sign is continuity. If this continuity is not realized, then neither the solemnity nor the mandate can make up for its lack. The service of adoration must have its origins in the conventual or parish Mass, and be as it were its necessary prolongation, continuing without interruption until its restoration in the conventual or parish Mass of the following day. Only at the price of such an effort will it be the expression, in terms of rites, of the interior attitude that each member of the Church should maintain from Mass to Mass.[30]

An Invitation

That is why at the present time, when it is not possible to establish perpetual adoration in parish churches with a rigorous continuity, this manifestation can no longer claim to be a sign of incessant prayer realized at the diocesan level.

The Assembly of French Cardinals and Archbishops suggested in March, 1960, that "the mode of organization [of perpetual adoration] be reconsidered, with a special effort to stress, according to new formulas, Parish Eucharistic Days." The question is to be realistic and to seek what is essential, and this consists in helping the faithful to understand the sacramental Presence in the tabernacle in its relation to the altar, and to honor it by the use made of it. These days, like all manifestations of Eucharistic worship, should be at once a lesson and an invitation.

If we want the time of prayer to be more than an hour during which we assure our material presence, we must take into account certain psychological and even physical conditions. This applies above all to the choice of hours, but it would also be wise to reduce the number of hours if this seems necessary, in order to assure the presence of groups of adorers. Even if they all pray in silence, the fact that they are together in a church in considerable numbers reminds them that our personal prayer is always a contribution to the eminently social work of Christ, who is the wellspring of our union.

A Communion

Whether Eucharistic prayer is organized in a permanent form or not, the fact of being associated in it gives to each one an opportunity to become aware once again of the state of intercession in which he finds himself by the very fact of his belonging to Christ, and to maintain or even increase the intensity of his interior participation by re-establishing or deepening his conscious union with him.

We should never lose sight of the fact that the purpose of Eucharistic prayer is not only to attract crowds to the chapel at the hour of solemn ceremonies. Rather, an effort should be made to dispose the faithful to open their souls sufficiently to the Holy Spirit during their hours of adoration so that they may reorient their faculties toward Christ and so that he may continue to guide their actions afterward. They should thus find in their adoration a stimulant that will bring their minds back to Christ at other hours of the day and night, making them commune in his thought wherever they may be, and share in his prayer by doing the will of his Father.

For at the center of each Eucharistic community, a cell of the Church, is the *sacramentum permanens,* as a sign and invitation. The Blessed Sacrament must be the magnet gathering around Christ, invisibly but in very truth, all the members of the parochial family who are consciously living by his life and participating in his prayer at a given moment.

It is evident that the Eucharistic Day alone will not suffice to make the thought of the sacramental Presence and its significance habitual for those who have participated in it. The intermediary step of personal prayer before the tabernacle must also be taken. Vital and attentive prayer to the Eucharistic Christ demands the ordinary effort to impose silence upon our faculties and to make ourselves present to Christ in a generous and selfless way. That is why the Church counsels that one of the two daily exercises of private mental prayer she requires of every priest be accomplished before the tabernacle.

In his radio message at the close of the Lyons Eucharistic Congress, Pope John XXIII expressed the wish that "all the participants in the Congress would return to their homes convinced of the excellence of the visit to the Blessed Sacrament and eager to make those around them love and esteem it." In former days it was one of the concerns of the confraternities of the Blessed Sacrament to promote visits to the Blessed Sacrament among their members. Several priestly associations also stress Eucharistic prayer, and various groups, such as the Association of the Most Blessed Sacrament and the Association of Daily Adoration, urge their lay members to make regular and relatively long visits.

Many confraternities are dead, and Eucharistic associations are not flourishing at the present time. But the importance of Eucharistic prayer remains as great as ever. It is good to consider that the need for it has not diminished, as is seen by the influence the spirituality of Father Charles de Foucauld exerts on the present generation—and not only in France.

We therefore feel we can affirm that the "enlightened and fervent worship of the divine presence of Jesus in the tabernacles of our churches," [31] which Pope Pius XII urged upon us, is more than just one means among many others of practicing incessant prayer. For our contemporaries, eager for personal contact, it is the means of knowing the nature and exigencies of this prayer, according to the teachings of the One who prays always.

When the Holy Father defined the visit to the Blessed Sacrament as "recollecting ourselves in silence before the tabernacle in order to fill our souls with the gifts of God," he reminded us that our participation in incessant prayer does not consist in "importuning God" but in offering ourselves to him in receptive silence so that he may flood our souls. It is our sacramental Communion prolonged and enriched by a spiritual Communion of every moment with the *sacramentum permanens*.

Since the "Sacrament of the Altar is the principal means of knowing Jesus Christ,"[32] and since Christ always reveals the Father (see Jn 14:9), we shall discover that it is by an ever more intimate participation in the vital movement of his own prayer that he wants to elevate us to the *simplex intuitus veritatis, sub influxu amoris*. If we actively accept his advances, he will associate us to his incessant prayer with the same enthusiasm, and open our souls up to contemplation. And therein lies the supreme development of the grace of our Baptism.

NOTES

Charles Michel-Jean, S.S.S., editor of *Parole et Pain,* a review of the Priest-Adorers in France and Belgium, organized the National Eucharistic Congress held at Bordeaux, France, in 1966. The above essay was published in *Cahiers de la Maison-Dieu,* No. 64 (1960), and was translated for *Emmanuel,* where it appeared in 1964.

1. "Hostia . . . clarificata in caelis (divinae bonitatis thesauros) ostensione vulnerum precumque effusione a Patre aeterno efflagitat."

2. Pope Pius XII, Discourse to the Congress of Assisi, September 22, 1956.

3. Cited by A. Boudinhon, "La Bénédiction du Saint-Sacrement," in *Revue du Clergé français* (1902), p. 264.

4. *Acta Sanctorum,* Oct. XIII.

5. Councils of Passau, Schwerin, Breslau (1416), and Cologne (1452).

6. We know that the Bishop of Paris ordered the celebrants not to elevate the host at the *Qui pridie,* but only after the words of the Consecration.

7. Text of decree establishing the singing of this motet at Notre-Dame-de-Paris in 1512 (Archives Nationales, LL, 294, fol. 104).

8. Alexander of Hales has written (*Summa Th*. IV): "Excitatur devotio frequenter aspicientis." Albert the Great applies the following principle in

this way: "Ostensio boni provocat ad bonum" (*Comm. in Sent.*, IV, 2. 70, a. 6).

9. In the ritual of Rodez (1514), we read: "Presbyter lotis manibus honorifice sumens hostiam infirmo ministrandam aliquantulum manutenens elevatam prope infirmum et ante oculos ejus sic dicat." Then follows an exhortation transcribed in the vernacular. Similar descriptions are to be found in the rituals of Paris (1574) and of Bourges (1588), as well as in a *Liber sacerdotalis* printed in Venice in 1512.

10. This prohibition is vigorously supported in the Roman Ritual: "Alicui ad adorandum solum devotioni seu cujus rei praetextu ad ostendendum non deferatur" (IV, c. IV, § 5).

11. *Archiv. für Litteratur und Kirchengeschichte des Mittelalters* (Berlin, 1886), II, p. 665: "Aliquando ivit ad ecclesiam sancti Fortunati ad videndum Corpus Christi extra positum." The words *extra positum* cannot be applied to the Elevation strictly speaking, and the context prevents us from restricting the fact to the Octave of Corpus Christi.

12. The first "Prayer of the Forty Hours" was celebrated in Milan in 1534. According to the Milanese chronicler Burigozzo, the exposition during this ceremony began during the month of May, 1537. It would seem that St. Philip Neri introduced it in Rome with an exposition in 1548. Until the time of Charles Borromeo this prayer took place at specific times and for specific needs, but not in an uninterrupted manner.

13. "Si facci oscura la detta capella, si che non habbi altro chiaro, che de i lumi . . . per accompagnare il mistero dell'istituto di questa orazione, e per eccitarsi piu a devotione" (*Avvertenza,* cited by De Santi, S.J., *L'Orazione della 40-Ore,* Rome, 1919). In the Clementine Instruction we read: "Ad effeto di reaccogliere la mente de' fedeli all' oratione" (§ 6).

14. "Di non amettere i poveri a vagar per le chiese . . . ma che stiano alle porte con modestia, per togliere con la loro opportunità il raccoglimento a i devoti." This prohibition was made by Innocent XI (1689), as cited by De Santi, p. 316.

15. The Instruction *Graves et Diuturnae* of Clement VIII, which established the Forty Hours in Rome in 1592, is almost entirely based on the *Avvertenza* of St. Charles. It was revised by Paul V, by Innocent XI, and finally by Clement XI in 1705. Clement XII also retouched it slightly, and published it in its present form in 1736.

16. The Code of Canon Law holds to the same point of view with regard to the decoration of the altar of reservation: "Ut ipso suo apparatu magis moveat fidelium pietatem ac devotionem" (Can. 1248, § 4).

17. In France this was above all the work of the Jesuits. Certain of these confraternities were specially dedicated to perpetual adoration.

18. When in 1661 the Chapter of Notre-Dame-de-Paris accepted the practice of weekly Benediction, it refused to allow exposition during the chanting of the prayers. The most important indictment against frequent exposition was published by J.-B. Thiers in 1663, and republished in 1673 under the title *Traité de l'exposition du Saint-Sacrement de l'autel.*

19. In answer to attacks against frequent exposition in 1683, Father Léon Augustin affirmed that "since heretics wanted as it were to annihilate this august sacrament . . . the Church took the opportunity to expose it more frequently in order to make its worship more public and more solemn" (*Conférences Eucharistiques* [Paris, 1683], p. 136).

20. Orlandini, *Hist. S.J.,* VI, year 1556. Cited in the periodical *Le Très Saint Sacrement* (Paris, 1880–1881), p. 523.

21. Commentary by the liturgist Wolfgang Mühlbauer, cited in the same periodical, p. 525.

22. In this same perspective, they even went so far as to give a new interpretation to more ancient usages. The carrying of torches at the Elevation and the additional candle lighted in certain places after the singing of the Sanctus were henceforth understood as honor rendered to the sacramental presence. These texts, however, are unanimous in affirming the purely utilitarian origin of these practices, as does this regulation of the General Chapter of the Carthusians in 1233: "Quando non potest videri Corpus Christi eo quod mane celebratur, possit diaconus tenere cereum bene ardentem a retro sacerdotis, ut Corpus Christi in hac parte possit videri."

23. Memorandum of the resolutions of the National Eucharistic Congress of Paris, 1923. Official minutes, p. 612.

24. The books of the Canonical Hours of the period frequently suggest ejaculatory prayers for this intention. See Gouda, *Expositio mysteriorum missae* (Argentinae, 1500): "Videntes hostiam . . . suspirio dicamus: Ave Salus, ave Vita."

25. "The tabernacle contains . . . the *sacramentum permanens*" (Discourse to the Congress of Assisi, September 22, 1956).

26. Radio message to the National Eucharistic Congress of Lyons, July 5, 1959.

27. There is no question here of an absolute maximum, but of a concrete personal maximum which depends both upon the psychological and spiritual development of each one and on the circumstances of his life.

28. Since we could not cite all the congregations practicing adoration, we preferred to name none of them. In limiting ourselves to the broad outlines of the diverse means used in our own day to stress the sacramental Presence and its significance for us, we believe we are putting our finger on the common basis of the task to which they all dedicate themselves. If we had

tried to analyze in detail the many and sometimes very subtle distinctions between their spiritualities, we should have gone too far afield.

29. The same would be true, we believe, in the case of communities that have received this mandate in their Rule but have become unable to assure strict continuity for lack of a sufficient number of valid adorers.

30. In the face of this problem, it may be preferable to maintain a longer service of adoration in a few houses of the community. The atmosphere adoration creates is a stimulant during the period of formation, on condition, of course, that a solid initiation to the life of prayer be given. The religious will be able to return to this life of adoration later on to regain their earlier fervor either on the occasion of their annual retreat or during their days of recollection during the course of the year.

31. Radio message of Pope Pius XII to the Eucharistic Congress of Rennes, June 25, 1956.

32. Radio message to the Eucharistic Congress of Caracas by Pope Pius XII, December 16, 1956.

12   On Visiting the
Blessed Sacrament

1. A discussion of "visits" would need to start from everything that applies to contemplation, meditation, recollection, silence, prayer and private devotion in general. All this must here, of course, be taken for granted. But it is possible to suspect that the specific concrete problems and difficulties brought up against "visits" (i.e., prayer "before" the reserved Sacrament of the Altar) are often apt to be, at bottom, problems and difficulties directed against private, prolonged, contemplative prayer in general; that the objections raised against visits as such are for the most part only a sort of ideological cover, supplied in retrospect, for a general withdrawal from the severe demands of meditation. Does one in fact know many cases of people who are really given to the practice of prolonged contemplative prayer and who also experience difficulties on the subject of visits? The question must at least be raised, with the man who is "anti-visit," of whether his objections are not in reality the protests of an activist against being called on to bring himself constantly into the presence of God, in quiet, calm, silent abandonment, and to endure the correction and purification of the silence of God.

2. It should be pointed out to the man who attacks the practice of visits as meaningless that he has no right to appeal to dubious theories drawn from the history of dogma and devotion, which are largely false interpretations of genuine facts, in order, whether theoretically or in tacit practice, to by-pass the teaching of the Council of Trent. But that

teaching asserts that it is actually plain heresy to say (in theory, and hence also in practice) that Jesus Christ in the Sacrament of the Altar is not to be honored with an external cult of adoration, that he is not to be celebrated in a special feast, that Eucharistic processions and "exposition" are to be rejected or that reservation of the sacrament on the altar is to be abandoned (see Denzinger 878, 879, 888, 889).

These dogmatic pronouncements do not, of course, clarify the inner meaning and ordering of this cult of Eucharistic adoration and of the reservation of the Sacrament within the totality of Christian life and liturgical action; and it is of course true, unfortunately, that in the course of the Church's history there have been periods and attitudes in Christian devotion in which (as it has been unkindly expressed) morning Mass was regarded as the consecration of a host for evening Benediction, thus bringing about in practice (and without any very strenuous efforts on the part of the official Church to counteract it) real and deplorable distortions of the perspective of enlightened Christian devotion. But in face of the definition of the Council (though reservation of the Eucharist as such is here regarded primarily as a necessity for Communion of the Sick) and of centuries of unanimous and spiritually fruitful practice on the part of the Church, including enlightened saints, it cannot be doubted that the honoring of the Sacrament even "outside" the sacrifice, both in private and in common (in paraliturgical forms such as Benediction and Exposition) is, as such and as a whole, an embodiment of genuine Christian life and faith. (This is in no sense to defend exposition *during* the holy Sacrifice, nor any exaggerated "visual hunger" for the sacred host, such as leads to an indiscreet proliferation of expositions, etc.)

What needs to be stressed is that the fact that there have been periods in which there was no actual Eucharistic devotion outside the sacrifice of the Mass cannot be a valid argument against such devotion's being genuinely Christian. It would be a severe loss to Catholic devotional life if a false romanticism about the early Church led to the abandonment of what has developed in the course of the history of devotion. Christianity is history. A practice with a thousand years of history behind it has its rights, even if they are not the first thousand years.

Those who exalt the early centuries into an absolute standard in matters of devotion ought to do it consistently (or abandon it, as an absolute, altogether): which would mean applying it to fasting, to a thoroughgoing preference and preeminence for the virginal state over marriage, to the length of the liturgy, to out-and-out monastic asceticism, and to many other things. It is only the mind of the whole Church of all ages that can pronounce on what is genuinely Christian, and humble reflection on the ultimate basic structures of Christianity, which are displayed in the Church in all periods but which do lead historically, both in theory and in practice, to conclusions which have not always been explicit and which yet, once given, become from then on part of the *permanent* self-fulfillment of the Church.

It is also a very unhistorical way of thinking, since it fails to recognize the "one-way" character of history, to suppose that everything that appears in the Church at some particular point in history has necessarily got to be traceable back to some more primitive stage of the same thing. On the contrary, in the Church as in the individual human life there are things that come into existence and then remain. And this not only in the sphere of theory.

Now, given the clarity of these general principles about the validity of what has come to be and is practiced in the Church; given the emphasis, long standing, universality and explicitness of the official Church's approval and encouragement of Benediction, etc., in Eucharistic devotion; and given that the Church refuses to abandon reservation of the Sacrament of the Altar and teaches that it is a legitimate object of latreutic cult, then there can be no doubt that there will always be (to a greater or lesser degree) a private cult of the reserved Sacrament. Accordingly, Pius XII in *Mediator Dei* defends not only adoration of the Eucharist but also "devout and daily visits to the sacred tabernacle"; and the Code of Canon Law commends *"visitatio Sanctissimi Sacramenti"* as a subject for the religious instruction of all the faithful (can. 125, no. 2; can. 1273; see also can. 1265–75: *de custodia et cultu sanctissimae Eucharistiae;* it should be noticed that for many churches there is a *duty* to reserve the Sacrament).[1]

3. Coming now to the inner ground on which rest the meaning and

content of "visits," it seems that it will not do to seek for it only and *exclusively,* as is usually done, in the real presence of Christ and the worthiness of the Sacrament to be adored. For it is questionable whether this traditional foundation (correct, but somewhat restrictedly formal) is capable, if left undeveloped, of fully overcoming the resistances to the practice of "visits" which are making their appearance today. After all, the basic theological difficulty is this: True, Christ is really present in the Sacrament. But what is he present *for?* So as to be there, to be with us? So as to be adored and honored as here present, as enthroned, as granting us audience? Even if we can answer "Yes" to this question—or, better, and with more dogmatic circumspection, "Yes, all this *too*"—nevertheless the primary thing is to say, with the Council of Trent, that the Sacrament is instituted by Christ *ut sumatur* (Denzinger 878). The basic structure of the Sacrament lies in its character as *food,* its availability for *eating*. This is the basic truth which must be our starting point.

Because this is so, and because here in Germany, in particular, we must not forget this truth, we do not want to set up, existentially and in terms of feeling, a barrier between us and Protestant Christians (whose theology and practice of the Lord's Supper proceeds from this truth) when the question does not, objectively, give rise to this barrier. Theologically, then, it is the sentence "Take and *eat,* this is my body" that is the first and basic proposition of Eucharistic theology, and not the sentence: Christ is here present. Hence Betz is right in saying [2] that the tripartite division of the tractate on this sacrament, beginning with the Real Presence and only then going on to deal with Communion and sacrifice, is unsatisfactory and misleading. *"Institutum est* ut *sumatur"* (Denzinger 878).

This basic principle should, then, also be our starting point for a theological explanation of the meaning of visits. This principle comprises within itself the real presence of Christ, for the food that is offered to us is the very body and blood of Christ, but it is more comprehensive, for it also says that what is given is given to us *to eat,* and we must, in our treatment of the question, do justice to this *totality* of its content.

But we come at once to an apparent difficulty. It might be said: Of course Christ is to be adored *in usu*,[3] for he is present when he is giving himself to us as the food of eternal life. But how can we be justified in going on from this basic principle to a further cult "outside" our reception of the Sacrament and independent of it, distinct from this presence as food and from the adoration of the Lord which is bound up with our reception of him? The Protestant Christian, for instance, shrinks from arguing further simply on a basis of formal logic, and considers that the Scriptures give him no license for such extensions.

It is also worth noting, in this connection, that the Council of Trent makes Communion of the Sick the justification for reserving the Eucharist and gives no other ground for it as valid, thus correctly representing the historical situation (for it was the necessity or reasonableness of having communion outside the common sacrifice that first gave rise to reservation, not the need to have Jesus present as the "silent dweller in the tabernacle") and thus also regarding reservation as a means to the *eating* of the Sacrament, which keeps the grounds for reservation well in line with the basic principle stated above (see Denzinger 879, 889).

If we are taking the primary biblical data as our point of departure in all this, then it must be said from the start that according to precise exegesis "body" and "blood" signify the whole of our Lord. What body and blood mean is the bodily person of Jesus, the somatically conceived Self of Jesus, one who is a living being by the bond of his life's blood and who, as the Servant of God, establishes the bond of the New Alliance in his blood.[4] It is *he* who is given. Hence it would be false to suppose that the biblical words are concerned only with his body and blood in some narrow modern sense of the words, so that we should have to have recourse to theological speculation and the notion of "concomitance" (Denzinger 876) in order to get from what is explicitly said by Jesus to the total reality of our Lord in the Sacrament.

This is not so: according to his actual explicit words, when rightly interpreted, according to their immediate sense, from the Aramaic, what he gives us is *himself,* so that in John 6:57 we have simply "I" for "flesh" and "blood." He thus truly gives the whole of himself as food.

Hence, adoration is here perfectly legitimate, because the food we encounter is not really something to be understood as a "thing" but is *himself*. To this extent, a certain treatment of the Eucharist almost as a *thing* in the early Church cannot by any means claim to be regarded as an exact and fully exhaustive interpretation of the biblical data. The medieval sense of encountering Jesus bodily as a person in the Sacrament is thoroughly biblical. And hence any act that is of its nature called for by encounter with a person—better, with *this* person—is fully legitimate in biblical terms.

We now have to go a step further. According to the simple, plain word of Scripture it is what is *offered* for eating, not strictly the food that is or has been eaten, that is the Lord in his bodily reality, causing salvation and establishing the Alliance. "Christ is present as food" cannot then mean, in biblical terms, that he is present by being eaten, but that he is present *in order* to be eaten. Realism in the Sacrament is the prerequisite, not the consequence, of the *usus*. On this point Lutheran Christians are at one with us Catholics as against Calvinists. Once this is grasped, then the following proposition can no longer present any insuperable difficulties: So long as this food is there as something *to be eaten,* Our Lord is there as approaching us to be received by us; and the meaningful possibility remains of encountering him as our Lord given for us and desiring to give himself to us.

Now it can safely be said that from the very earliest times Christendom has held and has freely acted on the view[5] that this food (by analogy with other foods) does not lose its character as food through having some relatively long interval elapse between the consecratory words that give it its meaning and the actual reception of it. Whenever the Eucharist is celebrated there is a certain lapse of time between consecration and reception, precisely as there was between the words of Jesus, as he handed it to them, and the Apostles' act of eating. So long as the bread remains bread according to the normal human sense—i.e., so long as its suitability as food persists (this being of its very essence, since what is involved here is an essentially human concept, not a physical one)—we have the presence of Christ offering himself as food, with all that this implies in an attitude of acceptance on man's side.

But what this implies is not only the justification of the cult of adoration of the Eucharist but also, conversely, that adoration of Christ in the Eucharist only corresponds adequately to its object when the Lord is adored *as* offering himself to us as food, *as* the "Servant of God," bodily present in his *soma,* who has established the new and eternal alliance in his blood and wills to give himself to us, as the ultimate reality of salvation, through the eating of this bread.

If the presence of Christ is conceived of thus, then wherever he is, he is there *as* the tangible presence of our salvation, pointing back to the sacramental event of sacrifice by which this presence has been established and forward to that event in which we shall appropriate that salvation in full measure, in its sacramental tangibility as well by reception of the Eucharist. It is not, I hope, necessary to say that the question of *which* particular sacramental particle is present in any particular case is *theologically* irrelevant: it is in any case the same Christ who is present and whom I shall be receiving; through which particular species this happens, in the concrete, is irrelevant.[6]

From this we now have the content and precise meaning of a "visit." It, too, is man's presence before the objective sacramental sign of Jesus' sacrificial death for our salvation; it is a subjective prolongation of Mass and a beginning of one's next communion. Hence everything that was said on the subject of thanksgiving applies to it, and everything that there is to say on the real meaning of preparation for communion.[7] It makes sense that they should take place before the objective sign of the cause and appropriation of salvation, the true body and blood of the Lord; in the presence of the Lord, present in his concrete bodiliness as sacrificial food for me in particular. Reservation of the Sacrament is reservation of the Lord made present in the Mass *as such,* and of the food to be eaten *as such.*

If adoration of the reserved Sacrament is to avoid turning into a strange, problematical duplication of our adoration of the omnipresent God and our actualization of the pneumatic self-communication of Christ, which can be done everywhere and at all times, then it needs to proceed from *that* aspect under which this presence is actually given, and guaranteed in its significance by God in spite of God's omnipresence and in spite of our inner union with Christ;[8] under the aspect, that is, of the Lord who has offered himself upon the cross, and who makes himself present *as such* in the Mass (and hence in the food that remains after the Mass) and offers himself *as such* to be eaten.

A person praying before the Sacrament might also remember that what he has before him is the sacramental sign of the unity of the Church. In the words of the Council of Trent, this Sacrament is the *"symbolum . . . eius unitatis et caritatis, qua Christianos omnes inter se coniunctos et copulatos esse* (*Christus*) *voluit"* (Denzinger 873a), the *"symbolum unius illius corporis, cuius ipse caput exsistit"* (Denzinger 875). Hence, in a visit, we also encounter him as the unity of the Church, and thus encounter the mystery of the Church itself, the Church in her most sacred visibility; and she, in turn, is, in her visibility, salvation made historical and tangible for us. This makes it easy to understand that the most private kind of "tabernacle devotion" is not by any means an occasion for mere religious individualism but, if rightly carried out, a realization of membership of the Church, of responsibility for her and prayer for her: an apostolate of prayer, we might also say, in a very genuine and profound sense.

4. It would be possible to arrive at the same result, for the basic meaning of "visits," approaching the matter from a different side. The starting point here is what one might perhaps call "altar devotion." It seems to be the case, throughout man's religious history, that wherever a sacrificial cult has existed the altar has been highly venerated, even apart from the actual act of sacrifice. It is the very spot where encounter with God takes place in the cult. Hence it is a constant reminder of this, man's highest possibility. It is a permanent promise of this event. Hence it is, quite simply, the holy place. It is the place of refuge; men lay their hands upon it when taking an oath; it is permanently, even outside the sacrifice, the seat of the Godhead.

All this is based on the strictly essential character of the altar, its relation to the sacrifice. But, precisely thus, it remains attached to it even outside the act of sacrifice. And this was also the case in early Christianity.[9] The altar is not merely a practical utensil for offering the Mass, used and then set aside; it is itself a permanent holy place. It is consecrated; it is held in the highest honor by the early Christians; angels stand about it; only the clergy are allowed to enter the area around the altar; people with scrupulous consciences never turn their backs on it; the unbaptized are not allowed to touch it; both clergy and laity reverence it by kissing it; oaths are taken touching it. People pray before it and, embracing it, know that they are thus embracing Christ. Hence it is also a place of refuge.

All this really means that the altar is thought of as the permanent form, in space and time, of the sacrifice, in which the Christ of God is present as our salvation (and hence as our real "altar" [10]). The practice of "visits" is in fact simply a legitimate, intensified continuation of this early Christian altar devotion. It is a legitimate culmination of it: the Sacrament that remains after the sacrifice (and it is legitimate for it so to remain, because this arises from the nature of food) points much more impressively and, because of the divine institution, much more objectively to the past sacrifice and the future sacrificial meal than does the altar alone. And when the two signs are combined, the altar and the sacrificial food resting upon it, then this gives us, in the most impressive possible way, a sign in space and time, of divine institution, that Christ has sacrificed himself and now approaches us as our salvation uniting itself to us.

It is before this sign that one prays. And the prayer one makes is the prayer that is the answer to this abiding, objectified Word: an ever-renewed realization of our self-surrender to the life-giving death of the Lord, acceptance of his grace, and readiness for his coming. So if anyone tries to reject "tabernacle devotion" by appealing to the fact that it did not exist in early Christian times, he must allow one to point out to him that, if he really does regard the devotional manners of the early Church as providing a standard for himself, then he must at least practice "altar devotion." But how is he going to be able to do this today, with the *sacramentum permanens* there resting on the altar, without finding his altar devotion turning into tabernacle devotion, as it has in fact done, rightly, throughout the Church? [11]

5. We can go on directly from this to grasp the connection between a "visit" and "spiritual Communion"; and the theological basis of the

"visit" is further strengthened by spiritual Communion. We must, of course, be able to assume that it is understood what spiritual Communion is.[12] If, contrary to the theology of John 6, to the whole of patristic theology, culminating in St. Augustine (but already clearly discernible in Origen), and to medieval theology up to and including the Council of Trent, spiritual Communion is seen merely as a pious "as if," a pious wish to receive sacramental Communion, then of course it cannot help us to see the meaning of visits. But in reality, according to the unanimous teaching of tradition, spiritual Communion is in very truth personal, actualized communication, in faith and love, with the Lord in his *pneuma*.

The *fructus* and *utilitas* of the sacrament are really received in it; the difference between sacramental and spiritual Communion is not that between the real and the merely notional, but (setting aside a possible difference of degree, in practice, in its effect) what is lacking to spiritual Communion in contrast to fruitful sacramental Communion is only that which is equally present in an unworthy communion; true though it is, of course, that spiritual Communion itself finds its fulfillment in the tangibility of sacramental Communion and hence, even when it is "only" spiritual (which does *not* mean only mental and notional), is in its essence, and in the *votum* of the recipient, related to sacramental Communion. Spiritual Communion is no more a matter of "as if" than perfect contrition is a mere wish to have one's sins forgiven, or baptism of desire a mere unfulfilled wish for justification. What happens in it is rather a real communication by grace, in the holy *pneuma,* with the person of Jesus; of this, contact with the body of Christ in the eating of sacramental Communion is only the tangible sign and sacramental means, wholly ordered to serve this pneumatic communication with Christ (see Denzinger 881).

Hence what happens in spiritual Communion is a conscious affirmation, in a personal act of faith, in love, and with reference to sacramental Communion, of that real pneumatic unity with Christ which is given by the sanctifying grace of the Holy Spirit; one's acceptance of it in the personal center of oneself is renewed, and thus its ontological reality is increased and deepened. When the Council says that what happens in spiritual Communion is a *"voto propositum illum caelestem panem edere"* (Denzinger 881), what this means, rightly translated, is not that what happens is a wish merely to eat the heavenly bread later on, but that in and with the wish to receive the Sacrament later there is *now* a true "eating of the heavenly bread." Just as the request for forgiveness, when made in real repentance, is not merely a hopeful expectation of a forgiveness that takes place later (in the sacrament), but is truly itself the event of that forgiveness (even when it happens "merely" in the examination of conscience).

Such is the genuine doctrine of spiritual Communion, which does not deserve the neglect which has widely befallen it today among the Christian people. The determining factor in this spiritual Communion is not its relation to the next sacramental Communion as such. We need not attach importance to the terminological question of whether we prefer to call the actualizing of our pneumatic communication with Christ-in-us "spiritual Communion" *only* when it includes this explicit relation to sacramental Communion, or whether this explicit relation does not have to be regarded as part of the concept of spiritual communion (*as explicit:* it is always present implicitly, if one simply cannot be spiritually united with Christ without also having the will to incarnate that union in the sacramental dimension, and so, again, to deepen it in oneself).

Whichever usage we follow, it is the actualization of our union with Christ by grace, our believing and loving acceptance and "realization" (in Newman's sense of the word) of this abiding unity with Christ, that is the determining factor in spiritual Communion. In the same way that what actually justifies in a *votum* for Baptism or the Sacrament of Penance is not the *votum* as such but faith and love, so spiritual eating, in John 6, is simply loving faith; but this truly and in full reality is a receiving of Christ in his Spirit, without which "flesh" avails nothing.

But where should we be able to achieve this realization by grace of pneumatic communication with Christ, truly present in us by his Spirit, more readily and with more meaning than when a man is kneeling before the Bread of Life, which is by its whole nature simply and solely (whether we consider the appearances or the body of Christ which they contain) the sign, the pledge and the promise of this pneumatic communication with the Lord? Here indeed the *"panis ille caelestis"* is *"propositus"* (Denzinger 881), which is the point of reference, in the words of the Council, of the *votum* of spiritual Communion. We can then surely say that the most appropriate context for spiritual Communion is when a man is kneeling before the altar of Christ, with the Bread of eternal Life lying upon it. But from this the converse also follows: if a valid tradition, with its roots in Johannine Eucharistic theology, shows that spiritual Communion is a meaningful thing to do, because it is truly an event of grace and not a pious fiction, then we have to say the same of "visits" as well, since they can, essentially, be nothing other than spiritual Communion [13] (even when they do not explicitly refer to sacramental Communion).

From what has been said, we now see that "visits" do not necessarily confront a person with the dilemma of either "conversing" with the "silent dweller in the tabernacle" and thus having to forget that we have "Christ *in* us the hope of glory" (though not in his physical, glorified bodily state), or else (if one does not want and is not able to do this) to be left wondering just why one is kneeling in front of the tabernacle at all.

As has already been said, it is not medieval but biblical for a Christian to realize, when considering the Sacrament, that we are here given the bodily self of the Lord, and that thus, simply by the gracious will of God, we are given the possibility of addressing ourselves in faith and love, in adoration and acceptance, to that Lord bodily present to us. It has also already been said, as part of this, that a Christian has, quite freely, to realize the inexhaustible abundance of the reality of the faith in a plurality of successive acts, one after the other; and that he can do this without giving way to that metaphysical scrupulosity which fears that what is, so to say, at the moment out of sight is also really out of mind and heart, merely because one is turning one's attention to something else.

All this alone is enough to show that there is nothing objectionable in a Christian's addressing himself here and now to our Lord in the

Sacrament, though at some other time he will find him in that Spirit which is poured out in his heart. But even apart from all this: if anyone has the charism of being penetrated through and through, right in his utmost depths, with the presence of Christ by his Spirit, then, so long as we are pilgrims who are traveling in the midst of *visible* things and must constantly *renew* our grasp of that by which we are grasped, there can be nothing but meaning and blessing in such a person's kneeling before this Sacrament which is the visible surety of that to which he clings by faith: namely, that the Lord is truly in us in his Spirit (more than if he were *only* near us in the flesh). However much he may plunge into the depths of his own being, to which grace has been given, there to hear the inexpressible groanings of the voice of the Spirit and to turn himself toward Christ dwelling in Spirit in the innermost center of his being, yet it still makes sense to do this before the sacrament which is precisely the tangible assurance of *that* which we bear within us, by faith, as the light of our interior selves.

6. The point made above as number 4 does not involve the assertion that every visit to a church is to be equated with a *visitatio Sanctissimi*. For a church is not only nor even primarily a place where the Eucharist is reserved. It is first and foremost a holy space, allotted and separated from this world for God, the place in which the community assembles and thus the symbol of it. Just as the Head of the community is Christ, whose body it is, so the church presents this body as a building and, if the Eucharist is reserved in it, the tabernacle is its keystone and cornerstone. But even where this is lacking, the church is still the sacred place of encounter with God, set apart by its own consecration (which, incidentally, makes no mention of the reservation of the Eucharist but only of its celebration); it is still "the church" in the sense of a symbol of the Body of Christ, "in" which a Christian can feel Christ's presence more nearly than elsewhere.

NOTES

The above chapter was originlly an essay in Father Rahner's collection entitled *The Christian Commitment,* translated by Cecily Hastings from *Sendung und Gnade,* copyrighted © and published by Sheed & Ward, Inc.

(New York, 1963), and reprinted by arrangement with the publisher.
Father Rahner currently holds the chair of dogmatic theology at the University of Münster, Westphalia.

1. See also I. de Guibert, *Documenta Ecclesiastica christianae perfectionis studium spectantia* (Rome, 1931), nos. 542 and 543; and Pius XI's address on July 24, 1929, to seminarians (*Enchiridion Clericorum* [Rome, 1938], no. 1467; see no. 351).

2. LTK III, p. 1135.

3. Lutheran Christians, too, regard the *usus* (during which Christ is really present) as comprising the *consecratio, distributio* and *sumptio,* not only the moment of actual eating.

4. Further precisions on this point can be found in J. Betz, *Die Eucharistie in der Zeit der griechischen Väter* I, 1 (Freiburg, 1955), and J. Betz, LTK III, 1141–7.

5. Without such "reflection" based on biblical data, giving the data a concrete interpretation for purposes of concrete action, the Church can never live at all. Even when they do not seem to be cogent by formal logic, nevertheless, seeing that they necessarily had to be made (either one way or the other), and that the Church has in fact, as a whole and over long periods, arrived at them as determining her theory and, even more, her practice, it can simply be said of them that they must have had the assistance of the Spirit of the Church and that they thus carry theological weight beyond that of their formal human conclusiveness.

6. This is not to say anything against the Church's desire that, when possible, the Lord should be received in species consecrated at the same Mass.

7. Preparation is to be understood in a wide sense: realization of the relation of the whole man to the crucified and risen Lord as him in whom alone we have God for our salvation.

8. Consider this point: There is a relation of man to the cross of Christ which is of grace, by which salvation is appropriated, and which is effective, even though it is not (as yet) mediated by the sacramental celebration of the Mass. Yet the Mass has meaning. For it has to be said in general that the basis of the sacraments is not that what they effect cannot be and is not effected otherwise, but that this thing that does happen *before* the sacraments and even "independently" of them constructs its own historical tangibility in space and time in the sacraments, because of the incarnational structure of the grace of Christ; and hence that it could not be received at all by someone who really, deliberately and radically shut himself against this incarnational dynamism in the grace that is offered him.

Hence it is a generally applicable law that grace and the actualization of grace are possible outside the sacrament, and yet that the sacrament retains its meaning. So if it were said that "visits" are meaningless because there is always the grace of our interior union with Christ, it would also have to be said, to be consistent, that the sacraments are meaningless, because there is always grace (even without the sacraments).

What should rather be said is that it is precisely that grace which already exists before the sacraments that gives the sacraments meaning, because it incarnates itself in them, and desires so to incarnate itself even where it is (in the first instance) being offered and accepted without this space-time tangibility. But precisely because the sacraments are the incarnational tangibility of grace and even, beyond this, of its acceptance, it is possible for man to gather, from this corporeal character of grace, what grace is and how he is to encounter and accept it. And hence if our spending time before the sacrament of the body of Christ, the sacrament of the death of the Lord and of the eternal Alliance, is to correspond adequately to that in whose presence we are, the way we do it needs to be determined by the special character of this sacrament. It needs to be more than merely being granted an audience and a friendly conversation with our Lord.

9. See material and references in T. Klausner, *RAC* I, 251–66; F. J. Dölger, *Die Heiligkeit des Altars, AuC* 2, 1930, 161–83; J. Braun, *Der christliche Altar,* 2 vols., Munich, 1924.

10. On the ancient theme that Christ is our altar, see Pauly-Wissowa I, 2, 1640–91; *DB* I, 1266–78; R. Galling, *Der Altar in den Kulturen des Alten Orients* (Berlin, 1925); M. Eliade, *Die Religionen und das Heilige,* Salzburg (1954), 415–37.

11. A note in passing: this could be the starting point for reopening the discussion of whether the efforts being made here and there to separate the tabernacle from the altar (i.e., to render its connection with the altar, as the place of sacrifice, architectonically and optically invisible) are really so obviously right as they sometimes think themselves; or whether the official stand being made in the Church against such attempts (see Code of Canon Law, can. 1268, § 2; Pius XII, in AAS 48, 711 ff., 1956; Decree of the Sacred Congregation of Rites, AAS 49, 425 f., 1957) is not keeping in sight something essential and of permanent validity. The various equally valid aspects involved are often hard to reconcile in practice. (The decree of the Congregation of Rites referred to above does itself indicate exceptions to the practice which it calls for, of having the tabernacle *on the high altar.*) But at least it should not be forgotten, when looking for theologically and pastorally desirable ways through this problem, that altar and tabernacle do have a close, positive relation to one another.

(Editor's Note: The authoritative Instruction on the worship of the

Eucharistic mystery, published April 13, 1967, contains the present definitive rules concerning the position of the tabernacle.)

12. On what follows, see H. R. Schlette, *Geistliche Kommunikation und Sakrament, Quaestiones disputatae* 8 (Freiburg, 1959), which gives complete references on spiritual Communion. See also H. R. Schlette, *Die Lehre von der geistlichen Kommunion bei Bonaventura, Albert dem Grossen und Thomas von Aquin* (Munich, 1959).

13. At least in the sense of an explicit realization, itself grace-given, of our objective unity with Christ in the grace of his holy Spirit.

13 The Eucharist
and Contemplative Prayer

A priest celebrating Mass does not have the leisure to adore the Blessed Sacrament, except for a few genuflections and a moment of silence after having communicated under the form of bread. He "celebrates," that is, he acts, he accomplishes an action that unfolds, involves him in the successive rubrics of its rites. Adoration at this juncture would impose an interruption that the dynamic qualities of the Eucharistic drama forbid; it would exact a passivity incompatible with the active function of the celebrant.

It is normal, however, to desire this adoration. If love wishes to act, it likes also to tarry, to become immobile, to contemplate while annihilating and forgetting self. Yet if, on the other hand, the authentic movement of the liturgy goes to the Father through Christ, the Christian soul itself tends to go directly to Christ taken as the end of its worship. Thus most of the psalms that are addressed to Yahweh have been referred to Christ by Christian tradition. Jesus himself authorized us to do so when, on Palm Sunday, he applied to his own Person the text of Psalm 8: *Out of the mouth of infants and sucklings, thou hast perfected praise* (Matt 21:16).

If it were necessary to justify speculatively this adoration of Christ in the Eucharist, which contains his human flesh ("This is my body"), it would suffice to recall the principle of concomitance universally admitted in Eucharistic theology. If, by virtue of the meaning of the words of consecration the transubstantiation causes only the body of Christ to appear under the appearances of bread, this body brings with it all the elements really united to it by the Resurrection, so much so that under each species there is present the entire Christ with his body and his blood, his human soul and his divinity. One may even extend this principle of concomitance: although the consecration brings on the altar only Christ in his passion (*Christus passus,* says St. Thomas), it makes him present also in all his mysteries and in all the stages of his life: nativity, childhood, adolescence, public life, agony, passion, death, resurrection and ascension. That is not all: the Eucharistic Christ is not only the historical, personal Christ: He represents and contains moreover the total Christ (although in another manner): Christ embodying his entire Church, all his members, all his elect in act and even in potency (sinners destined to be saved). Finally, the divine Person of the Word, present in the Eucharistic Christ, is inseparable from the other divine Persons: the Eucharist, if one may say so, gives us access to the entire Trinity. That is why the Eucharist is truly heaven begun, heaven here below.

Hence, the perfectly legitimate desire to adore the divinity of Christ in the Eucharist may be satisfied by the Eucharistic devotion that prolongs the Mass.

Must that also be justified? If the Eucharistic celebration is an action, this action is a transubstantiation, that is, it changes the entire substance of the bread into the entire substance of the body of Christ. Consequently, Christ is present in the Eucharist in a substantial manner, that is, in a permanent, lasting manner. As long as that which was bread keeps the appearance of bread, the species remain consecrated and Christ is present therein. Communion makes him disappear. But the hosts that remain after Communion keep the Real Presence. As Dom Lambert Beauduin has said so well: "We do not consecrate to adore, nor even to reserve [We consecrate to give thanks, to celebrate a sacrifice at which we will communicate.] . . . but we reserve and adore because we have consecrated." The Consecration, as an act, lasted only as long as it took to pronounce the words; but the Consecration, as an effect, lasts as long as the sacred species.

This review does not permit us simply to justify Eucharistic adoration, it enables us to direct it and to keep it within a just balance.

The Mass is first—not only chronologically, but in importance. It is the Mass that was instituted by Christ. Adoration is a practice of only the Latin Church, and a relatively modern one. But it is the legitimate consequence of the Mass. We do not celebrate Mass in order to have hosts, but the Mass gives us hosts that we may adore. The Mass is more honorable for God, more useful for the world than adoration—the more so, as far as the second point is concerned, since the Mass is offered by the entire Church for the entire Church, whereas adoration, even when made in common, remains in the individual order of exercises of piety.

Adoration flowing from the Mass is in a way qualified by it. In adoring the host, we must not forget that this host is always from a Mass, from a sacrifice.[1]

This Eucharistic devotion, no matter how contemplative it may be, must therefore keep a certain dynamic quality from the Mass with which it is connected. What I contemplate is neither a crucifix nor a relic. It is not God in his Essence, as we shall contemplate him in heaven, in the Word. It is the host from a sacrifice. I must then, in the very act of contemplating it, offer it to the Father and immolate myself with it. It is the host consecrated at the time of a sacrificial repast and destined to be eaten: I cannot contemplate it without desiring to be united with it, without being attracted to it by a movement of spiritual Communion, that is, by Communion in intention, by Communion that is prevented only by external circumstances.

Our visit to the Blessed Sacrament must in some way prolong the Mass and, like the Mass, it must have a universal scope. The sacrifice must be profitable for the entire world. While looking at this host, I must wish to break it and, at the same time, to distribute it for the profit of all men and, in some way, to gather all of them around it. This universal intention is imperative for all adorers in spirit and in truth, but even more especially for priests and apostles who have been consecrated and sent for the salvation of the entire world.

Finally, this contemplation of a host connected with the Mass must remain sacramental. That is, I must contemplate the thing signified through the sign and in the sign. The bread is not a veil behind which might be hidden Jesus in person, in his natural state. This bread is a sign of the "appearances," that is, something that makes us see, that reveals. What I see is bread, is the host. I do not see Jesus in himself, directly as a person, but Jesus in the sacrament, in a sacrament that is a gift, a sacrifice, a fraternal banquet, an ecclesiastical union. This fidelity to the sacramental condition in which I find Christ whom I adore requires my adoration to remain within the realm of faith. Thus it is stripped of, despoiled of, preserved from all excessive sentimentality, all childish imagination. On the other hand, this fidelity to the sacramental condition enriches my adoration with all the harmonics brought to it by the matter of the sacrament, its own finality, its biblical figures, the intentions Jesus had in instituting it and the intentions the Church had in celebrating it.

But once having recalled these principles and these doctrinal directives, it is nonetheless true that I enjoy a very great liberty. I am no longer subject to the beneficent but austere restraints of the liturgy. I am alone with Christ. I am there and he is there. He is really present in the host. I can then look at him through it, but really. It is he whom I see. I can speak to him, listen to him. I may very well say nothing precise, but repeat only: I am there and he is there. Undoubtedly I could do as much in the solitude of my room or in the hubbub of the street. His presence is not dependent upon a material reality. He is present in my soul by faith. He is present, according to his promise, in the assembly of the baptized. He is there in my brethren, especially the smallest, the poorest. He is there in still another way in the altar that symbolizes him (devotion to the Blessed Sacrament was prepared in the Middle Ages by devotion to the altar). There is, however, another mode of presence that is achieved in no other way: a presence that is more concrete, substantial, personal, human and, in the strict meaning of the word, more carnal.

This explains why the visit to the Blessed Sacrament will have a more special value for me in certain states of distress when the mysterious presence of Christ in my soul or in my brethren seems less evident to me and brings me less comfort. Especially does devotion to the

Blessed Sacrament have a particular efficacy for purifying and recti-
fying my sensitiveness because I have contact here with the very flesh of
Christ. In certain crises of sensuality, in certain storms of my anger,
pride or rancor, in the wake of a particularly bitter defeat, or else in a
period of discouragement or extreme weariness, Eucharistic adoration
will have an efficacy for comforting, relaxing, purifying, and calming
me that I cannot find in mental prayer too barren, too arid for the state
of confusion, trouble, or agitation I am experiencing.

Very free, not being constrained by any formula or ritual, my
contemplation will be able to go and come, to pass from the suffering
Christ (present here sacramentally) to the risen Christ, to the Christ
Child (we must not abuse the idea of "Little Jesus" present in the
tabernacle, but we are not forbidden to use it). Since all the mysteries
of Christ are present in the Eucharist, the great and unique "mystery of
faith," I can vary my adoration, if I feel so attracted, according to the
phases of the liturgical year. I can concentrate on his humanity, present
by virtue of the sacrament, as well as to his divinity present by
concomitance. I can, too, plunge myself into the entire Trinity, also
present by concomitance and by the circuminsession of the divine
Persons.

No matter how individual and personal this adoration may be, I shall
remember that I am a priest in order to give it an apostolic scope, a
Catholic value. I shall adore in the name of all, I shall intercede for all,
as at Mass, but with greater leisure. It will be quite natural for me to go
to the Blessed Sacrament in order to confide my pastoral cares, my
apostolic intentions to it. (Let us note, moreover, that there are other
occasions than a visit to the Blessed Sacrament for a priest's Eucharistic
devotion—among them a long distribution of Communion, the carrying of the Eucharist to a sick person.)

For a lay person a visit to the Blessed Sacrament will consist for the
most part in the preparation for and thanksgiving after Communion.
How could a priest forget, while adoring the Blessed Sacrament, that
he consecrated it in the morning and that he will consecrate it the next
day? I shall go so far as to say that a priest is bound to visit the Blessed
Sacrament (over and above the canonical recommendations) [2] by his

duty to prepare and prolong the celebration of Mass through an effort of personal piety and what the ancients called the "secret prayers." In our age of the liturgical revival, we must be on our guard against a certain liturgical craze, a certain abuse of "objective piety" which, under the pretext of according the primacy to liturgical celebration, would cast off as affective, late-come, or individualistic all practices of private devotion.

We must certainly distinguish between liturgical and personal piety, not to oppose one to the other, to depreciate one at the expense of the other, but to evaluate them justly, verify them and regulate one by the other. To be satisfied with liturgical celebration is to condemn it more or less rapidly to becoming an entirely exterior and desiccated practice. Liturgical celebration itself, in order to be truly religious and animated interiorly, requires the exercise of private adoration.

This private prayer is not exclusive. It can be joined to other practices, for instance, to the *lectio divina* (reading of the Scriptures). The traditional principle of the "two tables" may be applied here. We shall vivify our reading of the Scriptures by contemplating the Eucharist: both enable us to communicate with the same Word, the same God who is spirit and life. My contemplation of the Eucharist will be nourished, spiritualized, enriched by reading the Word of God in his presence. In this way my conversations with Jesus will not risk turning to an imaginary and sterile monologue. Then it will be really Jesus who speaks to me.

Finally, one will certainly be encouraged to recite the Divine Office before the Eucharist. The Church forbids our reserving the Blessed Sacrament in the altar of the choir. Why? Because in the choral recitation, the mind must lend itself above all to the collective celebration in which the two choirs look at one another, because the mystery of the presence of Christ is realized especially by the presence and ecclesiastical activity of the community of praise. But, on the other hand, the Church grants indulgences to those who recite the Office before the Blessed Sacrament.

By this granting of indulgences she wished undoubtedly to deter priests from reciting their Breviary, as they are only too prone to do, in a comfortable armchair or by walking up and down a shady path (if it is not while walking in crowded streets or traveling in a car full of chatter). If it is legitimate and even normal to recite the little hours at their time wherever we happen to be, the very places we are working, it is to be desired that we go to the church (we who have the good fortune to live so close to the church, indeed to dwell under the same roof) at least to say the long hours. This applies more particularly to Lauds, an essentially cosmic, missionary, conquering hour which ends with the *Benedictus,* hymn to the rising sun and reminder of our apostolic mission:

> For you will go before the Lord
> to prepare the way for him.
> To give his people knowledge of salvation
> through the forgiveness of their sins;
> this by the tender mercy of our God
> who from on high will bring the rising Sun to visit us,
> to give light to *those who live*
> *in darkness and the shadow of death.* . . .

We shall like especially to come before the Blessed Sacrament to recite Vespers, the evening sacrifice, a reminder of the hour when the Eucharist was instituted, an hour in which are found several of the Hallel psalms which Jesus sang with his Apostles on leaving the Cenacle and which end with the great thanksgiving hymn, *Magnificat.*

In reciting the psalms near the host, it will be easier for us to relate the Office with the Mass, to make of the psalms the voice of the Church speaking to Christ, and the voice of Christ speaking to his Father.

By these means we shall prevent more especially our Eucharistic devotion—even while remaining perfectly free and personal—from turning to sentimental reverie, to a selfish seeking of consolations without the will to progress and conquer self. We shall seek therein above all the gift of ourselves, our identification with Christ as a host—that is, at the same time as victim and food, since, according to the saying of Father Chevrier, we, too, must be "men that are eaten."

NOTES

1. It has been consecrated at Mass, during the sacrifice; and one might add that it will be consumed by the priest himself in the course of another Mass, because, in order to do away with certain superstitions, the Church has forbidden the distribution of the fragments to the faithful. There is only one exception: the host consecrated on Holy Thursday to be consumed on Good Friday during the "Mass" of the Presanctified, which was not a sacrifice and of course has now been suppressed.

2. Code of Canon Law, can. 125, § 2.

Raymond A. Tartre, S.S.S.

14 The New Instruction

The long-awaited Instruction on Eucharistic worship was approved by Pope Paul VI on April 13, 1967, dated May 25, feast of Corpus Christi, and became effective on August 15, 1967, feast of the Assumption of the Blessed Virgin. It bears three signatures: that of Cardinal Lercaro, President of Consilium, that of Cardinal Larraona, Prefect of the Sacred Congregation of Rites, and that of Archbishop Antonelli, secretary of that Congregation.

The Instruction, a document of some twelve thousand words, sets up authoritatively the various procedures concerning the celebration of Mass and of Holy Communion and the worship of the blessed Eucharist outside the liturgical celebration.

What is most striking about this Instruction is that it has not limited itself to stating new norms but in almost every instance has also given the doctrinal, pastoral, and ecclesial reasons for the changes. The first part, in fact, deals with the importance to be given to teaching the meaning of the new norms, for fear that they become merely a new set of rules, and not a means "to live the Eucharist more fully."

It is obvious that in this matter of practical legislation not every detail of worship could be covered in a world-wide church that includes every type of people with every degree of culture. Hence a number of norms deliberately leave latitude for adaptation to local conditions and circumstances. What counts, however, is the spirit and understanding of the Eucharistic mystery in the light of modern biblical, theological, and liturgical studies. Above all, the Instruction is to be interpreted as an instrument of the Holy Spirit, who never fails the Church at every moment of its history.

It is not within the scope of this essay to discuss all the new norms that will govern the Eucharistic mystery from now on. Rather, our interest will center on the underlying principles that call for the revision of the cult of the Eucharist. The Instruction is a rich mine of doctrine—much more so than is usual in documents of this sort, concerned chiefly with rubrical changes such as, for example, the procedures at Mass, genuflexions to be omitted, complex rubrics to be simplified or abbreviated. It is as though the Instruction were meant to serve as a source of theological guidance for the faithful concerning Eucharistic worship that they may "live the Eucharist more fully."

The new rules will have little effect beyond achieving a certain simplification unless they are readily intelligible as signs of the inner reality they are meant to convey. The Instruction affirms this role of the new norms in no uncertain terms: "The more intelligible the signs by which it [the Eucharist] is celebrated and worshiped, the more firmly and effectively it will enter into the minds and lives of the faithful" (Introduction, § 4).

Now, all the new norms for Eucharistic worship make it clear that although the Eucharist can be considered under various aspects, these norms must always take into account the essential unity and totality of the sacrament. Thus, although the sacrificial nature of the Mass is basic, this consideration cannot afford to ignore the loving presence of Christ. What chiefly concerns us here is to establish, along the lines laid down in the Instruction, the relations of dependence existing between the three aspects of the Eucharistic mystery—namely, that it is at once sacrifice, meal, and real presence.

The Instruction unites into one synthesis these three aspects: "The Eucharist contains the entire spiritual good of the Church, namely, Christ Himself [The Real Presence], our Passover and living bread [Holy Communion], offering through his flesh, living and life-giving in the Spirit, life to men [Holy Mass] who are thus invited and led on to offer themselves, their labors and all created things together with him" [Participation in worship with Christ] (§ 6, Para. 1).

Therefore we must assert that "the celebration of the Eucharist in the Sacrifice of the Mass is the *origin and consummation* of the worship shown to the Eucharist outside Mass" (§ 3e). Trent is quoted: "Nor is it [The Eucharist] any less to be adored because it was instituted by Christ to be eaten" (§ 3f). "Origin and consummation" means that a demonstrable link must be shown to exist between the Mass-sacrifice and Eucharistic worship and devotion outside the Mass. Only on this condition will the tendency to belittle devotion to the Real Presence be reversed and its orthodoxy justified. Hence the Instruction expounds at length the identity of Eucharistic worship whether liturgical or not, even as it describes the dependence of the one upon the other. The two complement each other, because each is needed to satisfy personal devotion and to fulfill community worship.

Pastoral in intent, the Instruction is concerned to relate Eucharistic worship to the whole Christian life. The opening words reflect this concern: "The Mystery of the Eucharist is the true center of the sacred liturgy, and indeed of the whole Christian life. Consequently, the Church, guided by the Holy Spirit, continually seeks to understand and to live the Eucharist more fully."

"To live the Eucharist more fully" was the purpose of several prior documents: the Decree on the Eucharist, Council of Trent (1638-1741); the encyclical *Mediator Dei* (1947); the Constitution on the Liturgy (1967); the Instruction on the Liturgy (May, 1967). The Instruction insists on this pastoral viewpoint of the "important role of the Eucharistic Mystery in the life of the faithful" (Introduction: § 1). It intends to "formulate practical norms which will show the Christian people how to act in regard to this sacrament so as to pursue that knowledge and holiness which the Council has set before the Church" (Introduction, § 2).

In fact, the Instruction insists that all aspects of the Eucharist must be considered, and "the real relationships which are known to exist between these various aspects of the mystery *should be so understood by the faithful as to be reflected in their lives*" (*ibid.*).

There is then a real pitfall to be avoided here: that of severing what must be one mystery, whenever one particular aspect of the Eucharist is treated. It would be a wrong idea, which the Instruction rejects, to impose one's limited view of the Eucharistic celebration by defining it as a community meal, or a sacrifice, while giving only lip service to Part III of the Instruction entitled "The Worship of the Eucharist as a Permanent Sacrament."

It has always been a temptation of theologians to attempt a synthesis of the Eucharistic mystery to accommodate their own theories. Formerly the sacrificial aspect of the Mass was deemed so central that nothing much was said about its being a meal. Likewise, the Eucharist was treated by certain authors mainly as a food, without relating it to the sacrifice of which it is an integral complement. Devotion to the Real Presence was also viewed principally as a Thou-I relation to be privately established between Christ and the soul, without reference to its being a spiritual communion within the context of the Sacrifice offering and an effective sign of unity and charity of the People of God.

We would stress the difficulty—or rather the impossibility, based on the universality of the Eucharistic Mystery—of trying to reduce it to a common denominator for every category of the faithful whose devotion to the Eucharistic mystery will be affected by their own mental or moral makeup, their state of soul, their spiritual attraction, their present needs.

The mystery of the Eucharist baffles the dialectic of theological speculation. A single formulation of its depth and extension is impossible—and indeed totally unwarranted, since the people for whom it is destined are as various as their personalities are distinctive. The figure of the manna is perhaps still the best description of what Christ intended the Eucharist to be: suited to every need, a remedy to weakness, spiritual strength and vitality, the perfecting of the Mystical Body, and a pledge of immortal life to men on their way to the Promised Land. The Eucharistic mystery cannot be contained in one or another of its aspects since it is co-extensive with the universal mystery of the Incarnation and Redemption, which it renews and applies to actual situations as the history of salvation unfolds itself.

Beyond the diversity of the Eucharistic mystery, however, a singleness of purpose is to be found in Christ's intention to gather his people together, a holy offering to the Father. The Eucharist is the sign of unity, the bond of love of the People of God. Therefore under all its diverse aspects, in the liturgy and in the loving presence of Christ, the purpose remains identical. We must never lose sight of Christian, ecclesial unity, as we celebrate the Eucharist, or receive it as the food of our soul, or worship the adorable person of Christ permanently, substantially present in the Sacrament.

The insistence on this unity in diversity is evident throughout the Instruction. In the Introduction (§ 3) the "origin and consummation of worship shown to the Eucharist outside Mass" is said to derive from the celebration of the Sacrifice of the Mass. Communion, distributed after Mass to those who cannot assist, is to be regarded as having the same effect of union with Christ's sacrificial offering at Mass. Farther on, under (g), the Instruction affirms that "the mystery of the Eucharist should be considered in all its fullness, not only in the celebration of Mass, but also in devotion to the sacred species which remain after Mass and are reserved to extend the grace of the sacrifice."

The Instruction in no wise intends to minimize the devotion and cult of adoration of the Eucharistic Christ, but it does definitely wish to put a stop to the notion that it is an aspect unrelated to "the grace of the sacrifice." *Mysterium fidei* (§ 67) brings this doctrine to the forefront:

As long as the Eucharist is kept in our churches Christ is truly the Emmanuel, that is, God with us. . . . He dwells with us "full of grace and truth." He restores morality, nourishes virtue, consoles the afflicted, strengthens the weak.

The whole point here is to reject the argument of those who imagine Christ's Eucharistic presence as passive or static. Christ continues his sacrificial action wherever He is really present; that presence cannot be conceived as anything but dynamic. There is nothing more efficacious for advancing along the road of holiness "than converse with Christ" in the Eucharist (*ibid.*). That can only be so because in his Eucharistic presence Christ unceasingly continues to bestow upon those who approach Him with devotion the fruits of the Sacrifice of the Mass.

To understand true devotion to the Real Presence, the Christian must perfect his knowledge of the Eucharistic celebration from which it flows as from its most authentic source. Because the liturgical celebration was off-center, Eucharistic piety lost its true purpose and balance. Centered on the Mass, viewed as its extension and pointed toward its celebration, Eucharistic worship and devotion will perpetuate all the blessings of the liturgical celebration. It will foster unitive, ecclesial, social virtues of Christian life that the liturgical celebration signifies and effectuates.

The aspect of the Eucharist that concerns us is elaborated in § 49 of Part III of the Instruction (The Reasons for Reserving the Eucharist outside Mass) and in § 50 (Prayer before the Blessed Sacrament). These two sections contain the principles from which are derived the norms concerning the structure of the church, the location of the tabernacle, the form of Eucharistic devotions, exposition of the Blessed Sacrament, and Eucharistic Congresses. It is in the light of these principles that the new norms have been drawn up. The doctrinal reasons for the adoption of the new ritual are to be kept in mind whenever questions of implementation come up concerning Eucharistic worship and devotion.

The Instruction is at pains to establish the true reasons the Church reserves the Blessed Sacrament after Mass. Primarily it is for pastoral reasons—specifically that the sick may receive Christ in Viaticum. This first reason for reservation of the Sacrament stems from a practice already evidenced in the custom of bringing the Eucharist to the early martyrs in prison before their confession of faith. But, as the Instruction remarks, "Belief in the real Presence of the Lord has as its natural consequence the external and public manifestation of that belief," and therefore "the reservation of the sacred species for the sick . . . led to the praiseworthy custom of adoring the heavenly food which is preserved in churches." Referring to *Mediator Dei,* the Instruction continues, "This practice of adoration has a valid and firm foundation."

How this adoration is to be understood according to the mind of the Church is clearly indicated in No. 5, entitled "Prayer before the Blessed Sacrament." We may set forth the doctrine of the Church in the following propositions:

Adoration of the Real Presence derives from the Sacrifice of the Mass.

Adoration is directed toward sacramental and spiritual communion.

Devotion to the Blessed Sacrament draws us to an ever deeper participation in the paschal mystery.

Devotion to the Real Presence leads us "to respond gratefully to the gift of Christ, who through his humanity constantly pours divine life into the members of his Body."

Eucharistic devotion enables us to "dwell with Christ our Lord."

Eucharistic devotion enables us to "enjoy Christ's intimate friendship."

In our visits we may "pour out our hearts before Christ for ourselves and our dear ones."

In visits we pray for the peace and salvation of the world.

During the visit "we offer our entire life with Christ to the Father in the Holy Spirit, and in exchange we receive an increase of the theological virtues of faith, hope, and charity."

In the visit, "we nourish those right dispositions which enable us with all due devotion to celebrate the memorial of the Lord."

We "dispose ourselves to receive frequently the bread given us by the Father."

Finally, we are exhorted "to worship Christ in the Blessed Sacrament in harmony with our way of life."

Pastors are asked to exhort the faithful to practice this worship of the Eucharist, and they should set the example. These propositions sufficiently reveal the mind of the Church concerning devotion to the Eucharist. They could be elaborated in a complete treatise of Eucharistic devotion according to the new perspectives of Vatican II's Decree on the Liturgy. The Christian who meditates upon these truths and who strives to apply them to his life will certainly "live the Eucharist more fully."

A final principle of Eucharistic devotion reiterates the one laid down in the Constitution on the Sacred Liturgy:

The liturgical seasons must be taken into account, and these devotions must harmonize with the liturgy, be in some way derived from it and lead the people toward the liturgy as to something which of its nature is far superior to these devotions" (Part III, § 58).

Thus the superiority of the liturgical act is maintained, for private devotions are wholly directed to its more worthy celebration. These devotions must be woven around the liturgical seasons; they must be inspired by the liturgy and lead to its fruitful participation.

"Devotion, both private and public towards the Sacrament of the Altar . . . is highly recommended by the Church" (*ibid.*). This is the solemn affirmation of the Instruction, the authoritative message addressed by the Supreme Shepherd to Christ's flock. If that message is accepted and its program followed by pastors and faithful, there will result the "holiness of life which the Council has set before the Church" (Introduction, § 2).

NOTE

Father Tartre, who holds degrees from Immaculate Conception College in Montreal and the University of St. Thomas (Angelicum) in Rome, is editor of *Emmanuel* and national director of the Priest's Eucharistic League for the United States. In addition to compiling the present volume, he has produced the well-received commentary on the Vatican II decree on the Ministry and Life of Priests, entitled *The Postconciliar Priest* (New York, 1966).

Appendix

Encyclical *Sacerdotii Nostri*

Excerpts on Priestly Eucharistic Piety. St. Jean Marie Vianney held it as certain that "the priest must first of all be dedicated to continual prayer." On this point it is well known that, when he had only recently been made the parish priest of a little village in which the Christian life was definitely languishing, he used to pass long and joyous hours of his nightly repose adoring Jesus in the Sacrament of his love. Thus the sacred tabernacle seems to have been the source from which he constantly derived heavenly strength by which he nourished and rekindled his own piety and provided for the effectiveness of his apostolic work. Thus, during this holy man's time, the beautiful words by which Our Predecessor of happy memory, Pius XII, described the Christian parish could most fitly be applied to the village of Ars. "The church is the center. The sacred tabernacle is the center of the church, and beside the tabernacle is the confessional in which the supernatural life or spiritual health is restored to the Christian people."

Devotion to the Holy Eucharist

The zeal for prayer of St. Jean Marie Vianney, who can almost be said to have spent the last thirty years of his life in church, where he was kept by the tremendous number of penitents, was distinguished by a special quality, in that it was directed particularly toward the Eucharist. His ardent piety toward Christ the Lord, hidden behind the Eucharistic veils, almost surpasses belief. "There," he said, "is the One who loves us so much. Why should we not love Him in return?"

227

He really had a burning charity toward the adorable Sacrament of the Altar. His soul was drawn by an irresistible impulse to the sacred tabernacle. He used to teach this method of prayer to his parishioners: "There is no need for many words in order that we may pray properly. By faith we believe that there, in the sacred tabernacle, the good God is present. We open our hearts to Him. We rejoice that He has admitted us into His presence. This is the best method of prayer." He left nothing undone to stir up the reverence and the love of Catholics toward Christ hidden in the Sacrament of the Eucharist and to urge them to receive Holy Communion. And, by the example of his own piety, he himself showed the way to the rest. "In order that anyone should be convinced of this," witnesses have reported, "it was enough that they should see him celebrating Mass or even see him genuflecting when he passed in front of the tabernacle."

The Eucharist and Priestly Life

"The marvelous example of St. Jean Marie Vianney," as Our immediate Predecessor testifies, "retains all its force even for our times." The long and continuous prayer of the priest before the adorable Sacrament of the Altar has a dignity and an efficacy which are such that the priest can obtain them in no other way. There can be no substitute whatever for such prayer. Thus the priest, when he is adoring Christ the Lord and thanking Him, when he is offering satisfaction for his own sins or for the sins of others, or finally when he is praying most fervently to commend to God the matters entrusted to him, burns with a more ardent love for the divine Redeemer to whom he has promised his fidelity, and for the men in whose favor he is exercising his pastoral care.

And from the Eucharistic piety which is ardent, zealous, and effective, it inevitably follows that he will feed and nourish the interior perfection of his own soul, and that the supernatural strength with which the strong workers for Christ must be equipped will come abundantly to him in the carrying out of his apostolic responsibility.

Likewise We do not want to pass over the benefits which come forth from this priestly Eucharistic piety to the faithful who are witness of the piety of the priests and are attracted by their example. For, as Our Predecessor of happy memory, Pius XII, rightly observed during one of his allocutions to the Roman clergy, "If you really desire that the faithful entrusted to you should pray piously and ardently, you must be an example to them in church, and they must see you praying. The priest who is on his knees before the sacred tabernacle in a reverent manner, and who prays attentively to God, is, for the Christian people, an example offering them an incentive and an invitation to rival such a priest in zealous piety." The parish priest assigned to Ars employed these resources when he started out in his apostolic ministry. There can be no doubt whatsoever that these same resources are always most effective, in every circumstance of place and time.

The Priesthood and the Holy Sacrifice of the Mass

Let us never forget that the principal form of Eucharistic prayer is completed and summed up in the holy sacrifice of the altar. It is Our belief, Venerable Brethren, that we must consider this more carefully, since it has to do with an especially necessary aspect of the priestly life.

It is not our purpose here to explain in any great detail the Church's traditional doctrine about the priesthood and the Eucharistic sacrifice. Our Predecessors of happy memory, Pius XI and Pius XII, in important and very clear documents, have dealt with these matters. We exhort you to take all care that the priests and the faithful under your direction may have adequate knowledge of these documents. For in this way the inaccurate statements of some men which are made occasionally when there are discussions on these points will vanish, and rash statements will be brought back to right order.

Now, on this very salutary point, We wish in this encyclical letter to show especially for what reason the holy Curé of Ars, who, as is fitting for a hero, was most observant of his priestly duties, is fully worthy to be proposed as an example of outstanding virtue for the directors of souls and is constituted as their heavenly Patron. If it be true that the priest receives the priesthood so that he may serve at the altar and that he has begun the performance of his ministry with the Eucharistic sacrifice, it follows that the Eucharistic sacrifice remains for the minister of God, as long as he lives, the principle and the source both of the sanctity which he acquires for himself and of the apostolic activity to which he has given himself. This is very well exemplified in St. Jean Marie Vianney.

For what is the summit of the priestly apostolate, if we now consider the highest point of its activity, other than this: wherever the Church lives, to gather around the altar the people joined together in the bonds of faith, reborn in holy Baptism, and cleansed from their sins? Then the priest, using the sacred power he has received, offers the divine sacrifice in which Christ Jesus renews that one and only immolation which He performed on Calvary for the redemption of the human race and for the glory of the heavenly Father. Then the Christians, uniting together, by the ministry of the priest offer the divine Victim to the sovereign and eternal God and offer themselves "a living sacrifice, holy, pleasing unto God." And here it is that the People of God, instructed in the teachings and the precepts of the faith, and nourished by the body of Christ, find what will endow them with supernatural life, advance them in that life, and, if need be, restore unity. Thus it is, moreover, that the Mystical Body of Christ, which is the Church, increases with spiritual growth everywhere on earth throughout the course of the centuries. . . .

It must especially be kept in mind that the priest, if he seriously intends, wills, and works to be holy, must find his model and his heavenly strength in the Eucharistic sacrifice he offers. So we are instructed by the exhortation of the *Pontificale Romanum: "Agnoscite quod agitis: imitamini quod tractatis."* On this point Our immediate Predecessor of happy memory was pleased to state in his exhortation *Menti nostrae:* "Just as the entire life of Our Savior was ordered to the sacrifice of himself, so likewise the life of the priest, who ought to bring out the image of Christ in himself, must be made a pleasing sacrifice with Him, in Him, and through Him. . . . For this reason he must not only celebrate the Eucharistic sacrifice, but even in a certain intimate way live it. For thus he can obtain that heavenly strength by which it comes about that he is entirely transformed and shares in the expiatory life of the divine Redeemer himself." And he likewise offers this instruction: "Thus it is necessary that the priestly soul should strive to reproduce in itself whatever is accomplished on the altar of sacrifice. For, just as Jesus Christ immolated himself, so His minister ought to immolate himself together with Him. Just as Jesus Christ expiated the sins of men, so the priest, by the lofty road of the Christian ascetical life, must attain to the purification of himself and of his neighbors."

The Church is looking at this point of heavenly doctrine when, with its maternal invitation, it urges its sacred ministers to cultivate the ascetical life and to offer the Eucharistic sacrifice most religiously. For is this not the reason why priests have fallen away little by little from the first charity they received in holy Ordination: that they have not been fully aware of the mutual bond by which the gift of self and the sacrificial offering must be joined to one another? St. Jean Vianney learned this by experience, and he thus stated it: "The reason why priests lose their fervor is that they do not say Mass attentively and piously." He, whose pious custom it was "to offer himself up in the way of expiation for sinners," used to shed tears "when he thought of the unfortunate priests who were devoid of the holiness necessary for their function."

With paternal exhortation We beg Our most beloved priestly sons to examine their consciences at a definite and stated time as to how they celebrate the Divine Mysteries, as to their attitude and state of mind when they go up to the altar, and as to the results they strive to acquire for themselves from the Mass. May the solemn centennial of the outstanding and marvelous priest, who, "from the consolation and the happiness of offering the divine Victim," drew the most ardent will to dedicate himself, be an incentive to them. And may his prayer, as We are sure it will, obtain for them an abundance of light and strength.

(English text from NCWC edition)

Encyclical *Mysterium Fidei*

Excerpts on Christ's Presence in the Sacrament of the Eucharist by Transubstantiation. 46. To avoid misunderstanding this sacramental presence which surpasses the laws of nature and constitutes the greatest miracle of its kind (see encyclical *Mirae caritatis, Acta Leonis XIII,* vol. XXII [1902–1903], p. 123) we must listen with docility to the voice of the teaching and praying Church. This voice, which constantly echoes the voice of Christ, assures us that the way Christ is made present in this sacrament is none other than by the change of the whole substance of the bread into his body, and of the whole substance of the wine into his blood, and that this unique and truly wonderful change the Catholic Church rightly calls transubstantiation (see Council of Trent, *Decree on the Eucharist,* ch. 4, and can. 2). As a result of transubstantiation, the species of bread and wine undoubtedly take on a new meaning and a new finality, for they no longer remain ordinary bread and ordinary wine, but become the sign of something sacred, the sign of a spiritual food. However, the reason they take on this new significance and this new finality is simply because they contain a new "reality" which we may justly term *ontological.* Not that there lies under those species what was already there before, but something quite different; and that not only because of the faith of the Church, but in objective reality, since after the change of the substance or nature of the bread and wine into the body and blood of Christ, nothing remains of the bread and wine but the appearances, under which Christ, whole and entire, in his physical "reality" is bodily present, although not in the same way that bodies are present in a given place.

47. For this reason the Fathers took special care to warn the faithful that in reflecting on this most august sacrament, they should not trust to their senses, which reach only the properties of bread and wine, but rather to the words of Christ which have power to transform, change, and transmute the bread and wine into his body and blood. For, as those same Fathers often said, the power that accomplishes this is that same power by which Almighty God, at the beginning of time, created the world out of nothing.

48. "We have been instructed in these matters and filled with an unshakeable faith," says St. Cyril of Alexandria, at the end of a sermon on the mysteries of the faith, "that that which seems to be bread, is not bread, though it tastes like it, but the body of Christ, and that which seems to be wine, is not wine, though it too tastes as such, but the blood of Christ . . . draw inner strength by receiving this bread as spiritual food and your soul will rejoice" (*Catecheses,* 22, 9; *Myst.* 4; PG 33:1103).

49. St. John Chrysostom emphasizes this point, saying: "It is not the power of man which makes what is put before us the body and blood of Christ, but the power of Christ himself who was crucified for us. The priest standing there in the place of Christ says these words but their power and grace are from God. 'This is my body,' he says, and these words transform what lies before him" (*De prodit. Iudae. homil.* 1, 6; PG 49:380; see *In Matth. Homil.* 82, 5; PG 58:744).

50. Cyril, Bishop of Alexandria, is in full agreement with the Bishop of Constantinople when he writes in his commentary on the Gospel of St. Matthew: "Christ said indicating (the bread and wine): 'This is my body,' and 'This is my blood,' in order that you might not judge what you see to be a mere figure. The offerings, by the hidden power of Almighty God, are changed into Christ's body and blood, and by receiving these we come to share in the life-giving and sanctifying efficacy of Christ" (*In Matth.* 26, 27; PG 72:451).

51. Ambrose, Bishop of Milan, dealing with the Eucharistic change, says: "Let us be assured that this is not what nature formed, but what the blessing consecrated, and that greater efficacy resides in the blessing than in nature, for by the blessing nature is changed." To confirm the

234

APPENDIX

truth of this mystery, he recounts many of the miracles described in the Scriptures, including Christ's birth of the Virgin Mary, and then turning to the work of creation, concludes: "Surely the word of Christ, which could make out of nothing that which did not exist, can change things already in existence into what they were not. For it is no less extraordinary to give things new natures than to change their natures" (*De myster.* 9, 50–52; PL 16:422–424).

52. However, there is no need to assemble many testimonies. Rather, let us recall that firmness of faith with which the Church unanimously opposed Berengarius who, yielding to the difficulties of human reasoning, was the first who dared deny the Eucharistic change. More than once she threatened to condemn him unless he retracted. Thus it was that our predecessor, St. Gregory VII, ordered him to pronounce the following oath: "I believe in my heart and openly profess that the bread and wine placed upon the altar are, by the mystery of the sacred prayer and the words of the Redeemer, substantially changed into the true and life-giving flesh and blood of Jesus Christ our Lord, and that after the consecration, there is present the true body of Christ which was born of the Virgin and, offered up for the salvation of the world, hung on the cross and now sits at the right hand of the Father, and that there is present the true blood of Christ which flowed from his side. They are present not only by means of a sign and of the efficacy of the sacrament, but also in the very reality and truth of their nature and substance" (Mansi, *Coll. ampliss. Concil.* XX, 524D).

53. These words are in complete accord with the doctrine of the mystery of the Eucharistic change as set forth by the ecumenical councils. The constant teaching of these councils—the Lateran, Constance, Florence, and Trent—whether stating the teaching of the Church or condemning errors, affords us an admirable example of the unchanging character of the Catholic faith.

54. After the Council of Trent, our predecessor, Pius VI, on the occasion of the errors of the Synod of Pistoia, warned parish priests, when carrying out their office of teaching, not to neglect to speak of transubstantiation, one of the articles of the faith (Const. *Auctorem fidei,* August 28, 1794). Similarly, our predecessor of happy memory,

Pius XII, recalled the limits to be observed in discussing the mystery of transubstantiation (Allocution of September 22, 1956, *AAS* XLVIII [1956], p. 720). We ourselves also, in fulfillment of our apostolic office, have openly borne solemn witness to the faith of the Church at the National Eucharistic Congress held recently at Pisa (*AAS* LVII [1965], pp. 588–592).

55. Moreover, the Catholic Church has held on to this faith in the presence of the body and blood of Christ in the Eucharist, not only in her teaching but also in her practice, since she has at all times given to this great sacrament the worship known as Latria and which may be given to God alone. As St. Augustine says: "It was in his flesh that Christ walked among us and it is his flesh that he has given us to eat for our salvation. No one, however, eats of this flesh without having first adored it . . . and not only do we not sin in thus adoring it, but we would sin if we did not do so" (*In Ps.* 98, 9; PL 37:1264).

Latreutic Worship of the Sacrament of the Eucharist

56. The Catholic Church has always offered and continues to offer the worship of Latria to the sacrament of the Eucharist, not only during Mass, but also outside of it, reserving consecrated hosts with the utmost care, exposing them to solemn veneration, and carrying them processionally to the joy of great crowds of the faithful.

57. In the ancient documents of the Church we have many testimonies of this veneration. The pastors of the Church, in fact, solicitously exhorted the faithful to take the greatest care in keeping the Eucharist when taking it to their homes. St. Hippolytus warns the faithful: "The body of Christ is meant to be eaten, not to be treated with irreverence" (*Tradit. Apost.* ed. Botte. *La tradition apostolique de St. Hippolyte* [Münster, 1963], p. 84).

58. In fact the faithful thought themselves guilty, and rightly so, as Origen recalls, if, after they received the body of the Lord in order to preserve it with all care and reverence, a small fragment of it fell off through negligence (*In Exod. fragm.;* PG 12:391).

59. The same pastors severely reproved those who showed lack of

reverence if it happened. This is attested to by Novitianus, whose testimony in the matter is trustworthy. He judged as deserving condemnation any one who came out of Sunday service carrying with him as usual the Eucharist, the sacred body of the Lord, "not going to his house but running to places of amusement" (*De spectaculis;* CSEL III, p. 8).

60. On the other hand, St. Cyril of Alexandria rejects as folly the opinion of those who maintained that if a part of the Eucharist was left over for the following day, it did not confer sanctification. "For," he says, "neither Christ is altered nor his holy body changed, but the force and power and vivifying grace always remain with it" (*Epist. ad Calosyrium;* PG 76:1075).

61. Nor should we forget that in ancient times the faithful, harassed by the violence of persecution or living in solitude out of love for monastic life, nourished themselves even daily, receiving Holy Communion by their own hands when the priest or deacon was absent (see Basil. *Epist.* 93; PG 32:483–486).

62. We say this not in order to effect some change in the way of keeping the Eucharist and of receiving Holy Communion which was later prescribed by Church laws and still remains in force, but rather that we may rejoice over the faith of the Church which is always one and the same.

63. This faith also gave rise to the feast of Corpus Christi, which was first celebrated in the diocese of Liège through the particular efforts of the servant of God, Blessed Juliana of Mount Cornelius, and which our predecessor Urban IV extended to the universal Church. From it have originated many practices of Eucharistic piety which, under the inspiration of divine grace, have increased from day to day and with which the Catholic Church is striving ever more to do homage to Christ, to thank him for so great a gift and to implore his mercy.

Exhortation to Promote the Cult of the Eucharist

64. We therefore ask you, venerable brothers, among the people entrusted to your care and vigilance, to preserve this faith in its purity

and integrity—a faith which seeks only to remain perfectly loyal to the Word of Christ and of the Apostles and unambiguously rejects all erroneous and mischievous opinions. Tirelessly promote the worship of the Eucharist, the focus where all other forms of piety must ultimately emerge.

65. May the faithful, thanks to your efforts, come to realize and experience ever more perfectly the truth of these words: "He who desires life finds here a place to live in and the means to live by. Let him approach, let him believe, let him be incorporated so that he may receive life. Let him not refuse union with the members, let him not be a corrupt member, deserving to be cut off, nor a disfigured member to be ashamed of. Let him be a grateful, fitting and healthy member. Let him cleave to the body, let him live by God and for God. Let him now labor here on earth, that he may afterward reign in heaven" (St. Augustine, *In Ioann. tract.* 26, 13; PL 35:1613).

66. It is to be desired that the faithful, every day and in great numbers, actively participate in the sacrifice of the Mass, receive Holy Communion with a pure heart, and give thanks to Christ our Lord for so great a gift. Let them remember these words: "The desire of Jesus Christ and of the Church that all the faithful receive daily Communion means above all that through the sacramental union with God they may obtain the strength necessary for mastering their passions, for purifying themselves of their daily venial faults and for avoiding the grave sins to which human fraility is exposed" (Decr. S. Congr. Concil., Dec. 20, 1905, approved by St. Pius X, *AAS* XXXVIII [1905], p. 401). In the course of the day the faithful should not omit to visit the Blessed Sacrament, which according to the liturgical laws must be kept in the churches with great reverence in a most honorable location. Such visits are a proof of gratitude, an expression of love, an acknowledgment of the Lord's presence.

67. No one can fail to understand that the divine Eucharist bestows upon the Christian people an incomparable dignity. Not only while the sacrifice is offered and the sacrament is received, but as long as the Eucharist is kept in our churches and oratories, Christ is truly the Emmanuel, that is, "God with us." Day and night he is in our midst;

he dwells with us, full of grace and truth (see Jn 1:14). He restores morality, nourishes virtues, consoles the afflicted, strengthens the weak. He proposes his own example to those who come to him that all may learn to be, like himself, meek and humble of heart and to seek not their own interests but those of God.

Anyone who approaches this august sacrament with special devotion and endeavors to return generous love for Christ's own infinite love will experience and fully understand—not without spiritual joy and fruit—how precious is the life hidden with Christ in God (see Col 3:3) and how great is the value of converse with Christ, for there is nothing more consoling on earth, nothing more efficacious for advancing along the road of holiness.

68. Further, you realize, venerable brothers, that the Eucharist is reserved in the churches and oratories as in the spiritual center of a religious community or of a parish, yes, of the universal Church and of all of humanity, since beneath the appearance of the species, Christ is contained, the invisible Head of the Church, the Redeemer of the World, the Center of all hearts, "by whom all things are and by whom we exist" (1 Cor 8:6).

69. From this it follows that the worship paid to the divine Eucharist strongly impels the soul to cultivate a "social" love (see St. Augustine, *De gen. ad litt.* XI, 15, 20; PL 34:437), by which the common good is given preference over the good of the individual. Let us consider as our own the interests of the community, of the parish, of the entire Church, extending our charity to the whole world, because we know that everywhere there are members of Christ.

70. The Eucharistic sacrament, venerable brothers, is the sign and the cause of the unity of the Mystical Body, and it inspires an active "ecclesial" spirit in those who venerate it with greater fervor. Therefore, never cease to persuade those committed to your care that they should learn to make their own the cause of the Church in approaching the Eucharistic mystery, to pray to God without interruption, to offer themselves to God as a pleasing sacrifice for the peace and unity of the Church, so that all the children of the Church may be united and think the same, that there be no divisions among them, but rather unity of

mind and purpose, as the Apostle insists (see 1 Cor 1:10). May all those not yet in perfect communion with the Catholic Church, who, though separated from her glory in the name of Christian, share with us as soon as possible with the help of divine grace that unity of faith and communion which Christ wanted to be the distinctive mark of his disciples.

71. This zeal in praying and consecrating oneself to God for the unity of the Church should be practiced particularly by Religious, both men and women, in as much as they are in a special way devoted to the adoration of the Blessed Sacrament, according it homage and honor on earth, in virtue of their vows.

72. Nothing has ever been or is more important to the Church or more consoling than the desire for the unity of all Christians, a desire which we wish to express once again in the very words used by the Council of Trent at the close of its decree on the Most Blessed Eucharist: "In conclusion, the sacred synod with paternal love admonishes, exhorts, prays and implores 'because of the loving-kindness of our God' (Lk 1:78) that each and every Christian come at last to a perfect agreement regarding this sign of unity, this bond of charity, this symbol of concord, and, mindful of such great dignity and such exquisite love of Christ our Lord who gave his beloved soul as the price of our salvation and 'his flesh to eat' (John 6:48 ff.) believe and adore these sacred mysteries of his body and blood with such firm and unwavering faith, with such devotion, piety, and veneration, that they can receive frequently that supersubstantial bread (Matt 6:11), which will be for them truly the life of the soul and unfailing strength of mind, so that fortified by its vigor (see 3 Kgs 19:8) they can depart from this wretched pilgrimage on earth to reach their heavenly home where they will then eat the same 'bread of angels' (Ps 77:25) no longer hidden by the species which now they eat under the sacred appearances" (*Decree on the Holy Eucharist,* c. 8).

73. May the all-good Redeemer who shortly before his death prayed to the Father that all who were to believe in him would be one even as he and the Father were one (see Jn 17:20–21), deign speedily to hear our most ardent prayer and that of the entire Church, that we may all,

with one voice and one faith, celebrate the Eucharistic mystery and, by participating in the body of Christ, become one body (see 1 Cor 10:17), linked by those same bonds which he himself desired for its perfection.

74. And we turn with paternal affection also to those who belong to the venerable Churches of the Orient, from which came so many most illustrious Fathers whose testimony to the belief of the Eucharist we have so gladly cited in our present letter. Our soul is filled with intense joy as we consider your faith in the Eucharist, which is also our faith, and as we listen to the liturgical prayers by which you celebrate so great a mystery, we rejoice to behold your Eucharistic devotion, and to read your theologians explaining or defending the doctrine of this most august sacrament.

75. May the most Blessed Virgin Mary from whom Christ our Lord took the flesh which under the species of bread and wine "is contained, offered and consumed" (*C.I.C.*, can. 801), may all the saints of God, especially those who burned with a more ardent devotion to the divine Eucharist, intercede before the Father of mercies so that from this same faith in, and devotion toward, the Eucharist may result and flourish a perfect unity of communion among all Christians. Unforgettable are the words of the holy martyr Ignatius, in his warning to the faithful of Philadelphia against the evils of division and schism, the remedy for which lies in the Eucharist: "Strive then," he says, "to make use of one form of thanksgiving, for the flesh of our Lord Jesus Christ is one, and one in the chalice in the union of his blood, one altar, one bishop" (*Epist. ad Philadelph.*, 4; PG 5:700).

76. Encouraged by the most consoling hope of the blessings which will accrue to the whole Church and the entire world from an increase in devotion to the Eucharist, with profound affection we impart to you, venerable brothers, to the priests, Religious and all those who collaborate with you and to all the faithful entrusted to your care, the apostolic blessing as a pledge of heavenly graces. . . .

(English text from Paulist Press Study-Club edition)

Peter Heynen, S.S.S.

The *Mysterium Fidei* and Its Antecedents

The Chief Themes of the Encyclical. The central ideas of the encyclical *Mysterium fidei* may be stated in the five following propositions:

1. The Eucharist is a mystery of faith; in fact, in the words of the liturgy, it is the supreme mystery of faith—a mystery difficult to believe, and according to St. Bonaventure, the most difficult to believe.

2. In the Eucharist Jesus Christ is sacramentally but also really and substantially present. This Real Presence is superior to the other modes of Christ's presence in the Church.

3. This Eucharistic presence is realized by transubstantiation, a term that no one may reject lightly, and one that the Council of Trent has deemed appropriate for expressing the mystery.

4. From these revealed truths there follows for the faithful the obligation to render worship of adoration to our Lord present in the Eucharist.

5. This adoration must be rendered to the Eucharist not only during the celebration of the Mass, but also at other times. It is fitting, and it is a duty for the faithful to make visits throughout the day to the Blessed Sacrament, which must be reserved in the churches in a place of great honor, and surrounded by all possible respect, in accordance with liturgical laws.

With these great affirmations before our eyes, let us now examine how this encyclical took shape in our Holy Father's mind.

BOMBAY

The Pope's sojourn in Bombay from December 2 to 5, 1964, was a meeting of the head of the Catholic Church with the vast non-Christian world; and from this point of view the journey proved of incalculable significance for the future. But amid the joy of this event there has been a tendency to forget, as the Pope himself has said, that this encounter with India took place "in the dazzling light that emanates from the Eucharistic mystery." (*Documentation Catholique,* 1965, col. 19)

The Pope went to India as a pilgrim to the Eucharistic Congress of Bombay, "as a pilgrim to venerate our Lord in the Holy Eucharist" (AAS, 57 [1965], 131 and 124). And upon his departure from Rome he declared:

As everyone has very well understood, our journey has no other purpose than to be a religious testimonial to our Lord, the immortal King of all peoples and all ages, on the occasion of the international Eucharistic Congress that will witness believing throngs from the whole world recollecting themselves in adoration at Bombay. (*Doc. Cath.,* 1965, cols. 1 and 2)

In addressing the members of the diplomatic corps, he affirmed:

It is indeed with a purely religious intent that we have undertaken this voyage. We have come among our sons of the Far East to worship our Lord Jesus Christ present in the Eucharist. That is truly the ultimate purpose of this International Congress, so graciously welcomed by India. (*Ibid.,* col. 9)

Likewise, in his letter to Cardinal Agagianian of November 11, 1964, the Holy Father declared:

God willing, We shall be present Ourselves for a brief visit at this Eucharistic Congress [of Bombay] for the purpose of adoring the august Sacrament of the altar, most solemnly exposed in India, and in order to bring to the men there assembled the good news of the Prince of Peace, hidden under the Eucharistic veils, and to confirm them in their faith. (AAS, 56 [1964], 975)

In another discourse Pope Paul called the Eucharistic Congress, "this universal act of worship and veneration of our most divine Savior in the sacrament of life for men" (AAS, 57 [1965], 120). And we find the same concern that was to be expressed in the Encyclical in his words to the acolytes of Bombay:

I have come from Rome to adore and praise, together with you, our Lord in the blessed Sacrament of the Eucharist. Always have a warm and deep devotion for the blessed Sacrament. Visit our Lord as often as you can. Receive him frequently in Holy Communion. Ask him to make you good, to make you holy, to make you resemble him more and more. (*Ibid.*, pp. 135–136)

The same ideas were developed also by Pope Paul in his discourse to the six bishops representing all the continents, immediately after he had consecrated them on the evening of December 3:

Venerable Brothers and beloved Sons, let us be fully cognizant of this reality that Jesus Christ is present.

Jesus Christ is alive.

Jesus Christ, who is the eternal and consubstantial Son of God, who is also the Son of Mary, true man, our brother.

He is here, in the mystery that this Congress celebrates. He is really present, and not merely represented, invoked, or commemorated. He is here himself, real and unique. It is only under the sacramental appearances that he is multiplied. And he is thus multiplied in order to communicate himself to each one of us.

How is this possible?

It is possible because divine powers have been communicated to certain ones among us. The priesthood of Christ was transmitted to certain of his disciples who have become the instruments of his action, heirs to his mission, vicars in his work. (*Doc. Cath.*, 1965, col. 11)

In the letter to Cardinal Agagianian, naming him the Papal Legate to the Congress of Bombay, the Pope returned even more forcefully to these ideas that were to be the fabric of his encyclical: the Real Presence and transubstantiation. Explicitly and repeatedly he appealed to the authority of the Council of Trent, and then went on to say:

To the One who is present in this most blessed Sacrament and who dwells among us, 'banished children of Eve,' we must render as his unquestioned right not only private but also social worship. That is what the Church understood when she instituted Eucharistic solemnities, sacred processions (*sacras pompas*), and these [Eucharistic] Congresses. (AAS, 56 [1964], 976)

ORVIETO

A few months before the Congress of Bombay, the seventh centenary of the Bull *Transiturus* was celebrated at Orvieto in August, 1964. On August 12, 1264, from Orvieto where he was then residing, Pope Urban IV had promulgated this bull extending to the entire Church the Feast of the Blessed Sacrament instituted at Liège in 1246 by Bishop Robert de Thorotte. Paul VI went to Orvieto by helicopter on August 11, 1964, and there pronounced a remarkable discourse on the subject: "The Christian Looks at the Eucharistic Mystery." Several of the principal themes of the encyclical were given very definite form in this discourse.

As Pope Paul said:

Let us be objective. Our modern mentality, taught to measure its certitudes with immediate sense knowledge and with pure scientific reason, cluttered with countless impressions and imaginings aroused by the literature and dramatic productions that now dominate and mold our psychology, finds it hard to accept with unshakable faith and sincere piety the ineffable Eucharistic announcement: This is my Body, this is my Blood. These words leave us, as it were, dumbfounded. We do not find the concepts, the reasons, the consequences of such an announcement. What is this all about? What does it mean? And above all, how can such a thing exist, when it seems to contradict the physical and biological laws we know? Why did our Lord, if he wanted to communicate himself to us, choose this mode that is so incomprehensible to us?

For us moderns, who have been trained to develop a rational and imaginative mentality, as We were saying, it is difficult to admit the reality that this Sacrament offers us. It requires faith on our part, simple and loving assent to the words that announce the Eucharistic mystery to us. And this assent demands that we relearn to think in a way that is as faithful and coherent as that of our ancestors. Their education was much more meager than ours, but they accepted the truth that came from God with greater simplicity and trust—not without difficulty, and certainly not without merit, but more easily than we do. Today, on the other hand we are better disposed to understand the "why" of this sacrament. The "how" demands an interior effort of us, but the "why" opens up admirable horizons to us. (*Doc. Cath.*, 1964, col. 1107)

In closing, Pope Paul developed the idea that there is no possibility of choice as between the bread of heaven and earthly bread: "Finally, let the man of today believe that the reason why Christ in the Eucharist demands of him an humble and fervent faith, is for his redemption, for his salvation, for his happiness. Such is the message of Orvieto."

ROME

On Holy Thursday of 1965, the Holy Father celebrated Mass in the Lateran basilica, as he had the preceding year. During the celebration he pronounced a homily in which we find a single constant element, a single leitmotiv: faith in the Eucharistic mystery:

May these words [of Christ], heard and accepted here, in this church which is the center of all churches, reach out to all the churches with a fraternal and joyous frankness, and return here as a faithful echo, as a choir, from all the churches in communion with this one, in order to tell us, and to tell the whole world: the living Christ is with us.

But, the Pope continued,

it is here that difficulties present themselves. We should like to understand, but our reason unaided does not suffice to make us understand. The words of Christ, so limpid and clear, become difficult for anyone who reflects on them. "This is a hard saying" (Jn 6:61). The human intellect rebels. And then some turn away shaking their heads, determined to save their respectable but paltry dignity, their precious but limited reason.

Still others want to diminish the full meaning of the divine words. For them, this is nothing but a ritual supper, there is only a symbolic and not a real presence; or else simply commonplace things to which a superior meaning has been attached. Then the mystery, in the sense of something obscure to the mind, remains and grows deeper; whereas the mystery, in the sense of divine reality present and hidden, disappears, as the words of Christ also disappear and vanish completely. (*Doc. Cath.*, 1965, cols. 873–876)

Only faith in the Lord's word, however, can give men certitude. This last thought was developed by the Pope with great conviction.

PISA

In June, 1965, when the 17th National Eucharistic Congress of Italy was held in Pisa, the Pope insisted on attending it in person. On Friday, June 10, he celebrated Mass there, and during it he delivered an important homily.

The theme of the Congress was "God with Us." In a letter to Cardinal Florit, Archbishop of Florence, appointing him Papal Legate to the Congress of Pisa, the Pope had written:

At Pisa, in this illustrious city, a voice will resound . . . affirming with new force the real and substantial presence among us, under the Eucharistic veils, of the Savior, God and Man. Does not everyone know that the Incarnation of the Word, this ineffable mystery of divine love, is perpetuated through the centuries in a certain respect by this most blessed Sacrament; in other words, that Jesus Christ who assumed a human body in order to suffer death for our salvation, will continue to perpetuate his presence and his sacrifice of the cross among us in the Eucharist, until he returns? (*Osservatore Romano,* French ed., June 18, 1965)

This homily is, as it were, a preliminary draft of the encyclical *Mysterium fidei,* for, as he says,

The sacred signs of the Eucharist are not only symbols or figures of Christ, or ways of indicating his love or his action toward those who are guests at his Supper; these signs actually contain him, the living and true Christ; they indicate that he is present as he is, living in eternal glory, but represented here in the act of his sacrifice. They are meant to manifest that the Eucharistic sacrament reproduces in an unbloody way the bloody immolation of Christ on the cross, and that this Sacrament makes those who worthily consume the body and blood of Christ under the appearances of bread and wine, participate in the benefits of his redemption. This is the truth. This is the truth.

The Holy Father continued:

Indeed, We know that in stating such a reality, We are proclaiming a mystery. While We are fully aware that when we affirm the truth, as the Catholic Church professes it, We are stating at the same time a whole constellation of other truths bound together in an extremely complex and yet wonderful way. These are truths essentially bound up with the Eucharistic mystery, and just as mysterious as it is, but likewise as firmly rooted in reality as it is.

Let us repeat: We know that We are stating a mystery. But that is the truth. That is the witness that We bear. It coincides with the testimony of this Congress, and it brings the full confirmation that is authorized by Our apostolic Magisterium—far more, it obliges us here—to profess that Christ is thus really present in the Sacrament of the Eucharist. We say this so that We may rejoice with you, faithful sons, who make the Eucharist your daily food. . . . We say this likewise to dispel certain uncertainties born of recent years from the efforts to give interpretations with regard to this important point, that might elucidate the traditional and authentic doctrine of the Church. We say it, furthermore, to invite you, all the men of our time, to fix your attention on this ancient and ever-new message, which the Church continues to repeat today: Christ, living and hidden under the sacramental sign that he offers us, Christ himself is really present. These are not meaningless words. This is no superstitious suggestion nor a kind of mythical phantasy. It is the truth, no less real than certain other truths, although of a much loftier order.

Here, as he had a year earlier at Orvieto, the Pope insisted on the difficulties modern man encounters in believing in the Eucharist.

We seem to hear certain among you murmur: How can this be? How can such a thing exist that is beyond all our usual experiences, beyond all the ordinary ways of knowing the physical world, beyond all possibility of control by means of the senses? The intellectual formation of our time accustoms the mind to concrete certitudes that do not transcend its cognitive faculty. And besides, the art of practicing doubt and negative criticism; the ease with which the mind turns to agnosticism and scepticism; the tendency to negation, both speculative and practical, in the realm of religion; and perhaps also a certain sloth deep within the souls of so many men who, in days gone by, have not been deprived of exact religious knowledge or of a certain satisfying experience of who Christ is and what his word is worth, a sloth that at a given moment paralyzes the act of honest and courageous reflection: all these typical forms of the modern mentality and culture sometimes make profane man obtuse to the announcement that We repeat here: Christ is with us.

We prefer to limit Ourselves to saying to you what We say to Ourselves: it is a mystery; in other words, a truth of a different order from that of common logic and of the knowledge that flows from sensible experience. But it is a truth guaranteed by the words of the Master, Jesus Christ. His words tend to create in our minds a unique way of apprehending the truth and of accepting it, superior to the normal capacity of the intellect. . . . The Eucharist is the *mysterium fidei,* the mystery of faith. A very brilliant light, a very gentle light for the one who believes; an opaque rite for the one who does not have faith. What a decisive theme is the Eucharist, when carried to such a point of free choice. He who accepts it, chooses. He chooses in union with the vigorous conclusion of Peter: "Lord, to whom shall we go? Thou hast words of everlasting life!" (Jn 6:68). (*Osservatore Romano,* French ed., June 18, 1965)

CONCLUSION

It is interesting and useful to place these declarations of the Pope side by side with the encyclical on the Eucharist, promulgated on September 3, 1965, on the Feast of St. Pius X. It is immediately clear that the same concern, the same thought lies at the origin of them all. We find in them a continuity that is a joy and a comfort. Besides, in his encyclical, the Pope himself refers to his discourse at Pisa (*Etudes Religieuses* [Brussels], p. 26, No. 58).

To anyone who will set this encyclical by the side of the above-mentioned discourses of the Holy father, it becomes clear that the encyclical and the discourses are addressed to modern man as such, formed by contemporary culture and technology, regardless of the country in which he lives. And every man of our time, whether he be a priest, a religious, or a layman, has the greatest interest in meditating deeply and assiduously upon the Eucharistic teachings of Paul VI. A profound sense of the Church urgently invites us to do so.

Certain attitudes with regard to the encyclical are incompatible with this sense of the Church. A Catholic cannot dissociate himself from the Pope's Eucharistic teaching, he cannot completely ignore it.

Nor, for that matter, can he be content to remain silent, respectful as he may want his silence to be, especially since the Pope expressly declares in the encyclical that he is speaking "in virtue of [his] apostolic authority." (*Etudes Religieuses,* p. 2, No. 12)

The teaching of the Council itself does not leave us in any uncertainty as to the path to follow. The Dogmatic Constitution of the Church is very clear:

They [the faithful] must offer religious submission of *the will* and *the intellect* in a special way to the "authentic" Magisterium of the Roman Pontiff, even when he is not speaking *ex cathedra,* in such a way that his supreme magisterium may be respectfully acknowledged, that his views may be *sincerely* accepted, in the measure that he makes his intention and his will known, which are manifested above all by the nature of the documents, either by the repeated presentation of the same doctrine, or by the manner in which he expresses himself. (Dogmatic Constitution on the Church, No. 25)

Do not the preceding pages prove factually this "repeated presentation of the same doctrine"?

In these declarations of the Council, no one should seek a pretext for declaring, as a priori impossible, any progress in theology on these precise points on the Real Presence and on transubstantiation. In the encyclical the Pope affirms explicitly that he "recognizes and approves" the laudable desire to scrutinize such a great mystery, to explore its inexhaustible riches, and to reveal its meanings to the men of our time," and to "give a clearer and more overt explanation of the dogmatic formulas approved by the Church." (*Etudes Religieuses,* p. 11, No. 19; p. 12, No. 22)

Nor can anyone claim the Pope is contradicting himself. The encyclical does not contradict in any way, nor can it contradict, the declarations of Vatican Council II. Did not the Pope himself approve and promulgate the constitutions and decrees of the Council, just as he, too, wrote the encyclical?

Now, the Decree on Ecumenism declares "that it is necessary to distinguish carefully the manner the doctrine is promulgated from the deposit of faith itself" (No. 6). True, the same decree tells us that "nothing is more foreign to ecumenism than the false irenism that injures the purity of Catholic doctrine and obscures its authentic and incontrovertible meaning." But it immediately adds: "At the same time, the Catholic faith must be explained in a deeper and more straightforward way (*profundius et rectius*), making use of a manner of speaking and terminology that are easily accessible even to the separated brothers" (No. 11).

Every Christian—whether he be a priest, religious, or layman—owes it to himself to want to attain in his own life this equilibrium toward which the Council strove in its decrees and constitutions. Then the encyclical *Mysterium fidei* will be a benediction for the Christians of our time, on condition that they accept it with a profound and genuine sense of the Church.[2]

NOTES

Peter Heynen, S.S.S., superior of the Blessed Sacrament Fathers in Brussels, was named by Cardinal Suenens to the commission charged with liturgical reform in the Brussels archdiocese. He is a frequent contributor to *Parole et Pain,* where the present study appeared in January of 1966.

1. The insistence and the accent of conviction with which the Pope repeated these last words, *"Cosi è. Cosi è,"* has been attested to by a number of those present on this occasion.

2. We need hardly call to mind the gesture of Paul VI, who decided that during the third session the Blessed Sacrament would be continually exposed in the Pauline Chapel for the adoration of the members of the Vatican household, of the Curia, and of the Council Fathers. Bishop de Smedt of Bruges has described in an article the stirring sight when, just before the opening of the Council sessions, the Fathers came and knelt in large numbers every morning before Christ in the Eucharist. (See *Kerkelijk Leven,* October 3, 1965.)

Selective Bibliography

Books

Bacciocchi, J. de, S.M. *L'Eucharistie.* Tournai, Desclee, 1961.

Casel, Odo, O.S.B. *The Mystery of Christian Worship.* Westminster (Md.), Newman, 1962.

Clark, F., S.J. *Adjumenta ad Tractatum de SS. Eucharistiae Sacramento.* Rome, Pontificia Universitas Gregoriana, 1966.

The Eucharist in the New Testament: A Symposium. Baltimore, Helicon, 1965.

Falardeau, N. R., S.S.S. *Eucharistic Literature: Books on the Eucharist in the English Language by Catholic Authors 1925–1955; also 1951–1961.* Cleveland, Western Reserve University, 1955 and 1962.

Jeremias, J. *Eucharistic Words of Jesus.* New York, Scribner, 1966.

Jungmann, J., S.J. *The Place of Christ in Liturgical Worship.* Staten Island (N. Y.), Alba House, 1965.

Kilmartin, E. J., S.J. *The Eucharist in the Primitive Church.* Englewood Cliffs (N. J.), Prentice-Hall, 1965.

Nicolas, M. J., O.P. *What Is the Eucharist?* New York, Hawthorn, 1960.

Powers, J. M., S.J. *Eucharistic Theology.* New York, Herder and Herder, 1967.

Rahner, Karl, S.J. *L'Eucharistie et les hommes d'aujourd'hui.* Paris, Mame, 1965.

Rouleau, M. A., S.S.S. *Eucharistic Literature: Books on the Eucharist in the English Language by Catholic Authors 1900–1924.* River Forest (Ill.), Rosary College, 1961.

Solano, J., S.J. *Textos Eucaristicos Primitivos.* 2 vols. Madrid, Biblioteca de Autores Cristianos, 1952, 1954.

Feuillet, A. *Johannine Studies.* Staten Island (N. Y.), Alba House, 1964. Chapter 3.

Tillard, J. M. R., O.P. *The Eucharist: Pasch of God's People.* Staten Island (N. Y.), Alba House, 1967.

Periodical Literature

Atkins, A., O.C.S.O. "The Eucharist: A Regenerative Sacrifice." *The Thomist,* 29 (1965), pp. 217–231.

> The Mass is Christ's sacrifice, which is the regeneration of mankind; it is the supreme human act, installing itself at the origin of all human activity.

251

Barosse, T., C.S.C. "The Eucharist: Sacrifice and Meal?" *Liturgical Studies,*
6 (1965).
A thorough examination of the New Testament data.

Baum, G., O.S.A. "The Manifold Presence of Christ at Mass." *The Ecumenist,* 3 (1965), pp. 69–72.

Bergh, E. "Nobiscum Deus." *Revue des Communautés Religieuses,* 37
(1965), pp. 208–215.

Bouesse, H., O.P. "Le symbolisme Eucharistique." *Année Théologique,* 13
(1952), pp. 191–203.
Christian unity is the Eucharist's main symbolism, but it does not
exhaust the richness of that complex notion.

Bourke, M. "The Eucharist in the Church." *North American Liturgical
Week,* 25 (1964), pp. 31–39.
By the Eucharistic covenant-renewal sacrifice, the Church, obedient
to the Word of God, enters into the ever-present and eternal sacrifice
of her risen Lord.

Brown, R. E., S.S. "The Johannine Sacramentary Reconsidered." *Theological
Studies,* 23 (1962), pp. 183–206.
Two relatively clear criteria for judging the presence of sacramental
symbolism in John are the following: There must be some internal,
contextual indication, although there need be no clear indication of
the symbolism. And this indication should be corroborated by the
external criterion of good sacramental attestation in the art, liturgy,
and literature of the early Church. For example, the symbolism of
the Eucharist is acceptable for the marriage at Cana (2:1–11), but it
is to be rejected in the cleansing of the Temple (2:13–22).

Buckley, M. J., S.J. "Holy Eucharist and Holy Spirit," *Worship,* 37 (1963),
pp. 332–341.
Through the Eucharist the mission of the Son continues in time;
through the Eucharist the mission of the Holy Spirit is renewed in
each communicant.

Burbach, M., O.S.B. "The Eucharist as Sacrament of Unity." *North American Liturgical Week,* 21 (1960), pp. 44–49.
Unity in Christ is Eucharistic unity, a unity signified by the Eucharist
and effected by the Eucharist.

"Controversy on the Real Presence." *Herder Correspondence,* 2 (1965),
pp. 388–395.
A theological debate and a pastoral letter in the Netherlands.

Cooke, B., S.J. "Eucharist: Source or Expression of Community." *Worship,*
40 (1966), pp. 339–348.
We cannot expect Christian unity to take place apart from the influence of the Eucharist.

———. "Synoptic Presentation of the Eucharist as Covenant." *Theological
Studies,* 21 (1960), pp. 1–44.

Jesus as depicted by the Synoptics recapitulates and fulfills in their various stages of evolution the priesthood, the Temple, and the sacrifices of Israel.

Crehan, J. H., S.J. "Christ's Action in the Mass." *Theological Studies,* 27 (1966), pp. 89–96.

The action of Christ in the Mass is his pleading at the heavenly altar for the ratification of this and each further renewal of his sacrifice.

Davis, Charles. "Episcopate and Eucharist." *Worship,* 38 (1964), pp. 502–514.

As the sacrifice of the People of God, the Eucharist produces its fruits when celebrated within the unity of the body of Christ, the Church, and in communion with the bishop.

De Haes, P. "The Presence of the Lord Christ." *Lumen Vitae,* 20 (1965), pp. 435–450.

Different modes of actualization in the liturgy.

Diekmann, G., O.S.B. "The Eucharist Makes the People of God." *Worship,* 39 (1965), pp. 458–468.

The distinctive Christian goal of fraternal charity has always been the same. Christ's gift of the Eucharist has always been ours. What is new is our new awareness of how essentially and inextricably these two belong together.

Duggan, G. H., S.M. "Transubstantiation in Catholic Tradition." *Australasian Catholic Record,* 42 (1965), pp. 73–80.

The term *transubstantiation* in Catholic tradition has a meaning which implies a doctrine regarding substance and accidents that is in substantial agreement with the metaphysics of Aristotle.

"Eucharist." *New Catholic Encyclopedia,* V, pp. 597–620.

Galot, J., S.J. "Prière Eucharistique et vie religieuse." *Revue des Communautés Religieuses,* 37 (1965), pp. 249–274.

Green, H. D. "The Eucharistic Presence: Change and/or Signification." *Downside Review,* 83 (1965), pp. 32–48.

Hanrahan, N. "Cardinal Vaughan and Priestly Devotion to the Eucharist." *Irish Ecclesiastical Record,* 103 (1964), pp. 101–107; 104 (1965), 27–36.

The priest's Eucharistic devotion illustrated by the Cardinal's personal life and apostolate.

Hawkins, D. J. B. "Reflections on Transubstantiation." *Downside Review,* 80 (1962), pp. 308–318.

Concludes that nearly the whole of the medieval Scholastic analysis may and should be upheld.

Jezierski, Sister Marie Caritas. "Catechesis and the Eucharist in Adolescence." *Lumen Vitae,* 21 (1966), pp. 190–198.

How catechetical presentation of the Eucharist can be made relevant to adolescent girls.

Jong, J. P. de. "The Eucharist as Symbolic Reality." *Review for Religious,* 25 (1966), pp. 853–859.
   In ancient times, symbol and reality were regarded as forming a unity composed of two elements that tolerated no separation.
Kilmartin, E. J., S.J. "The Eucharistic Cup in the Primitive Liturgy." *Catholic Biblical Quarterly,* 24 (1962), pp. 32–43.
   Though it seems reasonable to say that "breaking of bread" was the characteristic name given to the primitive Eucharistic celebration, this does not imply that the cup was placed in the background. Just the opposite seems to be true.
———. "The One Fruit or the Many Fruits of the Mass." *Proceedings of the Catholic Theological Society,* 21 (1966), pp. 37–70.
   There is no solid theological foundation to the supposition that there is a fruit (effect) of the Mass independent of the devotion of either the celebrating priest or the faithful assisting at Mass, and that it is this effect that is applied by the celebrant for the intention of the donor of the stipend.
Kinney, J. M. "Reservation of the Blessed Sacrament to the Time of Charlemagne." *American Church Quarterly,* 6 (1966), pp. 45–55.
   The early Church had a very strong belief in what came to be called the Real Presence.
Lash, N. "Eucharist." *New Blackfriars,* 48 (1967), pp. 172–185. Whatever other modes of Christ's presence in the world there may be, they are for the sake of his presence in us, his people.
———. "The Eucharist: Sacrifice or Meal?" *Clergy Review,* 50 (1965), pp. 907–922. The Eucharistic sacrifice is that sacrament which, as effective memorial of Christ's saving death and resurrection, is the covenant-sacrifice of the new people of God, recalling that covenant's sealing on Calvary, actualizing the covenant-union in the worshiping assembly, and anticipating the covenant's perfect fulfillment in the eschatological Messianic banquet.
Lussier, E., S.S.S. "The Real Presence." *Emmanuel,* 72 (1966), pp. 70–83.
———. "The Mystery of Christ's Eucharistic Presence." *Ibid.,* pp. 464–469.
———. "The Eucharistic Mystery in the History of Salvation." *Ibid.,* pp. 506–510. Meditative presentations stressing the basic unity of the Eucharistic mystery and its integration in the history of salvation. The Eucharist is the personal gift the risen and glorious Christ makes of himself to his Father and to his Church.
McAuliffe, C., S.J. "Transubstantiation and Eucharistic Theology." *American Ecclesiastical Review,* 155 (1966), pp. 361–373. Transubstantiation is a revealed truth that penetrates into every aspect of the Eucharistic mystery.
McBride, A., O.Praem. "A Catechesis of the Mass." *American Ecclesiastical*

Review, 152 (1965), pp. 414–421. An approach to the Eucharist stressing newer insights. The Mass is treated under seven topics: assembly, work, Word, Pasch, sacrifice, meal, and Parousia.

McCabe, H., O.P. "The Real Presence." *Clergy Review,* 49 (1964), pp. 740–759. Christ is present in the Eucharist not as a physical object that lies before us but as language in which we speak, the word in whom we pray and who speaks to us. The article occasioned several reactions: See 1965, pp. 388–394, 558–559, 721–723.

McGarry, C., S.J. "The Eucharistic Celebration as the True Manifestation of the Church." *Irish Theological Quarterly,* 32 (1965), pp. 325–337.

McGivern, J., C.M. "The Meaning of Eucharistic Piety." *Ecumenist,* 4 (1966), pp. 53–55. There is a way of viewing Christ's Eucharistic mystery that nullifies the meaning of the mystery of the Ascension and distorts the mystery of the Church.

Marcotte, E., O.M.I. "A propos de la Presence Reélle." *Revue de l'Université d'Ottawa,* 35 (1965), pp. 141–160. Study of the manner of Christ's real presence in the Eucharist. Suggests that the terminology *res et sacramentum* relative to the Eucharist is inadequate and needs updating.

Michel-Jean, C., S.S.S. "Le Sacrement a Demeure." *Parole et Pain,* No. 9, 1965, pp. 537–550. Study of the pertinence of Eucharistic devotion in our time of liturgical renewal.

Miller, J. H., C.S.C. "Until He Comes—The Eucharist and the Resurrection." *North American Liturgical Week,* 23 (1962), pp. 39–44. As we feast upon the flesh and blood of the resurrected victim in the Christian Passover, we are ourselves being resurrected bit by bit until we are ready for the fullest participation in the banquet of the heavenly mansion of our Father.

Neuner, J. "The Eucharist and the New Man." *Clergy Monthly,* 28 (1964), pp. 137–145, 161–166. If there is to be a renewal of man, and through man of the world, it can come only through the mystery that is revealed in Jesus Christ and continues to live in the Church, the mystery of divine love.

O'Connell, J. B. "Reservation of the Blessed Sacrament and Mass Facing the People." *Clergy Review,* 50 (1965), pp. 923–930. The Blessed Sacrament should have a special place of reservation, eliminating any possible confusion of mysteries and favoring the private, personal adoration of the sacramental presence by the people.

O'Neill, C., O.P. "What Is Transignification All About?" *Catholic World,* 202 (1966), pp. 204–210. Discussion of transignification in the light of *Mysterium fidei.*

Padovano, A. "Questions on the Eucharist." *Guide,* No. 200, 1965, pp.

7–14. Scriptural themes and the Eucharist, the Council of Trent, Protestant concepts, and some contemporary considerations.

Pousset, E., S.J. "L'Eucharistie: presence reélle et transubstantiation." *Recherches de Sciences Religieuse,* 54 (1966), pp. 177–212.

————. "L'Eucharistie: Sacrament et Existence." *Nouvelle Revue Théologique,* 88 (1966), pp. 943–965. Presentation of the new theology on the Eucharist, especially in relation to salvation history and the meaning of transubstantiation.

Powers, J. M., S.J. *"Mysterium fidei* and the Theology of the Eucharist." *Worship,* 40 (1966), pp. 17–35. Studies some deviations in the contemporary theology of the Eucharist, as pointed out by *Mysterium fidei,* and shows how the encyclical is meant to guide and not hinder theological thought and development.

Schillebeeckx, E., O.P. "Transubstantiation, Transfinalization, Transfiguration." *Worship,* 40 (1966), pp. 324–338. Factors that contributed to the re-evaluation of Eucharistic theology; the locale of the new theories; an examination of transfinalization and transsignification as interpretations of transubstantiation.

Schmidt, H., S.J. "Discussion on the Real Presence and Transsubstantiation." Systematic descriptive bibliography. *Information Documentation on the Conciliar Church,* August 27, 1967.

Schoonenberg, P., S.J. "Presence and the Eucharistic Presence." *Cross Currents,* 17 (1967), pp. 39–54. Penetrating study of the idea of presence as communication and of the different kinds of presences—spatial, personal, human. This is applied to the presence of God in the world and of Christ in the Eucharist.

————. "The Real Presence in Contemporary Discussion." *Theology Digest,* 15 (1967), pp. 3–11. Emphasizes the personal nature of the Real Presence. Draws some debatable practical conclusions.

Shaughnessy, J. D. "The Tabernacle and Reservation of the Blessed Sacrament." *Homiletic and Pastoral Review,* 65 (1965), pp. 680–683.

Sloyan, G. S. "Primitive and Pauline Concepts of the Eucharist." *Catholic Biblical Quarterly,* 23 (1961), pp. 1–13. New Testament evidence shows that the tradition Paul gave to the Corinthians was fully in the spirit of the first layer of the gospel tradition and was both eschatological and joyous despite its reference to the redemptive death.

————. "The Real Presence: Debate on the Eucharist." *Commonweal,* 84 (1966). pp. 357–361. Background and reflections on the encyclical *Mysterium fidei.*

Stanks, T. D., S.S. "The Eucharist: Christ's Self-Communication in a Revelatory Event." *Theological Studies,* 28 (1967), pp. 27–50. The Eucharist is considered as word, as event, and as a constituting action

of Christ and the assembly. Christ's purpose in the Eucharist: a
revelatory event for the sake of personal communication.

Vollert, C. S.J. "The Eucharist: Quests for Insights from Scripture."
Theological Studies, 21 (1960), pp. 404–443. Survey of recent articles
on the Eucharist by Catholic biblical scholars.

NOTE

Ernest Lussier, S.S.S., who compiled the Bibliography, is professor of
Scripture at the Blessed Sacrament Fathers' major seminary in Cleveland,
Ohio. He is also review editor of and a frequent contributor to *Emmanuel.*

Index

259

NOTE

Eugene LaVerdiere, S.S.S., who prepared the Index, is pursuing advanced studies in Sacred Scripture at "St. Stephen's" in Jerusalem, the Ecole Biblique conducted by the Dominican Fathers.